The Afterlives of Egyptian History

The Afterlives of Egyptian History

REUSE AND REFORMULATION OF OBJECTS, PLACES, AND TEXTS

A VOLUME IN HONOR OF EDWARD L. BLEIBERG

Edited by
Yekaterina Barbash and Kathlyn M. Cooney
With a Preface by Kathy Zurek-Doule

The American University in Cairo Press
Cairo   New York

First published in 2021 by
The American University in Cairo Press
113 Sharia Kasr el Aini, Cairo, Egypt
One Rockefeller Plaza, 10th Floor, New York, NY 10020
www.aucpress.com

Copyright © 2021 by The American University in Cairo Press

All rights reserved. No part of this publication may be reproduced, stored in a retrieval system, or transmitted in any form or by any means, electronic, mechanical, photocopying, recording, or otherwise, without the prior written permission of the publisher.

ISBN 978 1 6179 7992 7

Library of Congress Cataloging-in-Publication Data

Names: Barbash, Yekaterina, editor. | Cooney, Kathlyn, editor. | Zurek-Doule, Kathy, writer of preface. | Bleiberg, Edward, 1951- honoree.
Title: The afterlives of Egyptian history: reuse and reformulation of objects, places, and texts: a volume in honor of Edward L. Bleiberg / edited by Yekaterina Barbash and Kathlyn M. Cooney; preface by Kathy Zurek-Doule.
Identifiers: LCCN 2020029086 (print) | LCCN 2020029087 (ebook) | ISBN 9781617979927 (hardback) | ISBN 9781649030573 (epub) | ISBN 9781649030580 (pdf)
Subjects: LCSH: Egypt--Antiquities. | LCGFT: Festschriften.
Classification: LCC DT61 .A357 2021 (print) | LCC DT61 (ebook) | DDC 932–dc23

1 2 3 4 5   25 24 23 22 21

Designed by Jon W. Stoy
Printed in the United Kingdom

Contents

Abbreviations   vii
Notes on Contributors   xi
Acknowledgments   xv
Tabula Gratulatoria   xvi
Preface   xvii
Bibliography of Edward L. Bleiberg   xxiii
Exhibitions Organized by Edward L. Bleiberg   xxvii
Introduction   xxix

Section 1. Egyptian Afterlives in the Modern World

1. Egyptian Mummies at the Brooklyn Museum: Changing Attitudes and Perceptions   3
   Lisa Bruno

2. The Survival of Ancient Egypt in Modern Culture: A Never-ending Story   19
   Edmund S. Meltzer

3. The Ancient (Egyptian) Language of the *Children of Dune*   31
   Joachim Friedrich Quack

4. The Montuemhat Crypt in the Mut Temple: A New Look   37
   Richard Fazzini and Mary McKercher

Section 2. Egyptian Afterlives in Antiquity

5. A Visit with the Egyptian Statues of the Alexandria Serapeum and Iseum Campense — 57
   Paul Edmund Stanwick

6. The Various Lives of Statues in the City of the Sun — 77
   Simon Connor

7. Egyptian Stone Vessels Abroad: Reuse and Reconfiguration — 115
   Peter Lacovara

Section 3. Egyptian Afterlives in Pharaonic Egypt

8. A Late Old Kingdom Stela in the Royal Ontario Museum, Toronto (ROM 971.289) — 125
   Ronald J. Leprohon

9. A Case Study of Multiple Coffin Reuse in the National Museum of Scotland, Edinburgh — 143
   Kathlyn M. Cooney

10. A New Version of Book of the Dead 30B: Art Institute Chicago Heart Scarab 1894.1359 — 153
    Emily Teeter

11. The *Ba*-bringer and Other Fun(erary) Texts: pBrooklyn Museum 37.1783E — 165
    Yekaterina Barbash

Abbreviations

ADAIK	Abhandlungen des Deutschen Archäologischen Instituts Kairo
AH	Aegyptiaca Helvetica
AIC	Art Institute of Chicago
AJA	*American Journal of Archaeology*
AMS	accelerated mass spectrometry
AnOr	Analecta Orientalia
ÄOS	Ägyptisch–Orientalische Sammlung
Arachne	iDAI.objects arachne of the German Archaeological Institute (DAI) and the Archaeological Institute of the University of Cologne: https://arachne.dainst.org/
ArchVer	Archäologische Veröffentlichungen
ARCE	American Research Center in Egypt
ASAE	*Annales du Service des antiquités de l'Égypte*
ASE	Archaeological Survey of Egypt
BAR-IS	British Archaeological Reports, International Series
BCE	Before the Common Era
BCH	*Bulletin de correspondance hellénique*
BD	Book of the Dead
BdÉ	Bibliothèque d'Étude
BES	*Bulletin of the Egyptological Seminar*
BH	*Beni Hasan* (Newberry and Griffith) (4 vols.) Archaeological Survey of Egypt 1–2, 5, 7. London: Egypt Exploration Fund, 1893–1900.
BIFAO	*Bulletin de l'Institut français d'archéologie orientale*
BM	British Museum, London

BMMA	*Bulletin of the Metropolitan Museum of Art*
BSAE/ERA	British School of Archaeology in Egypt and Egyptian Research Account
BSEG	*Bulletin de la société d'Égyptologie Genève*
BSFE	*Bulletin de la société française d'égyptologie*
BSRAA	*Bulletin de la société royale d'archéologie d'Alexandrie*
ca.	circa
cat.	catalog
CdÉ	*Chronique d'Égypte*
CE	Common Era
cf.	*confer*, compare
CG	Catalogue général, Egyptian Museum, Cairo
cm(s)	centimeter(s)
col(s).	column(s)
CT	Coffin Texts
CT	computed tomography
diss.	dissertation
EA	*Egyptian Archaeology*
Ebers	*Papyrus Ebers, das hermetische Buch über die Arzneimittel der alten Ägypter* (Ebers) Leipzig: Wilhelm Eigelmann, 1875.
ed(s).	editor(s); edition
EEF	Egypt Exploration Fund
EES	Egypt Exploration Society
EJA	*European Journal of Archaeology*
ELTE	Eötvös Loránd University
ERA	Egyptian Research Account
ff	following
FIFAO	Fouilles de l'Institut français d'archéologie orientale
fig(s).	figure(s)
F.R.S-FNRS	The Fund for Scientific Research-FNRS
GC-MS	gas chromatography-mass spectrometry
GEM	Grand Egyptian Museum
GM	*Göttinger Miszellen*
HAUM	Herzog-Anton-Ulrich-Museum, Braunschweig, Germany
Hearst	*The Hearst Medical Papyrus: Hieratic Text in 17 Facsimile Plates in Collotype, with Introduction and Vocabulary* (Reisner). Leipzig: J.C. Hinrichs, 1905.
IAlexImp	*Recueil des inscriptions grecques et latines (non funéraires) d'Alexandrie impériale* (Kayser)

IFAO	Institut français d'archéologie orientale du Caire
JAEI	*Journal of Ancient Egyptian Interconnections*
JARCE	*Journal of the American Research Center in Egypt*
JAOS	*Journal of the American Oriental Society*
JdE	Journal d'Entrée, Egyptian Museum (Cairo)
JEA	*Journal of Egyptian Archaeology*
JEH	*Journal of Egyptian History*
JEOL	*Jaarbericht van het Vooraziatisch-Egyptisch Genootschap Ex Oriente Lux*
JNES	*Journal of Near Eastern Studies*
JSSEA	*Journal of the Society of the Study of Egyptian Antiquities*
Kmt	*Kmt: A Modern Journal of Ancient Egypt*
LÄ	*Lexikon der Ägyptologie*, 7 vols. (Helck and Otto, eds.) Wiesbaden: Otto Harrassowitz, 1972–92
Lacau, TR	*Textes religieux égyptiens*. P. Lacau. Paris: Honoré Champion, 1910.
LGG	*Lexikon der ägyptischen Götter und Götterbezeichnungen*. 8 vols. (Leitz, ed.), Dudley, MA, Peeters, 2002
m	meter
MÄS	*Münchner Ägyptologische Studien*
MDAIK	*Mitteilungen des Deutschen Archäologischen Instituts, Abteilung Kairo*
MMA	Metropolitan Museum of Art
MMJ	*Metropolitan Museum Journal*
MNR	Museo Nazionale Romano
MonAeg	Monumenta Aegyptiaca
MOM	Maison de l'Orient et de la Méditerranée
MRE	Monographies Reine Élisabeth
n, nn	note(s)
NINO	Nederlands Instituut voor het Nabije Oosten
NM	National Museum (Alexandria)
no(s).	number(s)
NSF	National Science Foundation
NYHS	New-York Historical Society
OBO	Orbis Biblicus et Orientalis
OIM	Oriental Institute Museum
OIP	Oriental Institute Publications
OLA	Orientalia Lovaniensia Analecta

OMRO	*Oudheidkundige mededelingen uit het Rijksmuseum van oudheden te Leiden*
p	papyrus
pl(s).	plate(s)
PM	*Topographical Bibliography of Ancient Egyptian Hieroglyphic Texts, Reliefs, and Paintings* (Porter and Moss)
P.Oxy	Oxyrhynchus Papyri
PSO	Ptah-Sokar-Osiris
PT	Pyramid Texts
RdÉ	*Revue d'Égyptologie*
RICIS	*Recueil des inscriptions concernant les cultes isiaques* (Bricault)
ROM	Royal Ontario Museum
SAK	*Studien zur Altägyptischen Kultur*
SAOC	Studies in Ancient Oriental Civilization
SCA	Supreme Council of Antiquities
SPBD	Saite through Ptolemaic Book of the Dead Studies
TÄB	Tübinger Ägyptologische Beiträge
TbT	Totenbuchtexte
TMO	Travaux de la Maison de l'Orient (Lyon)
TT	Theban Tomb
Urk.	*Urkunden des ägyptischen Altertums*
vol(s).	volume(s)
Wb	*Wörterbuch der ägyptische Sprache* (Erman and Grapow)
ZÄS	*Zeitschrift für Ägyptische Sprache und Altertumskunde*

The bibliographic abbreviations follow standard Egyptological conventions.

Notes on Contributors

Yekaterina Barbash received her PhD in Egyptian art and language from The Johns Hopkins University in 2005. She is currently curator of Egyptian, Classical, and Ancient Near Eastern Art at the Brooklyn Museum, where she has curated and co-curated several exhibitions. Prior to joining the Brooklyn Museum, Barbash taught ancient Egyptian art and Egyptian hieroglyphs. Her research interests include ancient Egyptian religion and philology, with a particular focus on mortuary texts and the Book of the Dead. Her publications include *The Mortuary Papyrus of Padikakem: Walters Art Museum 551*; catalogs of the exhibitions *Divine Felines: Cats of Ancient Egypt*; and *Soulful Creatures: Animal Mummies in Ancient Egypt* (co-authored with E. Bleiberg and L. Bruno).

Lisa Bruno has been a member of the Conservation Department at the Brooklyn Museum since 1993. In 2015, she became the Carol Lee Shen Chief Conservator. She received her master's degree in art conservation from the University of Delaware, Winterthur Museum Art Conservation Department, and specializes in objects conservation. Bruno has served as an adjunct professor at the New York University Institute of Fine Arts and at Pratt University, and has lectured on ancient Egyptian art collections and their research and care. Recent publications in the field of Egyptian art and archaeology include "The Scientific Examination of Animal Mummies," in *Soulful Creatures: Animal Mummies in Ancient Egypt*, and "Revisiting Restorations: The Re-treatment of Three Statues of Metjetji," in *Decorated Surfaces on Ancient Egyptian Objects: Technology, Deterioration, and Conservation*.

Simon Connor received his PhD in history, art, and archaeology at Brussels University in 2014. From 2014 to 2017, he worked as a curator of archaeology at the Museo Egizio in Turin. In 2017, he was awarded an art history fellowship at the Metropolitan Museum. He is currently *chargé de recherches* at The Fund for Scientific Research-FNRS (F.R.S.-FNRS) and the University of Liège. Recent publications include *Le statue del Museo Egizio* (2016), "Sculpture Workshops: Who, Where and for Whom?" in *The Arts of Making in Ancient Egypt* (2018), in *Perspective: actualité en histoire de l'art* (2018), and *Être et paraître: statues royales et privées de la fin du Moyen Empire et de la Deuxième Période Intermédiaire* (2020).

Kathlyn (Kara) Cooney received her PhD in Egyptian art and archaeology from The Johns Hopkins University in 2002. She is currently professor of Egyptian art and architecture and chair of the Department of Near Eastern Languages and Cultures at UCLA. She acted as co-curator of the exhibition *Tutankhamun and the Golden Age of the Pharaohs*, and produced the television series *Out of Egypt* on the Discovery Channel. She has published three books: *The Cost of Death: The Social and Economic Value of Ancient Egyptian Funerary Art*; *The Woman Who Would Be King: Hatshepsut's Rise to Power in Ancient Egypt*; and *When Women Ruled the World: Six Queens of Ancient Egypt*. She is currently working on a book about coffin reuse.

Richard Fazzini joined the Brooklyn Museum as assistant curator of Egyptian art in 1969 and served as the chairman of the Department of Egyptian, Classical, and Ancient Middle Eastern Art from 1983 until his retirement in June 2006. He is now curator emeritus of Egyptian art, but continues to direct the Brooklyn Museum's archaeological expedition to the Precinct of the Goddess Mut at South Karnak, a project he initiated in 1976. Richard was responsible for numerous gallery installations and special exhibitions during his thirty-seven years at the museum. An Egyptologist specializing in art history and religious iconography, he has also developed an abiding interest in the West's ongoing fascination with ancient Egypt, called Egyptomania. Well published, he has lectured widely in the United States and abroad, and served as president of the American Research Center in Egypt (ARCE), America's foremost professional organization for Egyptologists.

Peter Lacovara received his PhD from The Oriental Institute at the University of Chicago in 1993. Currently, he is the director of the Ancient Egyptian Archaeology and Heritage Fund and director of the excavation and restoration of the palace-city of Deir al-Ballas. He was senior curator in ancient Egyptian,

Nubian, and Near Eastern art at the Michael C. Carlos Museum. His collaborative publications include *The World of Ancient Egypt: A Daily Life Encyclopedia*; *Ancient Nubia: African Kingdoms on the Nile*; and *Nubian Gold: Ancient Jewelry from Sudan and Egypt*.

Ronald J. Leprohon received his PhD in Egyptology from the University of Toronto in 1980. He was the first director of the Canadian Institute of Egypt. For well over thirty years, Leprohon has been a professor of Egyptology at the University of Toronto. Recent publications include *The Great Name: Ancient Egyptian Royal Titulary*; "Self-presentation in the Twelfth Dynasty," in *Living Forever: Self-presentation in Ancient Egypt*; "Ideology and Propaganda," in *A Companion to Ancient Egyptian Art*; and "The Royal Titulary in the 18th Dynasty: Change and Continuity," in the *Journal of Egyptian History*.

Mary McKercher holds a BA in Ancient Near Eastern studies, concentrating on Egypt, from the University of Toronto. In 1979, after working for other archaeological expeditions, she joined the Brooklyn Museum's expedition to the precinct of the goddess Mut at South Karnak as photographer and archaeologist, roles she continues to fill. She has contributed to the Mut expedition's "Dig Diary" since it began in 2005, and her photographs have appeared in many publications about the Mut Precinct. With her husband, Richard Fazzini, she has also researched and written about the West's ongoing fascination with ancient Egypt, commonly known as Egyptomania.

Edmund S. Meltzer received his PhD in Near Eastern studies from the University of Toronto. He worked as a site supervisor on the Akhenaten Temple Project–East Karnak Excavation and as an ARCE fellow, and has held teaching positions at the University of North Carolina–Chapel Hill, The Claremont Graduate School, the Institute for the History of Ancient Civilizations in China, and Wisconsin public schools, and is currently at Pacifica Graduate Institute. Meltzer is a board member of the Society for the Study of Egyptian Antiquities based in Toronto, and one of the editors of its journal. His most recent publications include *The Edwin Smith Papyrus: Updated Translation of the Trauma Treatise and Modern Medical Commentaries* with Gonzalo Sanchez, MD; "Granite Statue Fragment Reg. No. HUJI X2 (Third Intermediate Period)," in *The Hebrew University of Jerusalem Archaeological Institute: Highlights of the Egyptian Collection* with Arlette David; and "Sinuhe Yet Again: Sinuhe and Moses," in *Egypt and the Mediterranean World: Studies in Memory of Sally L.D. Katary*.

Joachim Friedrich Quack received his doctorate from Eberhard Karls University in Tübingen in 1993, and his habilitation at the Free University of Berlin in 2003. Since 2005, he has worked as professor of Egyptology at Heidelberg University. In 2003 he received the Heisenberg Scholarship, and in 2011 he received the prestigious Gottfried Wilhelm Leibniz Prize from the German Research Foundation. A prolific writer and researcher, Quack has written *Anthologie der demotischen Literatur* with F. Hoffmann; *The Carlsberg Papyri 11: Demotic Literary Texts from Tebtunis and Beyond* with K. Ryholt; and *Einführung in die altägyptische Literaturgeschichte* III. He has also published over three hundred articles on a wide range of topics in Egyptology.

Paul Edmund Stanwick received his PhD in Egyptian and Roman art history and archaeology in 1999 from New York University's Institute of Fine Arts. He has held positions such as visiting scholar at the Institute of Fine Arts and, more recently, treasurer on the board of governors for ARCE. His publications include *Portraits of the Ptolemies: Greek Kings as Egyptian Pharaohs*; "New Perspectives on the Brooklyn Black Head," in *Offerings to the Discerning Eye: An Egyptological Medley in Honor of Jack A. Josephson*; and "Caracalla and the History of Imperial Sculpture in Egypt," in *The Art and Culture of Ancient Egypt: Studies in Honor of Dorothea Arnold*.

Emily Teeter (PhD, Egyptology) recently retired from the staff of the Oriental Institute Museum at the University of Chicago, where she was the coordinator of special exhibits. She is the editor of the *Journal of the American Research Center in Egypt*, and an Associate of the Oriental Institute. Her publications include *Baked Clay Figurines and Votive Beds from Medinet Habu*; *Scarabs, Scaraboids, Seals and Seal Impressions from Medinet Habu*; and *Religion and Ritual in Ancient Egypt*.

Kathy Zurek-Doule has worked at the Brooklyn Museum's Egyptian Classical and Ancient Near Eastern Art Department for twenty years. She holds a BFA in art history from the University of Illinois at Urbana–Champaign. Zurek-Doule has assisted with at least a dozen exhibitions and accompanying catalogs, including *Jewish Life in Ancient Egypt*; *Divine Felines: Cats in Ancient Egypt*; *To Live Forever: Egyptian Treasures from the Brooklyn Museum*; and *Soulful Creatures: Animal Mummies in Ancient Egypt*. An artist herself, her lifelong interests include artistic materials and processes, and she has research interests in ancient glass and faience production.

Acknowledgments

FIRST OF ALL, WE MUST EXPRESS GRATITUDE to Richard Fazzini for supporting Ed Bleiberg, first as curator of Egyptian, Classical, and Ancient Near Eastern Art at the Brooklyn Museum, and eventually as the deserved head of the department. We are further indebted to Richard and to Mary McKercher for their financial support of this volume, as well as their encouragement and participation. A particular thanks is extended to Mary for her tireless work in editing and formatting the footnotes and bibliographies. Kathy Zurek-Doule has been a tremendous help with the organization of this volume, contributing to it and graciously offering her time in its every step. We are indebted to the administration of the Brooklyn Museum, Brooklyn Museum Libraries and Archives (which include the distinguished Wilbour Library of Egyptology), and to the Brooklyn Museum's Digital Lab. We thank our families for their encouragement, and in particular our husbands/partners and children for bearing with us during the organization and creation of this volume for our dear friend, Ed. Last but not least, we are immensely grateful to the authors for their thoughtful contributions, and to the AUC Press.

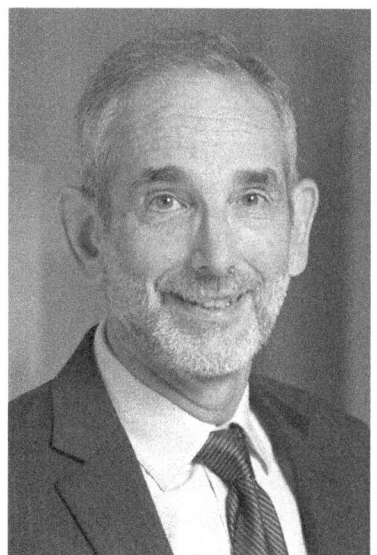

Fig. 0.1. Edward L. Bleiberg, Senior Curator of Egyptian, Classical, and Ancient Near Eastern Art, Brooklyn Museum, 2015. Photograph by Elena Olivo.

Tabula Gratulatoria

Betsy Bryan
Laurent Coulon
Diana Craig Patch
Rita Freed
Tom Hardwick
Salima Ikram
Deirdre Lawrence
James Leggio
Verena Lepper
Ann Russmann
Lisa Sabbahy

Preface

Kathy Zurek-Doule

IN THIS FESTSCHRIFT VOLUME, we celebrate Edward L. Bleiberg and his vibrant career in Egyptology. The occasion of his seventieth birthday gives us the opportunity to highlight his ever-present curiosity for Egyptology, as well as his youthfulness, sense of humanity, open mind, and humor. In addition to Egyptology, Ed has interests in literature, opera, contemporary culture, and current events, all of which have enriched his scholarly and curatorial work.

Ed has taught hundreds of students over the course of his academic career. Aside from his son Perry, in many senses I have been his student the longest; that is, I have benefited from his wise tutelage ever since he hired me as the department assistant for the Egyptian Classical and Ancient Middle Eastern art collections twenty years ago. I have seen Ed through many stages of his career trajectory, and I am elated to be able to contribute to this volume in his honor.

Ed was born in 1951 in the suburbs of Pittsburgh, Pennsylvania, where he attended Mt. Lebanon High School. He received his BA in history and history of religion from Haverford College in 1973. He then ventured off to the University of Toronto, where he received his master's degree in Near Eastern studies in 1977. He stayed on at the University of Toronto to write his dissertation, "Aspects of the Political, Religious, and Economic Basis of Ancient Egyptian Imperialism during the New Kingdom," earning his PhD in 1984. In addition to his studies at Haverford and the University of Toronto, Ed completed some coursework at Yale University and Hebrew University, excavated at Tell al-Amarna, found a short-term home at a kibbutz in Israel, and worked at a cafeteria in Switzerland to refine his German language skills.

Like many recent graduates, Ed moved around quite a bit after he completed his PhD. He lived for a short time with his brother in Baltimore; it was here that he met the love of his life, Betty Leigh Hutcheson, while on a dig. He and Betty Leigh bonded over their shared love of art and archaeology. In January 1986, he relocated to Memphis to work on the *Ramses II: The Great Pharaoh and His Time* exhibition with Rita Freed. The next year, he found work in Washington, D.C. He first took a position, in 1987, at the National Endowment for the Humanities as project director for awards to museums and historical organizations. The following year he worked at the National Endowment for the Arts, as project director for a conservation survey project, and in 1989 he joined the National Endowment for the Arts as project director for a conservation treatment project.

Although he considered his work in Washington, D.C. fulfilling, Ed yearned to work in Egyptology. After a brief stint working for these government agencies, he found his first teaching position as assistant director of the Institute of Egyptian Art and Archaeology at the University of Memphis (1986–89). He and Betty Leigh were married shortly after his appointment. After three years in Memphis, he was promoted to become the director and associate professor of the Institute of Egyptian Art and Archaeology (1989–98).

Their family grew with the arrival of their son Perry (Matthew). Ed often speaks fondly of his summers off with Perry; he and Baby Perry whiled away the days together at the Bard campus in upstate New York while Betty Leigh was doing her summer residencies. When Perry was nearing three years old, the Hutcheson-Bleibergs set off to New York for good, where Ed began his next career as curator.

Ed took a job at the Brooklyn Museum of Art as the associate curator in the Department of Egyptian, Classical, and Ancient Middle Eastern Art—ECAMEA, as it was informally called in-house, and still is by some of the veteran staff members—from 1998 to 2006. Here he worked under Richard Fazzini, the chair of the department, and alongside James F. Romano, Edna R. (Ann) Russmann, Paul F. O'Rourke, and Madeleine Cody.

When Ed came on in 1998, it was an energetic time in the office. Led by Jim Romano, the robust curatorial staff was executing a decade-long project in the making: the reinstallation of the Egyptian galleries. The galleries opened to much celebration and fanfare, but shortly after this came profound heartache as just a few months later we lost Jim to a tragic car accident. This was a huge loss to all of Egyptology but especially to our curatorial team. We speak of Jim often and have since turned his office into a small reference library in his memory.

After Richard retired in 2006, Ed became senior curator and head of the renamed Egyptian, Classical, and Ancient Near Eastern Art (ECANEA) collections. Soon after this, Yekaterina Barbash came on as assistant curator. Ann Russmann retired in 2009. Since then we have been a team of three. Our almost daily "staff meetings" consist of standing around my cubicle where we nosh on ever-present treats, and talk to one another about what we are working on and, these days, agonizing over the world's problems.

Being a curator gave Ed the opportunity to teach on occasion, which he missed doing on a regular basis. He really missed working with students. In 2009, Ed took a position as adjunct professor of history at Brooklyn College, teaching undergraduate coursework in the fall semester. The next year, in 2010, he started as adjunct professor of art history at Hunter College, teaching graduates and undergraduates during the spring semester.

In 2016, after a museum-wide reorganization, Ed's duties grew. He became the managing curator for ancient Egypt, Africa, Asia, and the Islamic world, overseeing the work of five curators specializing in different fields, two curatorial assistants (including myself), a contractual research assistant, one long-time volunteer, a curator emeritus and his research associate (Richard Fazzini and Mary McKercher), and a number of interns.

In the next year, heartache struck our work family again: Paul O'Rourke lost his battle with an aggressive illness. Paul was a very dear friend of Ed's. Their hours-long conversations about Egyptology, music, family, and current events, among many other topics, were really something to behold. He was a positive influence on us all and we miss him dearly. If Paul were alive today he would have at least fifty projects in the works to choose from for Ed's Festschrift, and to the delight of the editors of this volume, he would probably have submitted his manuscript weeks before the deadline.

Ed can boast of many accomplishments as a curator for more than twenty years, but as a humble man, he won't be doing this, so I will do it here for him in his Festschrift.

With a meager acquisitions budget and a storeroom full of wonderful objects, Ed has taken the Brooklyn Museum's famous ancient Egyptian collection and sent it across the globe, creating traveling exhibitions that have gone to nineteen distinct venues nationally, and two internationally, with more to come.

Ed's approach to exhibitions is the same as his approach to teaching. He takes ancient objects and makes them relatable to the contemporary world by identifying commonalities within the realms of society and economy. He enthusiastically teaches people from all walks of life that history is full of life lessons, and he makes history relatable and approachable by adapting his lessons to our current global and national conversations.

He has incorporated his life-long Egyptological interests and non-Egyptological passions into his work as a curator and as a professor. His personal research interests are broad, focusing on how people function within an economy and their various ways of organizing social life. *Jewish Life in Ancient Egypt*, which traveled to five venues, was an exhibition about practicing religious tolerance in a multicultural society and the value of family relationships. It addressed slavery and women's rights. (The catalog of this exhibition, a favorite in the Brooklyn Museum shop, was reprinted twice.) *Tree of Paradise: Jewish Mosaics from the Roman Empire* (2005), which traveled to four venues, shed light on the same Jewish religious minority in a broader global Mediterranean context. The tour-de-force exhibition *To Live Forever: Egyptian Treasures from the Brooklyn Museum* (2008), which traveled to eleven venues, demonstrated that those who were not fortunate enough to purchase golden grave goods, the same people largely ignored by history, also had rich ritual lives and religious practices. *Soulful Creatures: Animal Mummies in Ancient Egypt* (2013), which traveled to three venues, presented religious practices and their influence on the ancient temple and city economy. Most recently, Ed has worked on *Striking Power: Iconoclasm in Ancient Egypt* (2019), which is scheduled to travel to three venues. The exhibition shows how material culture is physically altered when people take back or establish power.

And what is an exhibition without a catalog? In addition to the ever-popular *Jewish Life in Ancient Egypt*, the museum's first catalog using digital photography, the following exhibition catalogs were issued: *Tree of Paradise: Jewish Mosaics from the Roman Empire*; *To Live Forever: Egyptian Treasures from the Brooklyn Museum*; *Soulful Creatures: Animal Mummies in Ancient Egypt* (with Yekaterina Barbash and Lisa Bruno); and *Striking Power: Iconoclasm in Ancient Egypt* (with Stephanie Weissberg).

The same ethos that Ed applied to traveling exhibitions was also evident in the in-house projects on which he worked. The exhibition *Pharaohs, Queens, and Goddesses* explored the richness of women's contributions to ancient thought and human progress. *A Woman's Afterlife: Gender Transformation in Ancient Egypt* highlighted the scholarship of a female Egyptologist, Kathlyn M. Cooney, and explored binary gender fluidity in Egyptian burial practice, showing that everyone, even women, could be reborn like Osiris. This exhibition was a contribution to the "Year of Yes" programming at the Brooklyn Museum, a commemoration of the tenth anniversary of the establishment of the Elizabeth A. Sackler Center for Feminist Art.

In 2016, Ed and Katya (Yekaterina) were tasked with reinstalling the Egyptian galleries with but a six-month turnover time. They used this project to engage with our local and national communities, taking into consideration the real, honest questions that people ask while interacting with the ancient Egyptian collection, and incorporating those questions into the permanent installation. Utilizing the user-generated questions from the Brooklyn Museum's ASK app to frame the Egyptian collection, racial identity and cultural connections were addressed by emphasizing that Egypt is an African country and society, and by incorporating works by the African-American artists Lorraine O'Grady and Fred Wilson into the installation, further engaging the museum's diverse audience on a more personal and equitable level.

Outside of his duties as curator and professor, Ed has worked on countless projects and presentations, some with popular appeal and others far more academic. It isn't every day you see an Egyptologist with an IMDb page: Ed was in the TV documentary "King Tut's Gold" in 2002. The project with the most student "street cred," however, took place at the University of Rochester on 13 April 2016, when Ed presented his lecture "From Scrolls to Screens: 5000 Years of New Media" as part of "New Media and Ancient Worlds: An Evening with Edward Bleiberg and David J. Peterson." Peterson is a language inventor and the creator of the Dothraki and Valyrian languages for HBO's *Game of Thrones*. Outside of museum publications and articles, Ed found time to publish academic texts and textbooks: *The Official Gift in Ancient Egypt* (1996); *Egypt 2625–323 BCE* (World Eras Volume 5) (2002); and *Arts and Humanities in Ancient Egypt* (2004). He has also been a guest in ten video conversations with Dr. Aaron Koller, associate professor of Near Eastern and Jewish Studies at Yeshiva University, on 929.org, a website dedicated to the teachings of the Hebrew Bible, or Tanach, the Book of Books. There, Ed and his former student, Koller, discussed ancient Egypt and the Hebrew Bible through the lens of the Brooklyn Museum's collection.

Ed was not dragged into the digital age kicking and screaming like some people we all know and love. On occasion, he and I walk through how to navigate updates and discuss poorly laid-out user interfaces (SAP Concur, Vena, all things budgetary), but he can hold his own, and was the favorite curatorial guinea pig for experimental technology when the Information Technology Department was run by Shelley Bernstein (who just so happened to be the department assistant before I came on). Ed has published many posts on the Brooklyn Museum's blog, *BKM Tech*, dealing with technology in the Egyptian galleries, as well as scientific testing on the Egyptian collection's human and animal remains. He has contributed widely to the social media content for the museum. He also worked with Katya and the ASK app team to vet the content that gets relayed to the public in the galleries, supplementing information that is displayed on the online object catalog pages.

Ed has been a great leader, mentor, and friend to both Katya and me over the years. People within the museum often compliment our strong working group. The three of us, with Ed leading at the helm, have been able to complete some of the most complicated projects within a six-month lead time: reinstalling a gallery, planning an international exhibition, executing a catalog from start to finish. These are just a few of the challenges Ed and our team have faced together. Try us!

As Ed's longest-running student, I can safely say that I have learned many lessons from him. First and foremost, he has taught me quite a bit about Egyptology. For someone with no formal training, I might be able to discuss the *sḏm.f* verbal forms with those of you who might be interested (I did say "might").

I have also learned a lot of important life lessons while working for him five days a week for the past twenty years. I will leave you with three of them.

Important lesson number one: be dynamic. Ed is a very dynamic lecturer. I can't tell you how many times people have come up to me with wide eyes to express how much they enjoyed Ed's tours. His RateMyProfessors.com ratings also indicate that even the teenagers are impressed.

Important lesson number two: be respectful. Ed sees people and pays attention to them, even to the youngest of people. I have seen him give his undivided attention to small children in a way that would make Mr. Rogers proud. His respect for other people makes him a great leader. He gives everyone credit for their ideas and efforts, he goes out of his way to extend a thank-you publicly as well as privately, and he identifies people's talents and lets people work to their potential.

Important lesson number three: be responsive. Ed responds to current events, in both the classroom and the gallery. People ask, "Why are the noses broken in ancient Egyptian statues?" and he delves right in to come up with thoughtful, well-researched reasons highlighting the significance of monuments past and present, and showing how such a question relates to the contemporary practice of replacing confederate statues in the American South. Ed even developed a course on the topic of iconoclasm in which, even after decades of teaching, he was still impressed by the students' papers.

Writing for Edward Bleiberg's Festschrift has been a great honor; it's the wordy, adult version of RateMyProfessors.com.

Bibliography of Edward L. Bleiberg

1982 "Commodity Exchange in the Annals of Thutmose III." *JSSEA* 11 (1981): 107–10.

———. Review of Percy H. Newby, *The Warrior Pharaohs: The Rise and Fall of the Egyptian Empire*. *Queen's Quarterly* 89, Kingston, ON: The Quarterly Committee of Queen's University, 878.

———. Review of A. Hoyt Hobbs and Joy Adzigian, *A Complete Guide to Egypt and the Archaeological Sites*. *Queen's Quarterly* 89. Kingston, ON: The Quarterly Committee of Queen's University, 877.

1983 "The Location of Pithom and Succoth." In *Egyptological Miscellanies: A Tribute to Professor Ronald J. Williams*, edited by James Hoffmeier and Edmund Meltzer, 21–27. The Ancient World 6. Chicago: Ares Publishers.

———. Review of Maria Theresia Derchain-Urtel, *Synkretismus in Ägyptisches Ikonographie: Die Gottin Tjenennet*. *Religious Studies Review* 9, no. 1: 68.

1984 Review of Karen Wilson, *Cities of the Delta* II. *JAOS* 104, no. 4: 768.

———. "Aspects of the Political, Religious, and Economic Basis of Ancient Egyptian Imperialism during the New Kingdom." PhD diss., University of Toronto. Microform: Ottawa: National Library of Canada.

1985 "The King's Privy Purse during the New Kingdom: A Study of *inw*." *JARCE* 22: 155–67.

1986 "Historical Texts as Political Propaganda." *BES* 7: 1–14.

1988 "Redistributive Economy in New Kingdom Egypt: An Examination of *B3kw(t)*." *JARCE* 25: 157–68.

———. "Thutmose III." In *Great Lives from History: Ancient and Medieval Series* 5, edited by Frank Magill, 2164–67. Pasadena, CA: Salem Press.

1991 Review of Geoffrey Martin, *Corpus of Reliefs from the Memphite Necropolis and Lower Egypt*. *JEA* 77: 219–20.

1993 (With Rita Freed) *Fragments of a Shattered Visage: Proceedings of the International Symposium on Ramesses the Great*. Monographs of the Institute of Egyptian Art and Archaeology 1. Memphis, TN: Memphis State University.

1994 "'Economic Man' and the 'Truly Silent One': Cultural Conditioning and the Economy in Ancient Egypt." *JSSEA* 24: 4–16.

1995 "The Economy of Egypt." In *Civilizations of the Ancient Near East* 3, edited by Jack Sasson et al., 1373–85. New York: Charles Scribner & Sons.

———. "The Pyramids of Giza." In *Oxford Companion to Archaeology*, vol. 2, 2nd ed., edited by Neil Silberman et al., 687–89. New York: Oxford University Press.

———. "Egypt: New Kingdom." In *Oxford Companion to Archaeology*, vol. 1, 2nd ed., edited by Neil Silberman et al., 473–77. New York: Oxford University Press.

1996 *The Official Gift in Ancient Egypt*. Norman: University of Oklahoma Press.

1998 Review of David O'Connor and David P. Silverman (eds.), *Ancient Egyptian Kingship*. Probleme der Ägyptologie 9. *JAOS* 118, no. 2: 286–87.

———. "Taxation and Conscription." In *Encyclopedia of the Archaeology of Ancient Egypt*, edited by Kathryn Bard and Steven Shubert, 761–63. London and New York: Routledge.

2001 Editor, "New Kingdom" and "Late Period." In *The Oxford Encyclopedia of Ancient Egypt*, 3 vols., edited by Donald Redford et al. New York and Oxford: Oxford University Press.

———. "Amenhotpe I," "Prices and Payments," "Storage," and "Thutmose I." In *The Oxford Encyclopedia of Ancient Egypt*, edited by Donald B. Redford et al., 1:71, 3:65–68, 3:327–29, and 3:400–401, resp. New York and Oxford: Oxford University Press.

2002 "Loans, Credit and Interest in Ancient Egypt." In *Debt and Economic Renewal in the Ancient Near East*, edited by Michael Hudson and Marc Van de Mieroop, 257–76. Bethesda, MD: CDL Press.

———. Editor, *Egypt 2615–323 BCE*. World Eras 5. Detroit: Gale Group: Thomson Learning.

———. *Jewish Life in Ancient Egypt: A Family Archive from the Nile Valley*. Brooklyn, NY: Brooklyn Museum of Art.

2004 *Arts and Humanities through the Eras: Ancient Egypt 2675–332* B.C.E. Vol. 1. Detroit: Gale Group.

———. "'East Is East and West Is West': A Note on Coffin Decoration at Asyut." In *Egypt, Israel, and the Ancient Mediterranean World: Studies in Honor of Donald B. Redford*, edited by Gary Knoppers and Antoine Hirsch, 113–20. Leiden and Boston: Brill.

2005 *Tree of Paradise: Jewish Mosaics from the Roman Empire*. Brooklyn, NY: Brooklyn Museum.

2007 "The Coffin of Weretwahset/Bensuipet and 'Scribal Errors' on Women's Funerary Equipment." In *Studies in Memory of James F. Romano*, edited by James Allen. BES 17: 29–46.

———. "State and Private Economy." In *The Egyptian World*, edited by Toby Wilkinson, 175–84. London: Routledge.

2008 "The Puzzling Stela of Userpehtynesu and Panetjer." In *Servant of Mut: Studies in Honor of Richard A. Fazzini*, edited by Sue H. D'Auria, 19–21. Boston: Brill.

———. *To Live Forever: Egyptian Treasures from the Brooklyn Museum*. Brooklyn, NY: Brooklyn Museum in association with D. Giles.

2010 "Re-used or Restored? The Wooden Shabti of Amenemhat in the Brooklyn Museum." In *Offerings to the Discerning Eye: An Egyptological Medley in Honor of Jack A. Josephson*, edited by Sue H. D'Auria, 39–43. Leiden and Boston: Brill.

2012 (With Jennifer Kurishima et al.) "Cats of the Pharaohs: Genetic Comparison of Egyptian Cat Mummies to Their Feline Contemporaries." *Journal of Archaeological Sciences* 39, no. 10: 3217–23. DOI: 10.1016/j.jas.2012.05.005.

2013 (With Yekaterina Barbash and Lisa Bruno) *Soulful Creatures: Animal Mummies in Ancient Egypt*. Brooklyn, NY: Brooklyn Museum in association with D. Giles.

———. "Animal Mummies: The Souls of the Gods." In *Soulful Creatures: Animal Mummies in Ancient Egypt*, edited by Edward Bleiberg, Yekaterina Barbash, and Lisa Bruno, 63–105. Brooklyn, NY: Brooklyn Museum in association with D. Giles.

2015 "Art and Assimilation: The Floor Mosaics from the Synagogue of Hammam Lif." In *Age of Transition: Byzantine Culture in the Islamic World*, edited by Helen C. Evans, 30–37. New York: Metropolitan Museum of Art.

———. "John Garstang's Three Kushite Jewels: How Many Reproductions?" In *Joyful in Thebes: Egyptological Studies in Honor of Betsy M. Bryan*,

	edited by Richard Jasnow and Kathlyn M. Cooney, with the assistance of Katherine E. Davis, 43–48. Atlanta: Lockwood Press.
2016	"Collecting and Exhibiting Late Antique Textiles at the Brooklyn Museum." In *Designing Identity: The Power of Textiles in Late Antiquity*, edited by Thelma K. Thomas, 96–103. New York: Institute for the Study of the Ancient World at New York University; Princeton, NJ: Princeton University Press.
2017	"The Brooklyn Museum Re-installs Its Egyptian Collection. Also at Brooklyn: 'Soulful Creatures' Animal Mummies Exhibit." *Kmt* 28, no. 3: 22–31.
2019	(With Stephanie Weissberg) *Striking Power: Iconoclasm in Ancient Egypt*. St. Louis, MO: Pulitzer Arts Foundation and the Brooklyn Museum.
———	. "What's in a Name? Iconoclasm and Damaged Inscriptions on Egyptian Sculpture." In *Patterns of Identity and Self-Presentation in Ancient Egypt. "The One Perfect in Years Who Has Sustained Minds": Essays in Honour of Ronald J. Leprohon*, edited by Christina Geisen, Jean Li, Steven Shubert, and Kei Yamamoto. Material and Visual Culture of Ancient Egypt. Atlanta: Lockwood Press, forthcoming.

Exhibitions Organized by Edward L. Bleiberg

Jewish Life in Ancient Egypt
15 February 2002–24 October 2004
Brooklyn Museum of Art, Brooklyn, NY, 15 February 2002–12 May 2002
Michael C. Carlos Museum, Emory University, Atlanta, GA, 18 October 2003–4 January 2004
Norton Museum of Art, West Palm Beach, FL, 24 January 2004–11 April 2004
Skirball Cultural Center and Museum, Los Angeles, CA, 30 April 2004–18 July 2004
Memphis Brooks Museum of Art, Memphis, TN, 8 August 2004–24 October 2004

Tree of Paradise: Jewish Mosaics from the Roman Empire
28 October 2005–24 January 2010
Brooklyn Museum, Brooklyn, NY, 16 September 2005–16 July 2006
Dayton Art Institute, Dayton, OH, 21 September 2007–6 January 2008
McMullen Museum of Art, Boston College, Chestnut Hill, MA, 15 February 2008–8 June 2008
Lowe Art Museum, Coral Gables, FL, 31 October 2009–24 January 2010

Pharaohs, Queens, and Goddesses
23 March 2007–16 September 2007
Brooklyn Museum, Brooklyn, NY

To Live Forever: Egyptian Treasures from the Brooklyn Museum
13 July 2008–7 January 2012

Indianapolis Museum of Art, Indianapolis, IN, 13 July 2008–7 September 2008
John and Mable Ringling Museum of Art, Sarasota, FL, 17 October 2008–11 January 2009
Columbus Museum of Art, Columbus, OH, 13 February 2009–7 June 2009
Chrysler Museum of Art, Norfolk, VA, 9 October 2009–3 January 2010
Brooklyn Museum, Brooklyn, NY, 12 February 2010–2 May 2010
Philbrook Museum of Art, Tulsa, OK, 6 June 2010–12 September 2010
San Antonio Museum of Art, San Antonio, TX, 15 October 2010–9 January 2011
Norton Museum of Art, West Palm Beach, FL, 12 February 2011–8 May 2011
Nevada Museum of Art, Reno, NV, 11 June 2011–4 September 2011
Frist Center for the Visual Arts, Nashville, TN, 7 October 2011–8 January 2012
Joslyn Art Museum, Omaha, NE, 10 February 2012–6 May 2012

Soulful Creatures: Animal Mummies in Ancient Egypt
22 March 2014–21 January 2018
Bowers Museum of Cultural Art, Santa Ana, CA, 22 March 2014–15 June 2014
Memphis Brooks Museum of Art, Memphis, TN, 18 October 2014–18 January 2015
Brooklyn Museum, Brooklyn, NY, 29 September 2017–21 January 2018

A Woman's Afterlife: Gender Transformation in Ancient Egypt
15 December 2016–2021
Brooklyn Museum, Brooklyn, NY

Egyptian Treasures from the Brooklyn Museum
1 February–August 2017; future tour dates are being arranged
National Museum of Korea, Seoul, South Korea, 20 December 2016–9 April 2017
Ulsan Museum, Ulsan, South Korea, 1 May 2017–27 August 2017

Striking Power: Iconoclasm in Ancient Egypt
22 March 2019–20 September 2020, co-organized with the Pulitzer Arts Foundation Pulitzer Arts Foundation, St. Louis, MO; future tour dates are being arranged
"World Art Gallery," long-term loan, National Museum of Korea, Seoul, South Korea, 16 December 2019–7 November 2021

Introduction

EGYPTOLOGISTS STUDY TEMPLES, TOMBS, AND CITIES built by the ancient Egyptians, along with the objects that were deposited in these places in antiquity. Most of that activity is focused on one period of time, not many. In other words, the study of the mortuary temple of Medinet Habu generally focuses on the time of its builder, Ramesses III, rather than its afterlives of use and reuse. Egyptological interpretation of structures and objects heavily relies on the understanding of historical situations surrounding their creation and use. Scholars have a natural tendency to flatten and simplify that use to one maker, one time, one purpose, rather than delving into the complicated and rich morass of alternative or even subversive uses. The temple of Medinet Habu was transformed into a church, for example, a subject that does not draw much Egyptological attention because it is perceived to be at odds with the temple's original purpose.

Ancient texts add another dimension. The wide range of texts produced by the ancient Egyptians and their contemporary neighbors sheds more light on the creations of the Egyptians. But again, most Egyptologists deal with the context of a text's creation rather than its afterlife, reuse, and reinterpretation.

It is natural that the intellectual space of Egyptological research, as well as the physical space of the eventual publications, are commonly taken up by the context and meaning of our subjects of study and the circumstances of their production. The religious and cultural trends prevalent at a given time; the social status of the craftsmen, artists, architects, and scribes; and the identity of the owners of buildings and objects when they were first made, are all essential to interpreting objects and texts alike. But the lamentable result of this single-pointed model of scholarship lies in the common omission/ignorance of secondary (and subsequent) lives of our objects of study.

Historical reality is continuous. It extends from a kind of pre-existence (the social context that created the demand for an object or idea to be created in the first place) to the moment of its creation, to its use and reuse (with all of the reinterpretation that these imply), and finally to our encounter with that object or idea today. There are frequently many stops in between. Some structures, images, and practices were reproduced (given another life) as part of movements like archaism, revival, classicism, and canonization. Others were moved, updated, revived, and reinterpreted, having fully lost their original purpose.[1] After the initial function of an object, or pertinence of a notion, had ceased, the object often acquired another life, a kind of afterlife. It is precisely this afterlife—the history of histories—that is the concern of this volume. Egypt has a particular *longue durée*, a continuity of preservation in deep time not seen in other parts of the world. Thus, objects and ideas could not only last but remain in use for millennia, demanding that buildings, objects, texts, and ideas needed to be continuously adapted for novel, alternative, or competitive functions, thereby redefining their purpose and place in a changing society.

After an object changed, or even lost, its original function, its use-life could continue. Such transformations also occurred during antiquity. Indeed, many scholars are currently identifying and addressing reuse and recycling performed by ancient Egyptians to maintain an object or building in their cultural sphere. What were presumed by past scholarship to be one-time objects have now been demonstrated as having been reused many times over. In addition to funerary equipment like coffins and tombs, sculpture and relief have also been shown to acquire new life and purpose soon after the demise of their original owners. Such reuse was applied to royal as well as private things. Materiality is finite and humans are resourceful. Materiality can also be perceived as powerful, and humans often reclaim older things and places for new uses.

Recent scholarship has also demonstrated the adaptation of texts throughout different periods and across textual genres, redefining documents that were previously thought to be strictly distinct to one time and place, and moving their use-lives into much broader contexts. Over the centuries, ancient buildings have been adapted for purposes that differed from the original. Temple sites have been transformed into places of worship for new deities or turned into houses and tombs. Already in the Late Antique, tombs were adapted to function as dwellings for the living. In more recent history, with the advance of colonialism and the ensuing documentation of antiquities and rise in public interest in antiquity, aspects and objects from ancient Egypt have become adopted by modern Western culture with different meanings and use-lives, reinterpreted by visitors to ancient sites and museums, as well as through television, film, and social media. Because appropriation often involves an object's movement from its original context, the question of provenance has emerged as a key puzzle, resulting in scholarship examining the original location and the use-lives of antiquities after they were removed from their original context. The appropriation and reappropriation of places, buildings, objects, and ideas define the rich use-lives of antiquity and shed light on the human tendencies to connect with their social lives through the materiality of objects, places, spaces, and texts.

Bleiberg's recent work develops exactly this avenue of research, as he considers the extensive history of Egyptian sculpture "beyond its original creation and context, through changing cultures and beliefs."[2] His research examines the patterns of purposeful destruction of ancient Egyptian statues, tombs, temples, and mummies in pharaonic and Late Antique Egypt. At the "border between the ancient polytheistic world and their new Christian world,"[3] pharaonic Egyptian creations were often violently and purposefully damaged in very specific ways that prevented a continuance of their original function. Bleiberg identifies the root cause of such drastic violence as the continuity of some beliefs regarding the function of these objects and the simultaneous reinterpretation of other beliefs. In other words, because these objects were still perceived as imbued with power, they had to be drastically altered to change their use-lives. Interestingly, as knowledge of the ancient system of beliefs and hieroglyphic language receded, the targeted destruction also stopped, to be replaced by the repurposing of ancient creations for their material value. Thus, for example, pharaonic buildings and sculpture acquired an entirely different use-life as reused blocks in buildings of Islamic Egypt. Indeed, no loss is ever complete, as the continued power of Egyptian monuments and objects is acknowledged by visitors to archaeological sites and museums today. Tracing the afterlives of ancient objects reveals the social and political trends of each step in the changing course of their history, making for a multiplicity of stories.

The first section of this volume concerns the persistence of ancient Egypt in the most recent times, from the nineteenth century CE until now. It covers the afterlives of Egyptian mummies, stories, concepts, and even language, and includes the interpretations and reinterpretations of archaeological sites. Lisa Bruno looks at the complicated relationship of museums with the mummified remains of the inhabitants of ancient Egypt. As the mummies were taken from tombs and transported across the seas and oceans into museums, they inevitably acquired new and unexpected use-lives. While the ancient Egyptians believed that keeping the memory of the deceased alive was integral to their survival in the afterlife, they surely never condoned the uncovering of carefully treated and wrapped bodies of their ancestors in the presence of the uninitiated. Mummification was developed to provide a resting place for the Egyptian spirits and was intended to last for millennia. And for millennia the mummies lasted, both hindered and assisted by modern intervention. By using the example of mummies housed in the Brooklyn Museum, Bruno traces early attitudes toward human mummies in the West and the shifting social biases and museum practices over time.

Edmund S. Meltzer examines the continuity of ancient Egypt in the present day, and outlines its influence on "high" and "mainstream" expressions of culture. Beginning with the nineteenth century CE, as the field of Egyptology was developing and its lore grew among the public, both writers and composers were inspired to incorporate elements of ancient Egypt into their work. Thanks to the active participation of Egyptologists themselves, Egyptian historical figures, events, and concepts found new use-lives in modern discourse through their manifestations in fantasy, mystery, and historical novels, as well as other media. Meltzer equates this reincarnation of Egyptian language, texts, religion, and visual culture in the past century to the concept of transformations *(ḫpr)* that was central to the Egyptians themselves.

The role of ancient Egypt in modern culture and literature is also pursued by Joachim Friedrich Quack, who directs his attention to its reincarnation in the cult-classic science-fiction novel *Children of Dune* by Frank Herbert. Quack uncovers and identifies the "ancient language" used by the two main characters of this novel as ancient Egyptian. He further pinpoints the origin of the author's description of the ancient language to Sir Alan Gardiner's *Egyptian Grammar*. He goes on to translate the mysterious language, tracing the sources of the novel's dialogue to several ancient Egyptian texts. Although some of Herbert's renderings of Egyptian texts are at times somewhat convoluted, his novel provides some well-known ancient compositions with a new mode of existence in an entirely new context.

The last essay of this section, written by Richard Fazzini and Mary McKercher, is concerned with the multiple lives of an important Egyptian site in antiquity, and the new use-life iterations in recent times as a part of Karnak's tourist world. The current understanding of this monument is a result not only of continual excavation, but also the updating of earlier copies of decoration and the addition of new ones; that is, the continuous work of Egyptologists and the changing conditions of the monument to the present day. This essay also discusses the restoration of the Montuemhat crypt and its surrounding temple, providing a new use-life to the complex and the objects found in it. Finally, their examination of the various lives of the crypt, from a temple treasury storeroom to a funerary chapel, connects this section of the book to the one that follows.

The second section of this book reviews the new use-lives that Egyptian objects acquired through reuse by later, and neighboring, cultures in antiquity. Paul Stanwick traces the many lives of Egyptian statues that were moved, altered, and reinterpreted in Greco-Roman times. He focuses on the Alexandria Serapeum and Iseum Campense in Rome of the imperial era. Covering the spread and adaptation of Serapis and Isis in Alexandria and abroad, Stanwick discusses the modification of Egyptian cults in response to new environments. Objects belonging to these cults largely remained unaltered while serving a new function in a reinvented Egyptian religion. They acquired a new function in Roman temples as objects of great value, helping to elevate the religious practices of Isiac dedicators.

Simon Connor's essay addresses the movement, reinterpretation, and mutilation of Egyptian sculpture from ancient Heliopolis during various phases of history. He places these within historical contexts and considers the ways that such practices might be understood. With a sweeping overview of Heliopolitan sculpture reused in a range of contexts, and found at a variety of sites in recent times, Connor partly reconstructs the sculptural program of ancient Heliopolis. He traces the reuse and movement of early Egyptian monuments to the new royal residences in Tanis. Citing the relative lack of alterations to earlier sculpture transferred from Heliopolis to the public spaces and temples of Alexandria, Connor argues for a cultic and decorative reinterpretation of these works in Greco-Roman times. His discussion of diverse motivations for the transfer and alteration of pharaonic Heliopolitan statues extends to their reuse in the masonry of medieval Cairo.

Peter Lacovara's essay examines the reuse and recycling of stone vessels by Egypt's neighbors in antiquity, as well as the later "interventions" of antiquities dealers. He argues that numerous Old Kingdom vessels, whether intact or fragmentary, were exported to Nubia, as well as to Egypt's neighbors to the north, during the Second Intermediate Period. Lacovara reviews the broad range of afterlives of stone vessels. After the original function of these vessels was abandoned, presumably with the passage of time and change of ritual, some were exported as gifts while others gained entirely new lives as they were transferred to other countries as valuable materials intended to be recycled.

The last section of this book focuses on the various lives that Egyptian objects, texts, and stylistic trends experienced before leaving the lands of Egypt or the pharaonic era. In this section, Ronald J. Leprohon reviews the tangible changes of tradition, image elements, and ritual formulae in Old and Middle

Kingdom Egypt, and utilizes these as criteria that enhance our understanding of objects created during these periods. His essay introduces a hitherto unpublished stela at the Royal Ontario Museum. Leprohon discusses the development of certain aspects of the grid used by craftsmen to lay out the decoration, the offering formula, as well as orthography and style, and determines the date and place of origin of the stela.

Kathlyn M. Cooney presents a coffin housed in the National Museum of Scotland, Edinburgh. This reused object had many use-lives. Possibly beginning from Ramesside or Twenty-first Dynasty origins, the coffin found further use-lives with the body of a mid-Twenty-first Dynasty man; thereafter, for that of a late-Twenty-first Dynasty woman; and after that as the container for a male mummy. When the coffin was modified for gender, artisans changed the fisted masculine hands to flat feminine versions, added earrings and breasts, and changed the names and titles. But such gender modifications were made only on the coffin lid, not the case. The case remained untouched, either because it was known that members of the funerary cortège would direct most of their attention to the lid, the focus of most ritual activity, or because the reusers wanted to connect these two individuals in death, possibly because they were family members. The chapter highlights the opaque nature of coffin reuse, a practice most reusers would have rather kept veiled and undiscussed, leaving current research tapping around in the dark to find possible motivations for certain reuse actions.

Emily Teeter focuses on changes in the life of religious compositions, focusing on Spell 30B of the Book of the Dead. In her essay, Teeter tackles an unusual example of this spell inscribed on a heart scarab at the Art Institute of Chicago. Her translation and discussion of the peculiarities of the text demonstrate the agency of both the object's artisan and commissioner within a meandering context of the constant redefinition of religious ideas and texts.

Yekaterina Barbash presents the first publication of an unusual mortuary manuscript from the Ptolemaic Period housed in the Brooklyn Museum. The peculiar selection of texts and challenging orthography are the result of the changing linguistic and religious practices of their time. While many of the texts in this composition are unique or rare, they all closely relate to the mortuary traditions that were initially recorded in the Old Kingdom. Barbash highlights the religious beliefs and textual sources that either survived or were revived and revised in order to serve the changing tastes of the Egyptians of later periods.

Notes

1. The fascinating *(Re)productive Traditions in Ancient Egypt: Proceedings of the Conference held at the University of Liège, 6th–8th February 2013*, edited by Todd Gillen (Aegyptiaca Leodiensia 10, Liège, Belgium: Presses Universitaires de Liège, 2017), offers a selection of very pertinent essays discussing the apprehensible changes in both productive traditions that stand in "dialectic relation to shifting social and historical circumstances," and the closed reproductive traditions that are meant to be passed down with precision but nevertheless fall under the influence of contemporary trends.
2. Edward L. Bleiberg and Stephanie Weissberg, *Striking Power: Iconoclasm in Ancient Egypt* (St. Louis, MO: Pulitzer Arts Foundation and the Brooklyn Museum, 2019), 27.
3. Bleiberg and Weissberg, *Striking Power*, 60.

1 Egyptian Afterlives in the Modern World

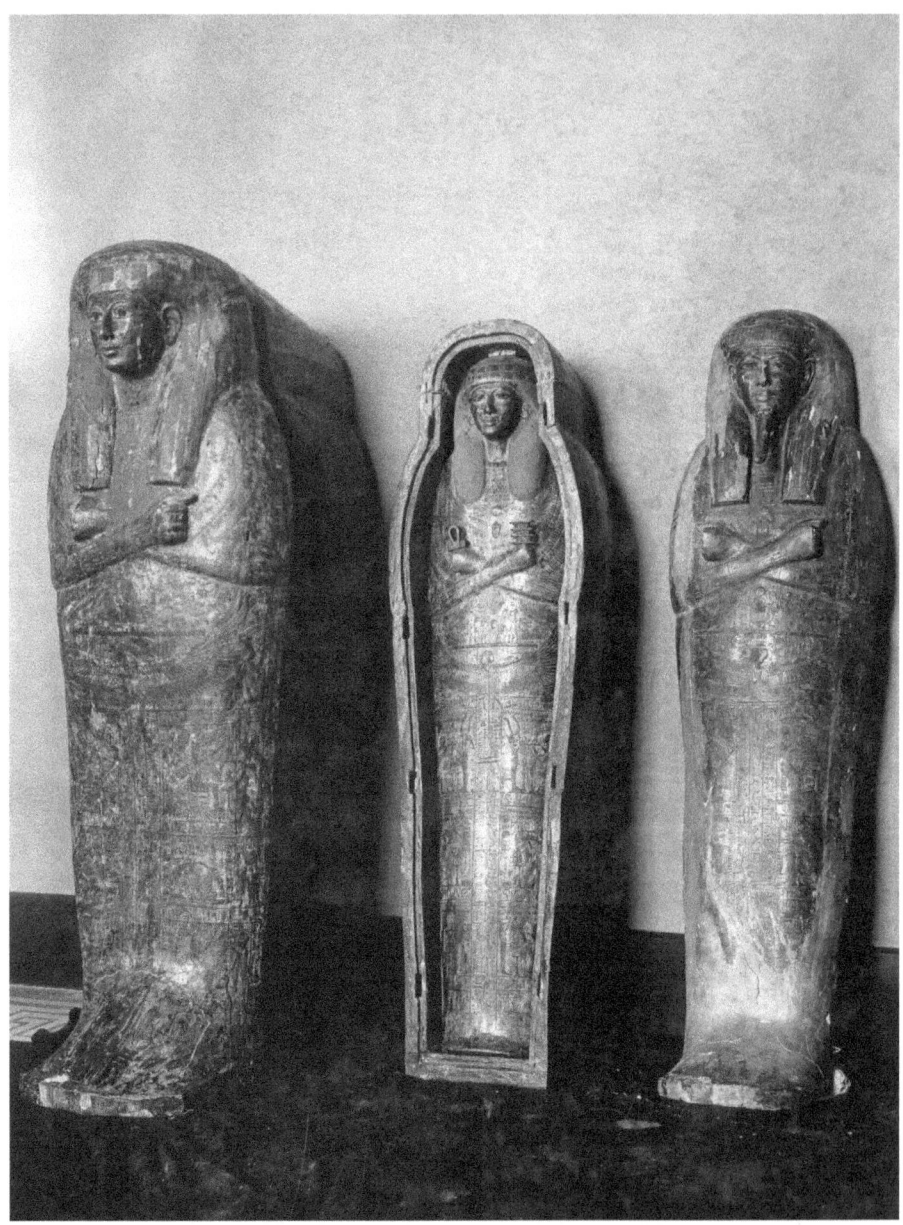

Fig. 1.1. Outer sarcophagus, coffin, and mummy board of the royal prince, count of Thebes, Pa-seba-khai-en-ipet, ca. 1075–945 BCE; wood (cedar and acacia), gesso, pigment; outer sarcophagus: 94 x 76.8 x 211.8 cm (37 x 30 1/4 x 83 3/8 in); coffin: 32 x 55 x 194 cm (12 5/8 x 21 5/8 x 76 3/8 in). Brooklyn Museum, Charles Edwin Wilbour Fund, 08.480.1a–b and 08.480.2a–c. Photograph courtesy of the Brooklyn Museum.

1 Egyptian Mummies at the Brooklyn Museum: Changing Attitudes and Perceptions

Lisa Bruno

THE BROOKLYN MUSEUM HAS COLLECTED OBJECTS from ancient Egypt since the early twentieth century.[1] An early acquisition of a complete human mummy was almost an unintended accident.[2] In 1908, the museum acquired the private collection of Armand de Potter. This was an early private collection built during the 1880s and 1890s. Included in the collection was a spectacular Twenty-first Dynasty sarcophagus consisting of an outer coffin (08.480.1ab), an inner coffin with a mummy board (08.480.2a–c), and the mummy of a man named Pa-seba-khai-en-ipet (08.480.2d). This was most certainly the coffin of an individual of some stature and note. He held the titles of royal prince and count of Thebes. An early glass-plate negative taken to record the new acquisition shows all components of the sarcophagus ensemble except one: the mummy itself (fig. 1.1).

While the sarcophagus was celebrated as an important work of art, the mummy was not. So it began, the complicated and at times ambivalent relationship that the Brooklyn Museum, along with many institutions, has had with ancient Egyptian mummies. They are what the general public first thinks of when discussing ancient Egyptian art and yet, while beautiful and often exhibiting the great deftness and skill of ancient artists and craftsmen, the mummies are not art objects. They are the remains of human beings.

The Brooklyn Museum and the curators of the arts of Egypt, starting with Dr. John Cooney and continuing with Dr. Edward Bleiberg, set the tone for care of the collections. Like any curator responsible for a collection, they are influenced by the prevailing attitudes of the time, as well as by colleagues in allied professions such as conservators. This chapter will outline some of the early perceptions and attitudes toward human mummies as illustrated by what happened to them, and how these practices changed over time as biases shifted and perceptions widened. In looking at the historic records at the museum, the physical mummy itself was not often valued beyond its artistic merit. This attitude was commonplace among the staff of art museums established in the nineteenth century. While natural history and university museums often did have an interest in the mummified remains, the mummies were merely looked at as specimens to be examined, sampled, and autopsied.[3]

The Brooklyn Museum has eight human mummies and several body parts, including severed heads, hands, and feet. The oldest of the museum's mummies is Pa-seba-khai-en-ipet (08.480.2d), with a date range of 1188–909 BCE. The most recent mummy is that of an anonymous man (52.128a–e) that dates from 244–419 CE.[4] There is a rare Roman Period red-shroud mummy known as Demetrios (11.600a–b) that dates from 50–100 CE.[5] A Late Period (791–418 BCE) mummy wrapped in crossed linen is named Thothirdes (37.1521Ec).[6] Another male mummy (37.14Ec–e) is not a mummy at all but rather skeletal remains, due to the history of its embalmment and circumstances. There are two mummies in the collection encased in cartonnage from the Third Intermediate Period, and the last is a partial mummy (37.47E) from 993–812 BCE.[7] Of the eight mummies, two were unwrapped, with one suffering damage beyond treatment at the time of this writing. Two suffered general neglect and two were subject to physical damage, while two remained undisturbed and intact.

While the mummy of Pa-seba-khai-en-ipet was accessioned at the time of acquisition by the museum in 1908, it was not fully cataloged.[8] Because its status was undefined as an associated but unrecognized component of the accessioned artwork, including the coffins and mummy board, it meant that there were no procedures or protocols in place for how to care for or study this mummy. This eventually led to its unwrapping by a curatorial researcher in the 1970s. Other mummies in the collection, including Demetrios, with its realistically painted portrait mask, and the Roman Period mummy of an anonymous man, with a painted plaster portrait mask that has a three-dimensional molded crown, were both separated from their face masks. The masks were displayed without an acknowledgment of their direct relationship to death and mummification because they were displayed without the mummified humans they were made for. The mummy of Thothirdes entered the Brooklyn Museum's collection by way of the New-York Historical Society (NYHS) from the early collection formed by Dr. Henry Abbott. Thothirdes arrived with a beautiful polychrome Late Period, Twenty-sixth Dynasty (ca.

664–525 BCE) coffin painted on both the interior and exterior. When the mummy of Thothirdes and, more importantly, his coffin, went on display in the newly constructed Egyptian galleries designed by Arata Isozaki in the early 1990s, the coffin was stabilized and treated but the mummy was not. The mummy's linen wrappings were exhibited in slight disarray for nearly twenty years until being conserved in 2010.[9]

The fact that mummies were considered peripheral or incidental to the decorative and artistic objects associated with them allowed them to be subject to at least indifference and at most violation and abuse. This lack of reverence was not unique to our contemporary Western society. The ancient Egyptians themselves practiced tomb robbing and creative reuse of coffins. This reuse is perfectly evidenced by the reinscription of an early Nineteenth Dynasty coffin of the Lady of the House, Weretwahset (37.47E), in the museum's collection.[10] The coffin was reinscribed and presumably reused for the Lady of the House, Chantress of Amun, Bensuipet, in the Twentieth or Twenty-first Dynasty.[11] When the coffin was examined by the Conservation Department in 2006, a pair of legs, tightly wrapped together with numerous layers of brown, now brittle, linen, was found. The legs were broken at about mid-femur and do not appear to have been cut. Before treatment of this coffin and the inner cartonnage, the fragment of the mummy was not properly titled. In 2008, Dr. Bleiberg submitted a title change: "Mummy of Bensuipet." While it is impossible to say for certain if this mummy fragment is in fact Bensuipet, a C14 (radiocarbon) test done on a linen sample indicated that it dates to between 993 and 812 BCE, which does put it within the Twenty-first Dynasty or the period of the second occupant of the coffin.[12]

Once the rediscovery of ancient Egypt took hold of the hearts and minds of Western audiences in the nineteenth century, and even into the early twentieth century, the public unwrapping of mummies became a popular activity at parlor parties and scientific societies. The museum has in its collection one mummy that suffered this fate, albeit before it was acquired by the museum. What is now titled "Contents of the Coffin of the Servant of the Great Place, Teti (37.14Ec-e)" is the completely disassociated skeletal remains and associated mummy wrappings, including linen, soil, plants, and the ring of an unknown man. Based on its style, the anthropoid coffin dates to the New Kingdom, mid- to late Eighteenth Dynasty (ca. 1339–1307 BCE). The coffin and its contents were collected in 1848 by Dr. Henry Anderson and given to the NYHS.[13] According to Dr. Anderson's notes, he discovered the mummy "in the house of a peasant on the bank of the Nile, opposite Thebes."[14] An X-radiograph of the sealed coffin was taken in 1937 upon coming into the museum's collection from the NYHS. The catalog record at the time noted of the mummy: "This is now nothing more than a very incomplete skeleton hopelessly mixed with the linen bandages. Several rather fine large towels were noticed among the wrappings." It should be noted that while the cataloger appears to have been somewhat disgusted with the mummy, he or she was complimentary about the "fine," large linen sheets.[15]

Minutes from the NYHS describe a public unwrapping of an ancient Egyptian mummy. On 15 December 1864, the *Evening Post* reported on the final lecture of a course given by the NYHS on the Egyptian mummy. One thousand people attended the event held at the Cooper Union in New York City.[16] In the account, the "unrolling" was performed by Dr. Weiss, a demonstrator of anatomy at Columbia University. The linens were soft and pliable, but what Dr. Weiss revealed through the unwrapping was not an intact, well-preserved human. A skeleton was found with a few ligaments, muscles, and some skin. Not much for the anatomist to demonstrate on. It is likely that this is what happened to the contents of the coffin of Teti.

After the mummy of Teti entered the museum's collection and was cataloged, the first conservation record was not until 1988. The brief report indicated that the coffin was in extensive need of examination and treatment due to structural instability.[17] The coffin and subsequently the skeletal remains inside were examined and conserved, starting in 2001.[18] The coffin was in a dire state of preservation, and it took several years to complete the treatment.[19] The skeletal remains were in much worse shape. As part of the treatment of the coffin, the carelessly discarded contents found within the coffin were systematically removed, sorted, and rehoused. To assist with this process, the museum invited Dr. David Minnenberg, emeritus director of pediatric urology at New York-Presbyterian Hospital,[20] and Dr. Pam Crabtree, professor of anthropology at New York University, to work with conservation staff. From the report provided by Dr. Minnenberg, dated 11 December 2001, "The bones of Tet(i) were quite well preserved, but were devoid of any soft tissue." The skeletal remains were estimated to be of a male, 5'4" (163 cm) and approximately 40±5 years of age upon his death. While no definitive evidence is stated in the report, it was surmised by Dr. Crabtree at the time that the bones may have been boiled to clean them of remnants of flesh.[21] The skeletal remains were reordered and packed with their linens in an archival housing. Further testing was done on the linens in 2009. A five-milligram sample was sent to the NSF AMS Laboratory at the University of Arizona for radiocarbon dating. The C14 results showed 95 percent of the data points being within the 997–821 BCE range, which is significantly later than the date given to the coffin.[22] This makes one wonder: to whom do the skeletal remains belong? Based on style, the coffin is firmly dated to the Eighteenth Dynasty, and the inscriptions[23] name the occupant as Teti, a tomb painter and "Servant of the Great Palace."[24] The materials used in the construction of the coffin are of high quality and include pistacia resin as the varnish.[25] Bleiberg wrote of the coffin and its occupant, "He paid nearly a year's salary for a coffin of this quality."[26] It is logical to presume that Teti's mummy would have been preserved with the highest quality materials in a manner indicative of thorough embalming. This would mean complete evisceration of the brain and interior of the torso before replacing organs wrapped or encased in linens and filling the interior of the body with resin. It would be unlikely that a mummy of such quality would have been in such a poor state of deterioration when unwrapped in 1864 as part of a lecture on mummification. As mummies were often switched or added to a coffin to increase the sale value during the nineteenth century, we will likely never know who this forty-year-old man, now cataloged as the contents of the coffin of Teti, once was.

While the intervention with the coffin set of Weretwahset and Bensuipet happened in Egypt, and while that of the unknown man in Teti's coffin happened before it arrived in Brooklyn, the mummies in the Brooklyn Museum's collection were certainly not spared at least some degree of intervention and indignity. The only two mummies in the collection to be spared neglect or intervention were those safely encased within sealed cartonnage cases. These include the cartonnage and mummy of Gautseshenu (34.1223)[27] and the cartonnage and mummy of the Priest, Hor (37.50E), both from the Third Intermediate Period.[28] Both cartonnage cases are elaborate, exquisitely constructed and crafted objects. Given that the cartonnage cases constructed from layers of linen and plaster are sturdy and beautifully painted with rich textures and pigments, the preservation of the mummy was likely secondary to the preservation of the sealed cartonnage. Even though the mummies remain undisturbed within their cartonnages, radiography, specifically computed tomography, or CT scanning, can reveal a wealth of information without the need to unwrap or disturb the mummy packages. Both mummies were scanned at North Shore University Hospital.[29] Gautseshenu has false eyes, and canopic packages, as well as uncontained viscera and models of the four sons of Horus inserted into her torso.[30] The main thing of note in regard to the mummy of Hor is that it had been cataloged as female before the CT scans.[31] This mummy was clearly found to be male after the scanning.[32] The mummy has a skull cavity filled with resin, and an interior torso filled with resin and desiccated viscera wrapped in resin-soaked linens, forming canopic packages.[33]

The first mummy to be unwrapped at the museum was that of the Roman Period anonymous man (52.128a-e), which lacked the complete encasement of the Third Intermediate Period style of mummy bundle. The mummy had been excavated by the Metropolitan Museum of Art during the 1928–29 excavation season at Deir al-Bahari.[34] The mummy was brought to New York in 1930 and sold to the Brooklyn Museum in 1952, presumably so that the curator at the time, Dr. John Cooney, could round out the Roman portion of the museum's Egyptian collection. While there was a conservation department at the museum, starting in 1934 with the appointment of paintings conservator Sheldon Keck, the focus was primarily on the examination and treatment of the paintings collection. The curatorial departments each had technicians who did a variety of activities for the curators such as art handling and installation, as well as conservation and cleaning. In the 1950s, the Egyptian Department had a very conscientious technician, Anthony Giambalvo, who performed several carefully done and well-documented treatments to unroll papyrus bundles.[35] In 1956, the curator directed his technician to remove the mummy mask and mount it on a linen-covered board for display, and unwrap the mummy. Cooney was curating an exhibition called *Five Years of Collecting Egyptian Art*[36] and wanted to use the face mask (without the mummy) for display.[37] While there are no written records or photographs describing or documenting the unwrapping, great care was clearly taken. After the painted mask and wood and fiber necklace were released[38] and removed, a single cut up the center of the outer wrapping revealed the inner layers of large linen sheets, sometimes cinched closer to the body with linen ties. Fifteen layers of linen, including two simple tunics, were carefully peeled away to reveal the mummified man. On 10 September 1957, the curator told the technician to throw the now-stripped mummy into the incinerator.[39] Giambalvo refused, based on his religious beliefs as a Roman Catholic. On 13 September 1957, the story landed on the front page of the *New York Times*.[40] The museum's anonymous man was pictured fully wrapped, with a caption that read: "This is the mummy of a man who died about 300 AD. Brooklyn Museum acquired it some years ago for its wrappings." The article goes on to ask how a museum in New York in 1957 could literally dispose of a body of an ancient man, but by then the desire to dispose of the body seems to have dissipated.[41]

Pa-seba-khai-en-ipet was unwrapped after both Dr. Cooney and Anthony Giambalvo had retired. Dr. Bernard Bothmer had become curator in 1963 after arriving as assistant curator in 1956. Pa-seba-khai-en-ipet was unwrapped at some point in the late 1960s or early 1970s. Before the unwrapping, the undated catalog card indicated that the mummy may have suffered an invasion of rodents.[42] There is no record of the unwrapping in the museum's files, but the unwrapping is described in a book by Mildred Mastin Pace, ironically entitled *Wrapped for Eternity* (1974).[43] Additionally, there is no record of the discussion or of the decision-making process in the curatorial, conservation, registrars, or archival files that gives any explanation as to why a researcher in the Egyptian Department was essentially allowed to tear apart a mummy.[44] The first memo that mentions the unwrapping is dated 1977. The memo, from curator Dr. Robert Bianchi to the Office of the Registrar, noted that "Kenneth Linsner unwrapped the mummy some time ago and during the process 2 earrings were removed and were floating around without numbers."[45] Note that this concern for the two earrings is not that dissimilar from the note from the 1930s that "fine large towels" were among the contents of Teti's mummy.

It wasn't only the curators who neglected to think of the mummies as humans, or at the very least complete entities unto themselves. The conservators in these early years also had a narrow-minded focus on only the artistic components of a mummy. Specifically, the Faiyum portrait of Demetrios was considered to be too fragile to remain attached to his mummy (fig. 1.2).

The wood onto which the portrait of this handsome gray-haired man with a hooked nose was painted is very thin, at 0.16 cm. The mummy had been excavated from Hawara in 1910 by the British School of Archaeology before being collected by the Brooklyn Museum in 1911.[46] Early photos of the complete mummy bundle show that the wood panel is cracked down the center. The mummy sat in its shipping crate from 1911 until it was rediscovered in a fifth-floor storage room in 1937. At that time it was felt that the portrait was in dire need of treatment. The portrait panel was removed from the mummy, in order to stabilize it, and it immediately changed shape, becoming "dished like a saucer."[47]

The treatment that transpired can only be described as highly interventive, and specifically focused on treating and stabilizing the panel painting as a work of art. Original resinous materials on the back of the panel which were used to attach the portrait to the mummy bundle were mechanically scraped off and not saved.[48] Since the portrait was painted in encaustic, the back of the portrait was coated in a thick layer of wax; it was thought that this might help stabilize the movement of the wood panel.[49] The face of the portrait was additionally varnished with "Rosin's mixture," probably a mixture of beeswax and rosin (a pine resin), making later analysis of the original materials compromised, if not highly problematic.[50] It is as if the conservators, and likely the curators, wanted to present the panel as a work of art akin to a finished Renaissance panel portrait.

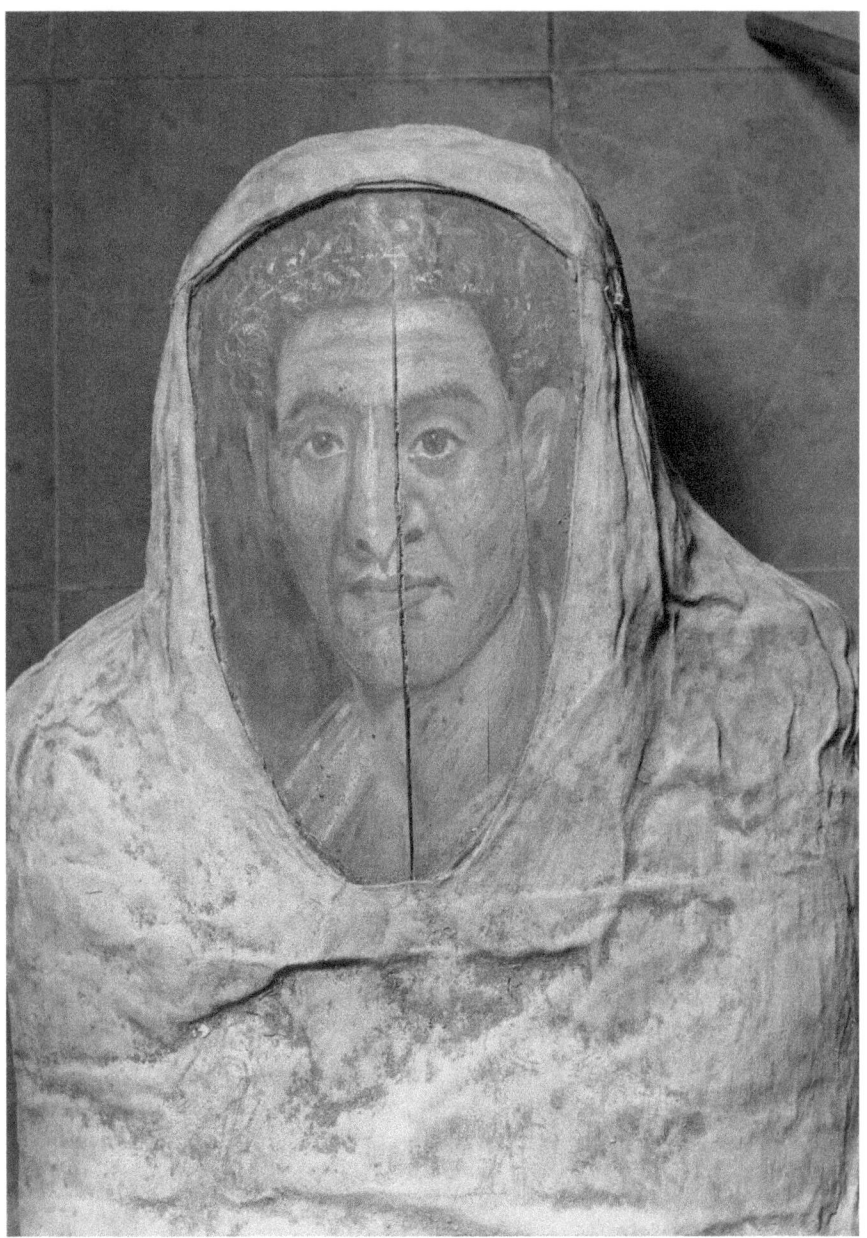

Fig. 1.2. Early black and white photograph of the portrait mask before removal. *Portrait of Demetrios*, from Hawara, Egypt, Roman Period, 95–100 CE, encaustic on wood panel: 37.3 x 20.5 x 0.2 cm (14 11/16 x 8 1/16 x 1/16 in). Brooklyn Museum, Charles Edwin Wilbour Fund, 11.600. Photograph courtesy of the Brooklyn Museum.

The wood remained unstable and mobile, while the mummy remained on the shelf. As early as 1967, conservators were considering making microclimates for the Faiyum portraits. An early attempt to create a microclimate was done on this and other Faiyum portraits that had arrived at the museum without their mummies. In 1971, Dr. Nathan Stolow, a conservation scientist from the National Conservation Research Laboratory at the National Gallery of Canada in Ottawa, constructed microclimate cases to protect the panels against changes in relative humidity (%RH).[51] Demetrios' portrait was kept in a microclimate, separated from his body, until 2008.

So why, after ninety-seven years, did the museum decide to return Demetrios's face to his mummy? In 2002, the Getty Museum started a research project centered around its red-shroud mummy, Herakleides.[52] With this project, the museum looked at a large portion of the surviving red-shroud mummies to compare materials used in construction. The findings showed definite similarities and pointed to an innovative use of waste products from silver mining production in southern Spain during the Roman Empire.[53] The other thing it showed was that of all the red-shroud mummies studied, that of Demetrios was the only one missing its face. At about the same time, Dr. Bleiberg began curating the exhibition *To Live Forever: Egyptian Treasures from the Brooklyn Museum*.[54] This exhibition explored the ancient Egyptians' thoughts of the afterlife and the practicality of getting there, no matter what one's economic status. For this exhibition, which traveled to eleven venues, Demetrios's face was finally reunited with his body and the conservation records from paintings and objects sections were combined into one.[55]

With the success of the exhibition *To Live Forever*, there was a newfound interest in the museum's mummies. Dr. Bleiberg helped allocate resources to study all the museum's mummies, including the approximately one hundred animal mummies in the collection. The study started with a project to sample and analyze the materials used in mummification for identification, specifically looking for links between mummification practices used on humans and animals, and to see how practices might have changed over time. Graduate student Lucy Cramp, working with Dr. Richard Evershed at the University of Bristol, sampled the Brooklyn Museum's entire collection and used gas chromatography mass spectrometry (GC–MS) for an initial identification.[56] Following the resin sampling, both the human and animal mummies were CT scanned.[57] This opportunity to promote scholarly study of these collection objects expanded the stories the museum could tell in a museum display. With these new directions, planning for an update of the museum's Egyptian galleries to include a room specifically addressing mummification was set in motion.⁵⁸ The question of whether or not anything could be done for the unwrapped mummies was raised early in the planning process.

The museum's oldest and highest-status mummy, Pa-seba-khai-en-ipet, with its spectacularly decorated inner coffin and outer coffin, was an obvious candidate for display, if only the mummy had not been interfered with. The researcher Robert Loynes, in his 2014 analysis of the CT scans, revealed that the level of mummification had been very involved. The brain had been completely removed and linen and other radio-opaque material were found in the skull. The eyes were removed and the sockets packed with linen and radio-opaque material. A hollow reed or stick had been inserted into the throat, likely as a device to hold the neck in place or aid in delivery of resin to the torso. The heart was found in the torso, along with amulets of the four sons of Horus: Hapi (ape), Duamutef (jackal), Qebehsenuef (falcon), and Imseti (human).⁵⁹ The CT scans were spectacular, but the mummy, in its current state of preservation, was not. Putting Pa-seba-khai-en-ipet on display covered with a sheer piece of linen was discussed,⁶⁰ but it was decided that this would be more like putting a corpse on display than a mummy.⁶¹

Happily, the mummy of the anonymous man proved a far better candidate for conservation treatment. Given that the mummification dated to later Egyptian periods and thus did not involve layers of resin-saturated linens, nor the numerous small strips of bandages, but instead large sheets,⁶² it was felt that the mummy could in fact be rewrapped. Because of the systematic approach and great care taken in the unwrapping, all layers were present in practically the same order that they were removed. Each layer was documented with photos, overall and details. Thread counts and descriptions of the linen sheets were made in the conservation report. Samples of the hair and linen were saved from the mummy bundle for possible analysis at a later date. A resin sample taken from the mummy's proper right big toe was found to contain *Brassicaceae*, also known as radish oil.⁶³ C14 was done on the linens and they were found to date to 244–419 CE, placing the mummy at the latter half of the Roman Period in Egypt.⁶⁴ The mummy had been placed on a thin board before wrapping, not unlike the board found within the mummy bundle of Demetrios, as seen in the CT scan.⁶⁵ Before rewrapping the mummy, a sample of the anonymous man's board was identified as *Ficus sycomorus*, which is native to Egypt (fig. 1.3).⁶⁶

The experience of rewrapping these human remains to turn them back into a mummy was a most profound one for all involved. Once objects are accepted into a museum's collection, especially sacred objects and human remains, the institution has a responsibility to care for them to the best of its ability. While

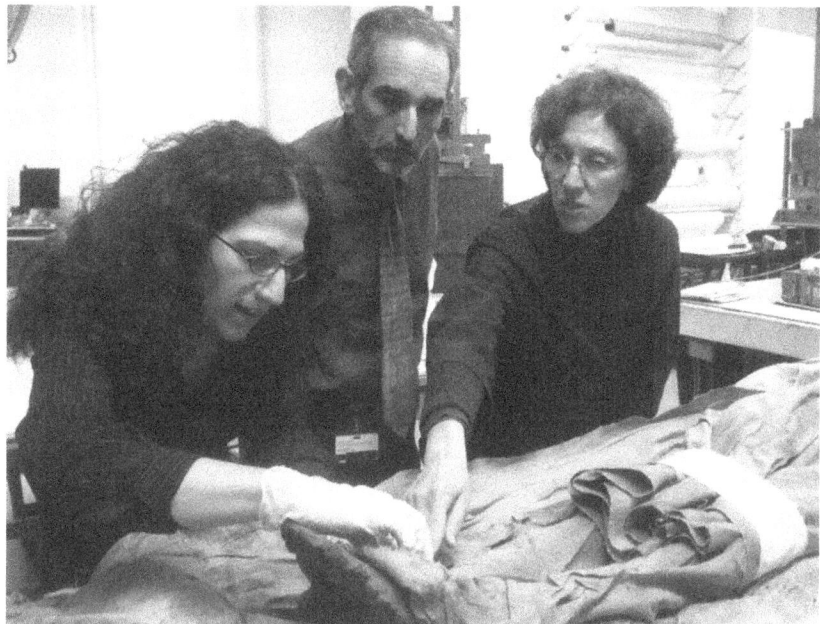

Fig. 1.3. Bruno, Bleiberg, and textile conservator Kathy Francis during the rewrapping of an anonymous man. *Cartonnage and Mummy of an Anonymous Man*, third century CE, human remains, wood (*Ficus sycomorus*, sycamore fig), grass, linen, plaster, pigment: 33.7 × 90 cm (13 1/4 × 35 7/16 in). Brooklyn Museum, Charles Edwin Wilbour Fund, 52.128a–e.

it is impossible to guarantee that all decisions will be considered the right choice in the future, it is only through discussions and careful thought with the various teams involved that an institution can make the best decisions possible. Finally, at least for now, the Brooklyn Museum has a supportive system of communication that at least ensures that all points of view are considered and recorded, especially when dealing with some of the more vulnerable members of the collection, the ancient Egyptian mummies.

Notes

1 Although cast plaster copies of statues and Roman glass vessels were part of the initial collection, the first ancient Egyptian object collected as a gift from the Egypt Exploration Fund appears to have been an unassuming terra cotta fragment of a female figure kissing an animal, thought to be of the Hellenistic Period (Brooklyn Museum 02.126).
2 Forty-one mummies or skeletal remains were received by the museum before 1936 but none was accessioned. One mummy was received from Rev. W.R. Ferris in 1901; four were excavated from Mamariya in 1907 and acquired from Henri de Morgan; and

thirty-six came from excavations by the Egypt Exploration Fund (EEF) at Sawama by Thomas Whittemore and Gerald Avery Wainwright in 1913–14. None of the mummies remain in the museum, although the objects found with them do.

3   The museum's initial incarnation, as The Brooklyn Institute of Arts and Sciences, included Natural History. Some of the early collected skeletal remains were in fact used in scientific experiments. See Candela, "Blood Group Reactions," 429–32.

4   The dates for both these mummies are based on C14 analysis done of samples from their linens. Testing was done at the National Science Foundation (NSF) Accelerated Mass Spectrometry (AMS) Laboratory at the University of Arizona. Testing for both samples was done in 2008–2009. See conservation files for reports.

5   C14 samples done on two samples of linen, one coarse and one fine, from the foot wrapping of Demetrios were taken by Dr. Marc Walton in 2007 and analyzed by Dr. Greg Hodgins at the NSF AMS facility.

6   Thothirdes' linens were sampled for C14 dating in 2009 and sent to the NSF AMS facility in Arizona.

7   The mummy of Bensuipet is not scientifically confirmed as being female, but the inscriptions on the coffin reference a woman. See conservation file.

8   Romano, "de Potter Collection," 702–706. Dr. Edward L. Bleiberg cataloged and made a separate entry in the museum database in 2000 during preparation for a gallery renovation, "The Mummy Chamber."

9   For details of the treatment, see the conservation report 37.1521Ec by textile conservator Kathy Francis, 3/29/2010.

10 Bleiberg, *To Live Forever*, 136–38.

11 For details on the examination and treatment of the coffin see Kariya, Bruno, Godfrey, and March, "Treatment of a Dynasty 18 Painted Coffin." For the inscriptions, see Bleiberg, "Coffin of Weretwahset/Bensuipet."

12 A five-milligram linen sample from the legs of the wrapped mummy was taken and sent for C14 analysis to the NSF AMS Laboratory at the University of Arizona. The sample was processed following standard protocols of washing with various organic solvents. See the report in the Brooklyn Museum conservation file.

13 A large portion of the Brooklyn Museum's Egyptian collection came through the purchase of the NYHS collection. See Fazzini et al., *Ancient Egyptian Art*. The acquisition of Teti's coffin is further discussed in Dodson and Raver, "Dr. Anderson's Mummy."

14 See curatorial file for catalog notation.

15 See Brooklyn Museum Curatorial File 37.14Ec–e.

16 At the time of the event, the NYHS was located on Second Avenue, just blocks from the Cooper Union.

17 See Brooklyn Museum conservation file for the report of 5/1988 by JC (Jane Carpenter).

18 See Brooklyn Museum conservation file for the report of 5/2001 by C Finch (Caroline Finch).

19 See Brooklyn Museum conservation file for the report of 3/2005 LB WN TM (Lisa Bruno, Won Ng, Tina March).

20 Dr. Minnenberg was also an intern in the Department of Egyptian Art at the Metropolitan Museum of Art, where he assisted in the examination of mummies.

21 See conservation file 34.14Ec–e.

22 See conservation file for the report from March 2009 from the NSF AMS facility at the University of Arizona.
23 Dodson, "Late Eighteenth Dynasty Necropolis," 89–100, pls. 15–16.
24 Bleiberg, *To Live Forever*, 46–47.
25 See analytical report in the conservation files on gas chromatography–mass spectrometry (GC–MS) from Richard Newman, Museum of Fine Arts, Boston, Scientific Research 7/24/2001.
26 See Cooney, "How Much Did a Coffin Cost?" for a discussion of the costs of burial.
27 Fazzini, *Dynasty XXII–XXV*, 28 and pl. XLVI, 1; Bleiberg, *To Live Forever*, 64–65 and fig. 54.
28 Twenty-fifth to Twenty-sixth dynasties (ca. 700–650 BCE) for Gautseshenu and the second half of the Twenty-fifth Dynasty (ca. 712–664 BCE) for Hor. For a discussion of the style and date of this cartonnage, see Payraudeau, "Harsiésis," pl. XIV.
29 The mummy of Hor was scanned on 23 July 2009 and that of Gautseshenu on 28 April 2011.
30 Robert Loynes, a researcher from the University of Manchester, examined the CT scans of Brooklyn's mummies in 2014. Details here are taken from his report on Gautseshenu.
31 Thothirdes, 37.1521Ec, was also cataloged as female before CT scanning proved otherwise.
32 Numerous press accounts at the time widely reported this finding.
33 See the well-described report of the mummy by Robert Loynes. Report in conservation file.
34 The mummy was found in the ground in a simple wooden coffin together with several other individuals. See excavation notes from the Metropolitan Museum of Art. See also Winlock, "The Egyptian Expedition 1928–1929," 14–34. Possibly one of the mummies found in the ravine is pictured in fig. 18. Godlewski, "Late Roman Necropolis," 111–16.
35 Kraeling, *Aramaic Papyri*, 126–27.
36 Cooney, *Five Years of Collecting*, 59–60, pl. 92.
37 The mummy was completely intact and the face mask would have been viewable by the public if displayed as a whole object, rather than separately as a portrait.
38 The stitches holding the face mask to the outer wrapping remained in the stitch holes.
39 While this might seem shocking, there are records in the archives of large mummified crocodiles being incinerated at the orders of Dr. Cooney.
40 See *New York Times*, 13 September 1957.
41 The discussion involved obtaining a death certificate for burial or transport across state lines. Apparently, one only needed to obtain a certificate from the Department of Health. As a certificate was never obtained and the mummy was never removed from the collection, one wonders if the museum's registrars did not have a positive role in all this.
42 See curatorial file, catalog card.
43 Chapter 8, "Unwrapping a Mummy in Brooklyn," is the most complete description we have of the process.
44 Patrick Cardon, researcher in the Egyptian Department from 1969 to 1979, recently recalled in a discussion with the author that he and other researchers were so upset by

NOTES 15

what had happened that they took the rest of the mummies and hid them within the museum's walls to prevent their unwrapping.

45 See memo in conservation file from 12/21/77. The two earrings now have accession numbers and are on view next to the coffin of Pa-seba-khai-en-ipet.
46 Petrie, *Roman Portraits and Memphis*.
47 See early conservation record in the file.
48 Resinous material was also removed off of the back of a Faiyum portrait panel (40.386) as a standard part of the conservation treatment; see conservation file. This portrait came to the museum without its mummy.
49 Dardes and Rothe, *Structural Conservation of Panel Paintings*.
50 Talk given at the APPEAR (Ancient Panel Paintings: Examination, Analysis, and Research) Conference held at the Getty Villa in Malibu, CA on 17–18 May 2018. Sabino, Sutherland, and Pozzi, "Challenges in the Characterization and Categorization of Binding Media in Mummy Portraits."
51 See documentation in the conservation file for 86.226.18.
52 Svoboda and Walton, "Material Investigations."
53 Walton and Trentelman, "Romano-Egyptian Red Lead Pigment."
54 Bleiberg, *To Live Forever*. See pages 20–21 for the portrait of Demetrios.
55 See conservation record for 11.600. The A, B numbering system to denote the separated face and body has now been classified as a secondary numbering system.
56 See conservation file report by Lucy Cramp and Richard Evershed (University of Bristol, 6/27/2011), "Analysis of Romano-Egyptian Human and Animal Mummy Balms from the Brooklyn Museum, New York."
57 The human mummies were scanned at various times at North Shore University Hospital on Long Island by Dr. David Minnenberg and Dr. Amgad N. Makaryus. The scans have been examined by medical doctors and mummy researchers alike. The animal mummies were scanned at the Animal Medical Center in New York City under the supervision of Dr. Anthony Fischetti, and have been analyzed by graduate students specializing in biology and ancient DNA. Micro-CT scanning on select animal mummies was done at the American Museum of Natural History under the supervision of Dr. Evon Hekkala of Fordham University.
58 Also, planning for the traveling exhibition *Soulful Creatures: Animal Mummies in Ancient Egypt* (see Bleiberg, Barbash, and Bruno, *Soulful Creatures*) had begun.
59 See Loynes' report in conservation file. There is some evidence of decay in the lower body which may have been the result of poor mummification of the lower limbs.
60 In 2008, the University of Manchester had to address a public outcry when several of their partially unwrapped human Egyptian mummies on display were covered. The museum responded to the outcry by removing the covers.
61 Lisa Bruno gave a talk titled "On Not Exhibiting a Corpse" at the "Understanding Egyptian Collections: Innovative Display and Research Projects in Museums" conference, https://podcasts.ox.ac.uk/not-exhibiting-corpse-mummy-chamber-brooklyn-museum
62 Not unlike the sizes evident from the remains of the contents found in the coffin of Teti.
63 See conservation file report by Lucy Cramp and Richard Evershed (University of Bristol, 6/27/2011), "Analysis of Romano-Egyptian Human and Animal Mummy Balms from the Brooklyn Museum, New York."

64 Analysis done by the NSF AMS facility at the University of Arizona. Report in conservation file.
65 See CT scan associated with the conservation file. The mummy was scanned at the North Shore University Hospital on 25 July 2007 on a GE LightSpeed VCT machine with a slice thickness of 0.6 mm.
66 Sample identified by Carolyn Cartwright at the British Museum; see email dated 07/07/2010 in Jakki Godfrey report of 04/30/2010 in conservation file.

Bibliography

Aufderheide, Arthur C. *The Scientific Study of Mummies*. Cambridge and New York: Cambridge University Press, 2003.

Bleiberg, Edward L. "The Coffin of Weretwahset/Bensuipet and 'Scribal Errors' on Women's Funerary Equipment." *BES* 17 (2007): 29–46.

———. *To Live Forever: Egyptian Treasures from the Brooklyn Museum*. Brooklyn and London: Brooklyn Museum, in association with D. Giles, 2008.

Bleiberg, Edward, Yekaterina Barbash, and Lisa Bruno. *Soulful Creatures: Animal Mummies in Ancient Egypt*. Brooklyn: Brooklyn Museum and D. Giles, 2013.

Bruno, Lisa. "On Not Exhibiting a Corpse: The Mummy Chamber, Brooklyn Museum," talk given at the "Understanding Egyptian Collections: Innovative Display and Research Projects in Museums" conference, 1–2 September 2014. Oxford: Ashmolean Museum, 2014. https://podcasts.ox.ac.uk/not-exhibiting-corpse-mummy-chamber-brooklyn-museum

Candela, P.B. "Blood Group Reactions in Ancient Human Skeletons." *American Journal of Physical Anthropology* 21, no. 3 (1936): 429–32.

Cooney, John. *Five Years of Collecting Egyptian Art: 1951–1956. Catalog of an exhibition held at the Brooklyn Museum, 11 December 1956 to 17 March 1957*. Brooklyn: Brooklyn Museum, 1956.

Cooney, Kathlyn M. "How Much Did a Coffin Cost? The Social and Economic Aspects of Funerary Arts in Ancient Egypt." In *To Live Forever: Egyptian Treasures from the Brooklyn Museum*, edited by Edward L. Bleiberg, 110–41. Brooklyn and London: Brooklyn Museum, in association with D. Giles, 2008.

Dardes, Kathleen, and Andrea Rothe. *The Structural Conservation of Panel Paintings: Proceedings of a Symposium at the J. Paul Getty Museum, 24–28 April 1995*. Los Angeles: The Getty Conservation Institute, 1998.

Dodson, Aidan. "The Late Eighteenth Dynasty Necropolis at Deir el-Medina and the Earliest 'Yellow' Coffin of the New Kingdom." In *Deir el-Medina in the Third Millennium AD: A Tribute to Jac. J. Janssen*, edited by Robert Demarée and Arno Egberts, 89–100. Leiden: Nederlands Instituut voor het Nabije Oosten, 2000.

Dodson, Aidan, and Wendy Raver. "Dr. Anderson's Mummy." *Kmt* 14 (2003): 39–46.

Fazzini, Richard. *Egypt, Dynasty XXII–XXV*. Leiden and New York: Brill, 1988.

Fazzini, Richard, et al. *Ancient Egyptian Art in the Brooklyn Museum*. New York: Thames and Hudson, 1989.

Gillen, Todd, ed. *(Re)productive Traditions in Ancient Egypt: Proceedings of the Conference held at the University of Liège, 6th–8th February 2013*. Aegyptiaca Leodiensia 10. Liège, Belgium: Presses Universitaires de Liège, 2017.

Godlewski, Wlodzimierz. "The Late Roman Necropolis in Deir el-Bahari." In *Graeco-Coptica: Griechen und Kopten im byzantinischen Ägypten*, edited by Peter Nagel, 111–19. Halle (Saale): Martin-Luther-Universität Halle-Wittenberg, 1984.

Kariya, Hiroko, Lisa Bruno, Jakki Godfrey, and Tina March. "Treatment of a Dynasty 18 Painted Coffin 37.47a–e (Abbott Collection 405A)." In *Decorated Surfaces on Ancient Egyptian Objects: Technology, Deterioration, and Conservation*, edited by Julie Dawson, Christina Rozeik, and Margaret Wright, 97–105. London: Archetype Publications, 2010.

Kraeling, Emil G. *The Brooklyn Museum Aramaic Papyri: New Documents of the Fifth Century BC from the Jewish Colony at Elephantine*. New Haven, CT: Yale University Press, 1953.

Pace, Mildred Mastin. *Wrapped for Eternity: The Story of the Egyptian Mummy*. Guildford and London: Lutterworth Press, 1974.

Payraudeau, Frederic. "Harsiésis, un vizir oublié de l'époque libyenne?" *JEA* 89 (2003): 199–205.

Petrie, Flinders. *Roman Portraits and Memphis (IV)*. British School of Archaeology in Egypt and Egyptian Research Account, seventeenth year. London: School of Archaeology in Egypt, 1911.

Romano, James F. "The Armand de Potter Collection of Ancient Egyptian Art." In *Studies in Honor of William Kelly Simpson* 2, edited by Peter Der Manuelian and Rita Freed, 697–711. Boston: Museum of Fine Arts, 1996.

Sabino, Rachel, Ken Sutherland, and Federica Pozzi. "Challenges in the Characterization and Categorization of Binding Media in Mummy Portraits." In *Mummy Portraits of Roman Egypt: Emerging Research from the APPEAR Project*, edited by Marie Svoboda and Caroline R. Cartwright, 8–15. Los Angeles: J. Paul Getty Museum, 2020.

Svoboda, Marie, and Marc Walton. "Material Investigations of the J. Paul Getty Museum's Red-shroud Mummy." In *Decorated Surfaces on Ancient Egyptian Objects: Technology, Deterioration, and Conservation*, edited by Julie Dawson, Christina Rozeik, and Margaret Wright, 148–55. London: Archetype Publications, 2010.

Walton, Marc, and Karen Trentelman. "Romano-Egyptian Red Lead Pigment: A Subsidiary Commodity of Spanish Silver Mining and Refinement." *Archaeometry* 51, no. 5 (2008): 845–60. https://onlinelibrary.wiley.com/doi/10.1111/j.1475-4754.2008.00440.x

Winlock, Herbert. "The Egyptian Expedition 1928–1929: The Museum's Excavations at Thebes." *Metropolitan Museum of Art Bulletin* 24, no. 11 (Nov. 1929): 1, 3–34.

2 The Survival of Ancient Egypt in Modern Culture: A Never-Ending Story

Edmund S. Meltzer

IT IS A PLEASURE AND AN HONOR to offer these observations and reflections on the *Nachlass* and reception of ancient Egyptian culture to my friend, colleague, and fellow student Edward L. Bleiberg, whose fascination with the continuing survival and influence of ancient Egypt over the centuries and millennia I share, and who most worthily presides over my boyhood haunt, the Egyptian Department at the Brooklyn Museum. We met when we were fellow graduate students at the University of Toronto, and from the beginning I have been impressed by his kindness, decency, and helpfulness, and by his perceptive and engaging ideas on subjects of mutual interest. I fondly remember that one year we were both part of the "road trip" that often set out from Toronto to ARCE meetings, and we weary travelers enjoyed his family's welcoming hospitality.

More recently, I have been extremely grateful for his helpfulness and that of his staff, when Dr. Gonzalo Sanchez and I were working on the Edwin Smith Papyrus. These efforts led to the rediscovery of the then unpublished, and long unseen, handwritten translation by Edwin Smith himself.[1] I hope that Ed will enjoy the following excursion into the legacy, recycling, and reincarnation of ancient Egyptian literature in the modern world.

The persistence of ancient Egypt is a theme that I have explored over the years in several lectures and articles, and that has increasingly engaged Egyptological scholarship. Important contributions include Erik Hornung's *Secret Lore of Egypt: Its Impact on the West*,[2] Steve Vinson's magnum opus on First Setne, *The Craft of a Good Scribe*[3] (as well as the papers that preceded and accompanied it), Jan Assmann's *Moses the Egyptian*,[4] and Terence DuQuesne's erudite discussion of "Egypt's Image in the European Enlightenment."[5]

Some of the material, in literature as well as music and a range of other media, does not simply continue or perpetuate elements or associations of ancient Egypt. The best of this material can be felt to incorporate these elements in such a way that it has a new gestation and birth or a renewal of life. I find especially significant those works that encapsulate and transmit or, one might say, sometimes transmute, the actual content of ancient Egyptian texts, religion, and visual culture, as well as language. But in these remarks I would like to cast my net more widely, to convey some idea of the extent to which Aegyptiaca have permeated our so-called modern culture. As I examine these cultural manifestations, I ponder the question: Is it possible to say in this context "Plus ça change, plus c'est la même chose"? As we begin our sampling, one thought I would like us to hold on to is the centrality of transformation *(ḫpr)* for the ancient Egyptians, both in the nature and relationships of the deities and the afterlife capabilities of the blessed dead, who are, after all, a subset of the former.

In the nineteenth century, as the field of Egyptology was taking shape and experiencing major growth and expansion, and Egyptian discoveries were capturing many people's imagination, the use of ancient Egyptian themes and content in literature, art, and music also became a significant phenomenon, with the active participation of Egyptologists. This of course was not a brand-new development, but had precedents in works such as the Mozart-Schikaneder *Magic Flute* and Masonic romances such as *Sethos*. Still, the breakthrough of the decipherment of hieroglyphs and the rise of Egyptology as a field provided a new substance and concrete history which had been lacking. The reincarnation of the ancient Egyptian legacy entered a qualitatively new phase with first-hand access to the wealth of actual ancient Egyptian sources. Looking for the legacy of ancient Egypt in literature and the arts, a legacy informed by that documentation, one thinks immediately of fantasies, mysteries, and historical novels, categories that sometimes overlap and converge. This, however, represents far from the complete picture. Therefore, along with those obvious destinations, we shall look at some other attractions.

The Egyptologist Georg Ebers was one of the primary contributors to the nineteenth-century wave of Egyptianizing literature and other cultural productions, with novels such as *An Egyptian Princess* and *Uarda*.[6] He supplied these works with copious footnotes providing both documentation and verisimilitude; for instance, in a footnote in *An Egyptian Princess*, Ebers refers to the Wedjahorresnet inscription to illuminate Cambyses' policies in Egypt.[7] The other major Egyptological participant in this cultural movement who comes immediately to mind is Auguste Mariette, who played an important role in the genesis and early productions of Verdi's opera *Aïda*, including the writing of the scenario that caught Verdi's imagination and finally moved him to accept the commission.[8] Thomas Schneider has argued the influence of inscriptions discovered by Mariette himself.[9] I have long been impressed by the close resemblance of the hymn to Ptah ("Fthà," also referred to as "Vulcano") sung by the chorus of priests to the ancient Egyptian theology of Ptah the self-created Creator.[10]

This role of the Egyptologist as a major participant in the revivification of Egypt's legacy in writing and the arts has been represented in more recent times by Dr. Barbara Mertz and her novels, written under the pen names Elizabeth Peters and Barbara Michaels. Dr. Mertz's Egyptologically themed novels are set in the (recent) present, rather than in ancient Egypt itself; the only story of hers that she actually set in ancient Egypt, to my knowledge, is a short story with a characteristically witty and playful title, "The Locked Tomb Mystery,"[11] in which the sleuth is the famous historical sage Amenhotpe Son of Hapu. "Elizabeth Peters" and Kristen Whitbread, with the assistance of *Kmt* founder Dennis Forbes and other contributors, have provided a detailed companion to the major series of Amelia Peabody and Radcliffe Emerson novels.[12]

The Nobel Prize–winning author and literary giant Thomas Mann was not an Egyptologist but was possessed of considerable Egyptological erudition and a longstanding interest in the subject, which he drew on masterfully in *Joseph and His Brothers*, his novelistic treatment, in four parts, of the biblical narrative of Joseph. In company with some previous, and a great deal of later, writing, Mann placed the narrative in the Amarna Period, with Akhenaten as the pharaoh who elevated Joseph to the position of vizier. Erik Hornung thinks that the discovery of the vizier ꜥpr-iꜣ (the West Semitic theophore Aper-El or Abdu-El) "appears to justify Thomas Mann's position."[13] There is also a book-length treatment by Jan Assmann,[14] a scholar who has been greatly concerned with the influence of ancient Egypt on biblical traditions. This is indeed an area that has been of great interest to the honoree of the present volume, whose publications include the book *Jewish Life in Ancient Egypt*[15] and an article discussing toponyms mentioned in the Exodus account, "The Location of Pithom and Succoth."[16] It can be noted that in the chronology of Bleiberg's book, the honoree parts company with Thomas Mann, not to mention Hornung, on the chronological position of Joseph, writing in his table: "Circa 1650 BCE Joseph enters Egypt."[17]

One major aspect of ancient Egyptian culture that has found its way into general and popular literature is the central cultural concept of *maat* (or *maʿat*, *ma'et*; Egyptian, *m3ʿt*). In Howard Fast's biblical-historical novel *Moses, Prince of Egypt*,[18] which in a manner of speaking continues the narrative begun in Thomas Mann's opus, Moses, raised in the Egyptian court, speaks in the first person, in an ironic, bitter, and disillusioned tone, about the principle that he calls *macaat*. One might wonder whether the "c" introduced into that word might be an attempt to represent the phonetics of the Egyptian *'ayin*, or some sound intervening between the vowels. My suspicion is that the explanation is more graphic or visual, and that Fast transcribed as "c" the superlinear diacritic found in the transliteration and many printed transcriptions of the word "*m3ʿt*." Another, and more culturally fundamental, way that *ma'at* has been adopted into modern culture and discourse is in Maulana Karenga's book *Maat, the Moral Ideal in Ancient Egypt: A Study in Classical African Ethics*,[19] with an enthusiastic endorsement by Assmann[20] and more widely known in the African-American community.

In the realm of popular literature, ancient Egypt sometimes turns up in unexpected places. Among the many humorous classics written by P.G. Wodehouse, the first entry in the Blandings Castle saga, centering on Lord Emsworth, *Something Fresh* (American title, *Something New*), describes him as a collector of Egyptian scarabs whose prize piece is a "Fourth Dynasty Cheops." When Wodehouse's novel was published in 1915, the most widely accessible work on royal-name scarabs was Petrie's *Historical Scarabs: A Series of Drawings from the Principal Collections, Arranged Chronologically*,[21] which primarily dates the scarabs according to the dates of the rulers named. Subsequently, it was ascertained that examples of scarabs (not cylinder seals) with names of Archaic and Old Kingdom rulers were carved later, and thus a "Cheops" scarab would not actually date to the Fourth Dynasty.

Another popular genre of British fiction is represented by Arthur Ransome's series of novels centering on the Swallows and Amazons and their friends, children who engage in highly independent, largely nautical adventures, ranging from England as far as China. Ransome was a folklorist, a literary historian, and a foreign correspondent with wide international experience who was fluent in Russian and knew Chinese. The named pairs or groups of children, Swallows and Amazons et al., have boats which they pilot expertly and tend devotedly. One brother and sister who join up with the Swallows and Amazons are the Ds, the son and daughter of a husband-and-wife team of archaeologists who work in Egypt. Their boat is called the Scarab.

We have now arrived at the realm of what some readers and critics like to term "high fantasy." We will begin with an author who is not usually highlighted in these contexts but who probably deserves to be: the journalist, magazine editor, and fantasy writer Abraham Merritt ("A. Merritt" in the usual byline of his books), who was the author of vividly atmospheric and intensely romantic narratives such as *The Ship of Ishtar*, *The Face in the Abyss*, *The Moon Pool*, *Seven Footprints to Satan*, *Dwellers in the Mirage*, and *Burn, Witch, Burn!*

As its title suggests, the allusive context and cultural trappings of *The Ship of Ishtar* relate to Mesopotamian rather than Egyptian civilization. Egypt is, however, involved in Merritt's oeuvre. In *Seven Footprints to Satan*, the protagonist, who has been recruited, or coerced, into the vast criminal network headed by the so-called Satan, is given the task of stealing "the necklace of Senusert the Second" from the Metropolitan Museum. The master criminal explains to the protagonist, James Kirkham, that the king had the necklace made for his daughter.[22] The reference is to the pectoral of Sit-Hathor that bears the cartouche of her father, Kha'kheperre' Senwosret II, which is not in New York but in Cairo.[23]

A much more extensive involvement of ancient Egyptian myth and literature appears in Merritt's luridly titled novel *Burn, Witch, Burn!* published in 1933.[24] (Rather confusingly, the movie of the same title was actually a dramatization of a totally different novel by a different author, *Conjure Wife* by Fritz Leiber.) Merritt's tale is a harrowing and horrifying one of an enchantress who makes dolls, perfect minute portraits of people, into which she imprisons their souls, thereafter to do her bidding. The author sets the stage with a preface describing, in vivid language, a worldwide magical tradition reaching back into prehistory and encompassing cultures across the globe. The frame of the narrative is completed with the final chapter, in which the protagonists look back on their unbelievably harrowing ordeal and reflect on folk-magical practices, especially the use of magical dolls and their attendant paraphernalia, emphasizing the vast age and universality of the forces with which they contended. The narrator quotes a clay tablet from "the days of Assur-nizir-pal" recounting a case of sorcery in which the perpetrators made an image of their intended victim. This is followed by a rather extensive selection of Egyptian material: the creation by Khnum, who is described as "the first recorded Maker of Dolls"; the fashioning of the wife of Bata in the story of "The Two Brothers," to which some scintillating detail is added; and the recounting of the use of magical dolls in the conspiracy against Ramesses III.[25]

In reviewing the presence of ancient Egypt in modern literature, there is one item that at first I hesitated to include but which I just couldn't resist, so here it is: a historical novel by James Busbee Jr., entitled *Son of Egypt*.[26] The cover blurb reads: "Glory, Passion, and Intrigue in an Ancient Empire." When I came across this novel in a secondhand bookstore as a high-school student, I bought it, as I bought pretty much any ancient Egypt–themed title I encountered. As I read it, two things became apparent: that its genre could probably be described as a macho equivalent of something like today's "Silhouette Desire" romance novels, and that the author had considerable Egyptological knowledge, including at least some familiarity with hieroglyphs. It was published by a respectable mainstream mass-market publisher that proudly advertised its fiction list as a "Who's who in fiction," including works of such luminaries and cultural icons as Pearl S. Buck, John Dickson Carr,[27] Noel Coward, William Faulkner,[28] Edna Ferber, Ben Hecht, Ernest Hemingway, Christopher Isherwood, Sinclair Lewis, John O'Hara, Damon Runyon, John Steinbeck, and Thornton Wilder,[29] as well as an anthology of fantasy stories from *The Saturday Evening Post*. To make a long story very short . . . Aahmes, an Egyptian soldier, experiencing tragic events and overwhelming injustices in his life, defects, follows more or less in Sinuhe's footsteps (while finding some solace in every port—Sinuhe's "land gave me to land" seems to become something like "I'm a travelin' man . . ."), and joins the Babylonian (Kassite) army. The king is impressed with him and entrusts him with a very important and delicate mission: to escort a young princess to Egypt where she is to become the bride of the young king Amenhotpe III. Not much imagination is needed to come up with a hypothesis about what happens on the way to Egypt, where they are received by Amenhotpe and a dour, officious priest and official named Eye. Amazingly, as is the case with Sinuhe, Aahmes' reunion with Egypt—and his union with the Babylonian beauty—is a happy one and, as in Shakespeare's *Midsummer Night's Dream*, "Jack shall have Jill. Nought shall go ill."

Not yet satiated with this literary material, or with high culture such as opera, we will now move on to other, more visual media. Much of this material is generally pigeonholed under the heading of "Egyptomania," but I think that the label mischaracterizes some of the material and generally devalues it, and marginalizes it from the mainstream cultural discussion, where I think it belongs.

One sphere in which the visual impact and general fascination of ancient Egypt have sometimes been given expression is the comic book. When I was growing up in New York and becoming a confirmed future Egyptologist, I hungrily collected any comic that had a story featuring ancient Egypt. There was a Supergirl story in which, to the best of my somewhat hazy memory (I parted with my comic collection years ago, a decision about which I sometimes have belated second thoughts), our heroine is being pursued by a mummy bent on her destruction, who is motivated by a hieroglyphic inscription warning of dire consequences "unless you destroy her." It turns out that the end of the inscription was actually a lacuna (though that word was not used), and the mummy desisted when he realized that it was a matter not of her person but of a particular amulet that she possessed—"unless you destroy her *scarab*." Armed with a recently purchased copy of Samuel Mercer's *An Egyptian Grammar*, I ascertained that the object pronoun in "destroy her" was not the same as either of the possible possessive constructions that could be used in "her scarab," and I called the editorial offices of DC to point out the error.

To convey an idea of the variety of directions from which some permutation of ancient Egypt could come at one through popular culture, an equally inaccurate but more amusing example occurred in an episode of the "Peabody and Sherman" time travel segment of *The Adventures of Rocky and Bullwinkle and Friends*. Peabody and Sherman went to Egypt in the time of Khufu and saw the Great Pyramid built, upside-down, balanced on its apex. The pyramid was restored to its familiar orientation when Khufu's naughty son (who was not named; could it have been Hardedef?) took some gunpowder, which he had acquired on a recent trip to China, and ignited it, whereupon the pyramid was launched into the air and landed on its proper base. I am fairly sure that the Old Kingdom trade in Chinese gunpowder is otherwise unknown.

And an episode of the old Superman cartoon series explained the disparity in the sizes of figures in Egyptian art with a plot narrating how a king had created gigantic robots.

Another "blast from the past" can be found on the old *Batman* live-action TV series, the one with capitalized words followed by exclamation points, such as "POW!" and "BAM!," appearing on the screen, with Robin exclaiming excitedly, "Holy *sḏm.f*, Batman!" (No, I have to admit that the last quotation came from wishful thinking or my fevered imagination.) Anyway, the reality was almost as good. Victor Buono played a professor of Egyptology who was knocked out when a window sash fell on his head and awoke as a deranged villain called "King Tut" who dressed in a bizarre costume that was supposed to be ancient Egyptian. His rampage ended when a window sash fell on his head a second time. When the professor awoke, as himself this time, apparently wondering how anyone could have come up with such a ridiculous costume, Batman said softly and respectfully, "Professor, it's time to get back to class."

More recently, devotees of "The Doctor," as in the British TV series *Dr. Who*, have seen how he encountered Nefertiti held prisoner by an unscrupulous intergalactic trader who added her to his cargo of illicit dinosaurs and other contraband. But Dr. Who to the rescue! The fact that she referred to her not very beloved husband as "Amenhotep" might enable us to place this incident before his name change to "Akhenaten."

In a sense, this selective, perhaps even capricious whirlwind tour comes full circle with the role of an Egyptologist, John L. (Jack) Foster, in revivifying the literary legacy of ancient Egypt and making it accessible to a much wider audience through his work on Egyptian verse texts.[30] Another Egyptologist who published verse translations of ancient Egyptian poems is Margaret A. Murray.[31]

But there is yet another poetic translator of ancient Egyptian literature who, we think, deserves to be mentioned: the Pulitzer Prize–winning poet Robert Silliman Hillyer, who published a book entitled *The Coming Forth by Day: An Anthology of Poems from the Egyptian Book of the Dead Together with an Essay on the Egyptian Religion*.[32] A substantial section of his translations is included in *An Anthology of World Poetry*, edited by Mark Van Doren.[33]

Hillyer was a formalist and one of the "Harvard Aesthetes" who did not accept the approach of the modernists (Ezra Pound, T.S. Eliot, et al.). He objected to the awarding of the Bollingen Prize to Pound, on account of Pound's fascist sympathies.[34] To give a flavor of his translations, I will quote from his rendering of one of the solar hymns from the Book of the Dead.[35]

> Homage to thee, O Ra, at thy tremendous rising!
>
> Thou risest! Thou shined! The heavens are rolled aside!
> Thou art the King of Gods, thou art the All-comprising,
> From thee we come, in thee are deified. . . .
>
> O Thou Perfect! Thou Eternal! Thou Only One!
>
> Great Hawk that fliest with the flying Sun!. . . .
>
> Homage to thee, O Ra, who wakest life from slumber!
> Thou risest! Thou shined! Thy radiant face appears!
> Millions of years have passed, we can not count their number,
>
> Millions of years shall come. Thou art above the years!

I hope that my friend and colleague Ed Bleiberg will find these reflections and meanderings of interest and that reading them will bring an occasional smile. *Ankh, Wedja, Seneb!*

Notes

1. Sanchez and Meltzer, *Edwin Smith Papyrus*, Appendix 5.
2. Hornung, *Secret Lore*.
3. Vinson, *Craft of a Good Scribe*.
4. Assmann, *Moses the Egyptian*.
5. DuQuesne, "Egypt's Image."
6. Ebers, *Uarda*.
7. Ebers, *Egyptian Princess*, vol. 1, n150.
8. Simpson, "Mariette and Verdi's *Aida*"; Graefe, "Addendum."
9. Schneider, "Gebel Barkal Stelae."
10. Meltzer, "Mariette and *Aïda* Once Again"; for the Italian text of the hymn and an English translation, see Bleiler, *Aïda*, 75–76.
11. Anthologized in Ashley, *Mammoth Book*, 182–98.
12. Peters and Whitbread, *Amelia Peabody's Egypt*. For historical information and references pertaining to Amenhotpe Son of Hapu, see Kozloff, *Amenhotep III*. For my review of the first "Amelia," *Crocodile on the Sandbank*, see Meltzer, "Review of Elizabeth Peters."
13. Hornung, "Thomas Mann, Akhnaten, and the Egyptologists," 102.
14. Assmann, *Thomas Mann und Ägypten*.
15. Bleiberg, *Jewish Life*.
16. Bleiberg, "Location of Pithom and Succoth."
17. Bleiberg, *Jewish Life*, 44.
18. Fast, *Moses, Prince of Egypt*.
19. Karenga, *Maat*.
20. Karenga, *Maat*, xvii–xxii.
21. Petrie, *Historical Scarabs*.
22. Merritt, *Seven Footprints*, http://gutenberg.net.au/ebooks06/0601971h.html
23. As seen, for example, in Aldred and Shoucair, *Jewels of the Pharaohs*, pl. 33; and Müller and Thiem, *Gold and the Pharaohs*, 110, 253, with pl. 219.
24. Merritt, *Burn, Witch, Burn!*
25. For recent discussions of the tale of "The Two Brothers" and the conspiracy against Ramesses III, see Hollis, *Tale of Two Brothers*; Katary, "Two Brothers as Folktale" and "Concerning Bata"; Di Biase-Dyson, *Foreigners and Egyptians*; Jay's review of *Foreigners and Egyptians*; Dodson, *Poisoned Legacy*; and Redford, *Harem Conspiracy*. I attempted a fictional treatment of the "Harem Conspiracy" in a short story entitled "To Kill a King," which won Erasmus Hall High School's Richard Young Short Story Medal in 1968 and is posted on my Academia page.
26. Busbee, *Son of Egypt*.
27. Diamond, "'Supernatural' as a Marginalizing Force," discusses Carr's novels from the standpoint of gender studies as well as the role of Egyptology.
28. Faulkner also distinguished himself by writing the screenplay for an atrocious movie about Khufu called "Land of the Pharaohs."
29. Wilder is the author of the quite fascinating historical novel *The Ides of March*, in which Cleopatra plays a prominent role.
30. For a bibliography, appreciations, and discussion, see Foster, "Appreciation" and "Bibliography."

31 Murray, *Splendour That Was Egypt*, 210–11. Her version of one of the love songs, beginning "Lost! Lost! Lost!," is used as the epigram for an Egyptian-themed fantasy novel, *Recreated*, by Colleen Houck, the second volume of the "Reawakened" series, 1.
32 Hillyer, *Coming Forth by Day*.
33 Van Doren, ed., *Anthology of World Poetry*, 235–51.
34 Poetry Foundation, poetryfoundation.org/poets/robert-hillyer
35 Van Doren, ed., *Anthology of World Poetry*, 235–36.

Bibliography

Aldred, Cyril, and Albert Shoucair. *Jewels of the Pharaohs*. London: Thames & Hudson, 1971.

Ashley, Mike, ed. *The Mammoth Book of Egyptian Whodunnits*. New York: Carroll & Graf, 2002.

Assmann, Jan. *Moses the Egyptian: The Memory of Egypt in Western Monotheism*. Cambridge, MA and London: Harvard University Press, 1997.

———. *Thomas Mann und Ägypten: Mythos und Monotheismus in den Josephsromanen*. Munich: C.H. Beck, 2006.

Bleiberg, Edward L. *Jewish Life in Ancient Egypt*. Brooklyn: Brooklyn Museum, 2002.

———. "The Location of Pithom and Succoth." In *Egyptological Miscellanies: A Tribute to Professor Ronald J. Williams*, edited by James K. Hoffmeier and Edmund S. Meltzer, 21–27. Ancient World 6. Chicago: Ares, 1983.

Bleiler, Ellen H. *Aïda*. Dover Opera Guide and Libretto Series. New York: Dover, 1962.

Busbee, James Jr. *Son of Egypt*. New York: Avon Books, 1953.

Diamond, Kelly-Anne. "The 'Supernatural' as a Marginalizing Force in the Fiction of John Dickson Carr." *JSSEA* 44 (2017–18): 183–204.

Di Biase-Dyson, Camilla. *Foreigners and Egyptians in the Late Egyptian Stories: Linguistic, Literary, and Historical Perspectives*. Probleme der Ägyptologie 32. Leiden: Brill, 2013.

Dodson, Aidan. *Poisoned Legacy: The Fall of the Nineteenth Egyptian Dynasty*. Cairo: American University in Cairo Press, 2010.

DuQuesne, Terence. "Egypt's Image in the European Enlightenment." *Seshat* 3 (1999): 32–51.

Ebers, Georg. *An Egyptian Princess*. 2 vols. Trans. Eleanor Grove. New York: William S. Gottsberger, 1880.

———. *Uarda*. Stuttgart: Eduard Hallberger, 1877.

Fast, Howard. *Moses, Prince of Egypt*. New York: Bantam, 1960.

Foster, Ann L. "John L. Foster 1930–2011" and "Bibliography." *JSSEA* 42 (2015–16): xii–xxii.

Graefe, Erhart. "Addendum" (to Simpson article). *BES* 4 (1982): 79.

Hillyer, Robert Silliman. *The Coming Forth by Day: An Anthology of Poems from the Egyptian Book of the Dead Together with an Essay on the Egyptian Religion*. Boston: B.J. Brimmer, 1923.

Hollis, Susan Tower. *The Ancient Egyptian Tale of Two Brothers: A Mythological, Religious, Literary, and Historico-Political Study*. 2nd ed. Oakville, CT: Bannerstone Press, 2008.

Hornung, Erik. *Secret Lore of Egypt: Its Impact on the West*. Trans. David Lorton. Ithaca, NY and London: Cornell University Press, 2001.

———. "Thomas Mann, Akhnaten, and the Egyptologists." Trans. Terence DuQuesne. In *Hermes Aegyptiacus: Egyptological Studies for B.H. Stricker on His 85th Birthday*. Discussions in Egyptology, Special Number 2, edited by Terence DuQuesne, 101–13. Oxford: DE Publications, 1995.

Houck, Colleen. *Recreated*. New York: Random House, 2016.

Jay, Jacqueline E. "Review of Di Biase-Dyson, *Foreigners and Egyptians*." *CdÉ* 90 (2015): 74–80.

Karenga, Maulana. *Maat, the Moral Ideal in Ancient Egypt: A Study in Classical African Ethics*. New York and London: Routledge, 2003.

Katary, Sally L.D. "Concerning Bata and the Doomed Prince: Their 'Afterlives' in the Classical Literature." *JSSEA* 42 (2015–16): 25–41.

———. "The Two Brothers as Folktale: Constructing the Social Context." *Papers presented in memory of Ronald J. Williams. JSSEA* 24 (1997): 39–70.

Kozloff, Arielle P. *Amenhotep III: Egypt's Radiant Pharaoh*. Cambridge, UK and New York: Cambridge University Press, 2012.

Meltzer, Edmund S. "Mariette and *Aïda* Once Again." *Antiquity* 52 (1978): 50–51.

———. "Review of Elizabeth Peters, *Crocodile on the Sandbank*," with trans. from Cairo Ostracon #25218 on page 26. *JSSEA* (then called *The Newsletter*) 7, no. 2 (1977): 24–25.

Merritt, Abraham. *Burn, Witch, Burn!* New York: Avon Books, 1933.

———. *Seven Footprints to Satan*. New York: Boni & Liveright, 1928. http://gutenberg.net.au/ebooks06/0601971h.html

Müller, Hans Wolfgang, and Eberhard Thiem. *Gold of the Pharaohs*. New York: Barnes & Noble, 2005.

Murray, Margaret A. *The Splendour That Was Egypt*. Rev. ed. London: Sidgwick & Jackson, 1964.

Peters, Elizabeth, and Kristen Whitbread, eds. *Amelia Peabody's Egypt: A Compendium*. New York: Harper Collins, 2003.

Petrie, W.M. Flinders. *Historical Scarabs: A Series of Drawings from the Principal Collections, Arranged Chronologically*. London: D. Nutt, 1889.

Redford, Susan. *The Harem Conspiracy: The Murder of Ramesses III*. DeKalb, IL: Northern Illinois University Press, 2002.

Sanchez, Gonzalo M., and Edmund S. Meltzer. *The Edwin Smith Papyrus: Updated Translation of the Trauma Treatise and Modern Medical Commentaries*. Atlanta, GA: Lockwood Press, 2012.

Schneider, Thomas. "The Gebel Barkal Stelae and the Discovery of Ancient Nubia: Auguste Mariette's Inspiration for *Aïda*." *Near Eastern Archaeology* 78, no. 1

(2015): 44–51.

Simpson, William K. "Mariette and Verdi's *Aïda*." *BES* 2 (1980): 111–19.

Van Doren, Mark, ed. *An Anthology of World Poetry*. New York: Albert & Charles Boni, 1921. https://archive.org/stream/in.ernet.dli.2015.102654/2015.102654. An-Anthology-Of-World-Poetry_djvu.txt

Vinson, Steve. *The Craft of a Good Scribe: History, Narrative and Meaning in the First Tale of Setne Khaemwas*. Harvard Egyptological Studies 3. Leiden: Brill, 2017.

3 The Ancient (Egyptian) Language of the *Children of Dune*

Joachim Friedrich Quack

THE SUCCESSFUL SCIENCE FICTION NOVEL by Frank Herbert, *Children of Dune* (1976),[1] depicts the twins Leto and Ghanima who, in their private conversation, fall back into an ancient language, long extinct at the time the action is set. The children are able to make full use of the memories of their ancestors and thus bring back this specific language. Concerning the language as such, the novel reads: "They had been speaking for some time in a language so ancient that even its name remained unknown in these times."[2] Two interesting remarks are given about the syntax of this language: "He used the special infinitive of the ancient language, a form strictly neutral in voice and tense but profoundly active in its implications,"[3] and, "In the ancient language it was an extremely convoluted statement, employing a pronominal object separated from the infinitive. It was a syntax which allowed each set of internal phrases to turn upon itself, becoming several different meanings, all definitive, and quite distinct but subtly interrelated."[4]

It has already been noted in internet contributions that the term for the "Golden Path," *Secher Nbiw*, which Leto propagates, goes back to the Egyptian language.[5] The aim of the following contribution is to analyze in detail the short sentences in the ancient language given in this novel, to demonstrate that they are somewhat garbled renderings of ancient Egyptian, and to look for possible sources. As a matter of fact, with all the subtlety of a sledgehammer, the novel's author pinpoints the cultural origin of the language by having Ghanima address Leto with "You are not Osiris."[6] Also, in "And Isis had been the demon-goddess of death to the people whose tongue they now spoke,"[7] mention of the goddess leaves no doubt as to the language's origins.

If Herbert made use of ancient Egyptian for his "ancient language," it of course has to be asked which sources were used. An obvious candidate would be a grammar of the Egyptian language with quoted examples, and indeed I think that there is good evidence that Herbert made use of what was the standard grammar of Egyptian at the time of writing: Alan Henderson Gardiner's *Egyptian Grammar*.[8] All of the specific sentences given in the novel, as well as some syntactical remarks tallying with Herbert's indications about the qualities of the ancient language, can be matched with material in one single lesson of that grammar: Lesson XXIa, which treats the infinitive.

A first case is spoken by Ghanima: *Mohw'pwium d'mi hish pash moh'm ka*, which is rendered as: "The capture of my soul is the capture of a thousand souls."[9] This sentence is an adaptation of a passage from the annals of Thutmose III, having in the original text *mḥ pw m dmi ḫ3 p3 mḥ m Mkti*: "The capture of Megiddo is the capture of a thousand towns,"[10] which is actually cited by Gardiner.[11] The adaptation shows, even beyond the question of vocalization, some errors. The noun *dmi* (town) is left standing in the first part of the sentence where it should also have been replaced by the *ka* used in the second part. With *hish* and *pash*, an unjustified *sh* has crept in,[12] and *hish* for *ḫ3* is also otherwise phonetically inexact. *Ka* is left in the "ancient language" without any indication of the possessive pronoun by way of a suffix or possessive article.

Almost directly afterward follows the next sentence in this language, this time spoken by Leto: *Wabun 'k wabunat*, with the translation "Rising thou risest."[13] As already recognized by others,[14] quite obviously this renders *wbn=k wbn.t* as "you rise a rising." The passage in itself might seem to be too short to pinpoint a specific source with certainty. However, when discussing briefly the complementary infinitive, Gardiner cites the example *wbn.k wbn.t*, "you rise a rising,"[15] the very same phrase taken up in the novel. It should also be noted that the Egyptian text is in the second-person singular masculine, implying that Leto is soliloquizing here, provided we can be sure that the poet was aware of the fact that the ancient Egyptian language also distinguishes masculine and feminine forms in the second person singular, contrary to English. The direct answer to this by Ghanima is *muriyat*, translated as "It must be done lovingly."[16] Quite obviously, Egyptian *mry.t* (beloved) is intended. Indeed, Gardiner indicates concerning the infinitive 𓌻𓇋𓇋𓂝𓁐 *mryt* (love) for the usual *mrt* (loving),[17] thus providing a good source for *muriyat* in the novel.

Somewhat more problematic is *L'ii ani howr samis sm'kwi owr samit sut*, which is supposed to mean, literally: "We will accompany each other into deathliness, though only one may return to report it."[18] For the final part one can at least recognize *šm.kwi . . . r smi.t st*, "I went . . . to report it," and it is not unlikely that the *ow* which is not explained is intended to be Egyptian *wꜥ* (alone), even if a syntactically correct construction would require it to be also in the first person of the pseudoparticiple, thus *wꜥ.kwi*.

For the first part, the presence of the verb *ii* (to come) is probable, and there is some likelihood that *samis* is a rendering of Egyptian *šms* which basically means "to follow," but is found in the English–Egyptian glossary of Gardiner's *Grammar* for "to accompany," although this implies that the crucial part of the sentence—"into deathliness"—is altogether omitted in the "ancient language" version. By counterchecking with what Gardiner would offer in terms of examples, I propose that the first part was inspired by *iy.n=i ḥr šms=f*, "I returned accompanying him," *BH* 1: 8, 10, and the second part by *ꜥḥꜥ.n šm.kwi r smi.t st*, "I went to report it," of Shipwrecked Sailor 157, both cited by Gardiner on the same page.[19] This would imply that there was no real effort spent to transpose the first part into the first person plural.

Ultimately, the passage is quite unsatisfactory and shows how someone with rather limited competence tried to render a phrase in Egyptian that was so central to his poetic intentions that he felt an urgent need to give it in the "ancient language." Perhaps, in the indication "literally" for the correspondence between the English version and the "ancient language," which is given only here in the whole chapter, there is some hint at the bad conscience of the author, who was well aware that he had failed to produce a really convincing text in the "ancient language."

More easily clarified in its origins is *Alia darsatay haunus mʾsmow*, spoken by Ghanima, which is not directly translated but taken up in its contents by Leto's feeling that "indeed Alia's actions did give off a foul smell"; a little later, *mʾsmow* is explained as "the foul odor of summer."[20] The sentence can be understood as Egyptian *ꜥly3 (ḥr) dr sti ḥnš m šmw*, strongly inspired by the heading of the recipe *dr sti ḥnš m šmw*, "to remove a foul odor in the summertime," in the medical papyrus Hearst (2,17) and Ebers (86,6), actually cited by Gardiner.[21] Syntactically, the construction with a substantival subject (a personal name) and an uninflected form of the verb directly following would only be acceptable from advanced Late Egyptian onward (when the present-tense periphrastic constructions had lost the preposition *ḥr* in pronunciation), even though the inspirational passage is in Classical Egyptian. The limits of competence of the author concerning verbal syntax and precise lexical meaning of the verb chosen (it would have been better to construct the phrase as *dd ꜥly3 sti*)[22] are, however, obvious. He did not get beyond the level of a genuinely interested but, ultimately, minimally competent dilettante.[23]

Also, the remark about the syntax of the infinitive must be suspected of referring back to Gardiner, where we can read: "Though strictly neutral in voice, as also in tense, the Egyptian infinitive has usually an active implication."[24] The similarity with Herbert's "form strictly neutral in voice and tense but profoundly active" is obvious. At the same time, Herbert's "profoundly active in its implications" somewhat twists Gardiner's statement in order to make it fit better with his poetic intentions.

Gardiner also discusses the question of separating a pronominal object from the infinitive,[25] thus giving a point of contact with the second description of the syntactic specialties of the "ancient language." When Herbert writes: "It was a syntax which allowed each set of internal phrases to turn upon itself, becoming several different meanings, all definitive, and quite distinct but subtly interrelated," it rather builds up claims which are useful for his poetic intentions but are not obviously borne out by the facts.

Ultimately, we can see that the author felt a real need to put some central parts of the dialogue between Leto and Ghanima into a special language to which he could ascribe syntactic properties different from English, and beyond the specific cases given in that language. Also, he could imbue the rest of the conversation with the poetic notion of being delivered in a language with such properties. As a matter of fact, these supposed qualities (which to me seem rather mystifying) certainly were a major appeal for the author when choosing the language. Indeed, it is striking that in the passage where this supposed subtlety of the "ancient language" is stressed most, no actual text in this language is given. I fail to see how anything could be constructed in ancient Egyptian which even remotely carried all the implications that Herbert ascribed to the linguistic quality of the ancient language.

In any case, the deficits of his approach are obvious. All diacritics of the transliteration of the Egyptian text get completely lost in the transcription of the sentences, even if there would have been meaningful ways to transpose them into English orthography (for example, to print *sh* for *š*). The method of vocalization chosen remains quite unclear to me. When adapting the primary sentences for the desired content, blatant errors can be observed. It should also give food for thought that all examples come from the chapter about the infinitive, which stands at the beginning of the section about verbal morphology and syntax. This gives the impression that Herbert started optimistically but did not get very far before giving up his attempt to acquaint himself more deeply with the "ancient language," and ultimately relied for most of the conversation between Leto and Ghanima on the simple claim that what he gave as English text was in fact delivered in that mysterious ancient language.

One could even ask whether the ancient language, with its supposed qualities, was just a convenient ploy for the author, who could thus, in a sort of metatext, provide a desired deeper level of meaning to the conversation, a level that he would have failed to achieve in a purely English version.

Ultimately, what we have here is a special case of the afterlife of Egyptian texts which are picked up not so much for their intrinsic qualities but for their possibility to be adapted into quite a new meaning. I hope that Ed Bleiberg enjoys reading about it and, in any case, I would like to thank him for his many kind welcomes to me at the Brooklyn Museum over the years.

Notes

1. For what follows, I have used the New English Library edition of 1992 in 426 pages.
2. Herbert, *Children of Dune*, 71.
3. Herbert, *Children of Dune*, 71.
4. Herbert, *Children of Dune*, 79.
5. For example, see https://en.wikipedia.org/wiki/Golden_Path_(Dune) with an explicit reference to Faulkner, *Concise Dictionary*, and the terms *nbw* and *shr* (pages 129 and 242, respectively).
6. Herbert, *Children of Dune*, 79.
7. Herbert, *Children of Dune*, 80.
8. Gardiner, *Egyptian Grammar*. In order to better demonstrate my argument, in the text that follows I use the same transliteration system for the Egyptian language as that used by Gardiner.
9. Herbert, *Children of Dune*, 71.
10. *Urk.* 4: 660, 8.
11. Gardiner, *Egyptian Grammar*, 223, marginal 11.
12. This may have arisen from a misunderstanding of the Egyptian *ꜣ*.
13. Herbert, *Children of Dune*, 71.
14. As indicated at https://www.reddit.com/r/dune/comments/5oim2m/ancient_language_used_by_leto_ii_and_ghanima_for/. *"Wabun 'k wabunat"* (translated as "Rising, thou risest!") is clearly, to anyone who has studied the language, ancient Egyptian, just somewhat tweaked.
15. With a reference to Lacau, TR 47, 24; Gardiner, *Egyptian Grammar*, 223 with marginal 6.
16. Herbert, *Children of Dune*, 72.
17. Gardner, *Egyptian Grammar*, 223.
18. Herbert, *Children of Dune*, 78.
19. Gardiner, *Egyptian Grammar*, 225, marginal 3 and 4.
20. Herbert, *Children of Dune*, 79f.
21. Gardiner, *Egyptian Grammar*, 229; marginal 10.
22. The verb *dr* means "to drive away," "to get rid of," which would be quite contrary to the intended meaning in the novel.
23. Obviously, my description of the author as an incompetent dilettante only refers to his handling of the ancient Egyptian language and does not imply any judgment

upon his poetic qualities, as such. In any case, Herbert's interest in languages is documented; see Touponce, *Frank Herbert*, 4.
24 Gardiner, *Egyptian Grammar*, 222.
25 Gardiner, *Egyptian Grammar*, 226f.

Bibliography

Faulkner, Raymond O. *A Concise Dictionary of Middle Egyptian*. Oxford: Griffith Institute, 1986.

Gardiner, Alan. *Egyptian Grammar: Being an Introduction to the Study of Hieroglyphs*. 3rd rev. ed. Oxford: Oxford University Press, 1957.

Herbert, Frank. *Children of Dune*. London: New English Library, 1992.

Touponce, William F. *Frank Herbert*. Boston: Twayne Publishers, 1988.

4 The Montuemhat Crypt in the Mut Temple: A New Look

Richard Fazzini and Mary McKercher

In 1998 I (Richard) recommended that the Brooklyn Museum hire Edward Bleiberg as associate curator of Egyptian, Classical, and Ancient Near Eastern Art. It was one of my better decisions as he is a superb curator. I was even more pleased when he was named to succeed me as department head, and I value our years of friendship. Mary and I are honored to contribute to this Festschrift marking his seventieth birthday and his many achievements as senior curator before his retirement in 2020. We hope he finds our chapter informative and entertaining.

In 1859, Auguste Mariette discovered a small chamber (ca. 210 cm × 100 cm) built into the east wall of the Mut Temple, off the hypostyle hall (fig. 4.1a).[1] It is preceded by an uninscribed antechamber (ca. 60 cm × 50 cm wide) and was probably closed by a double-leaf door that rested against the antechamber walls when open (fig. 4.1b), the doorway being about 45 cm wide. It is called the Montuemhat Crypt or the Taharqa Crypt because its rear (east) wall bears a relief of Taharqa, Nesptah A (Montuemhat's father), Montuemhat, and his son Nesptah B offering to Mut. The side walls have texts by Montuemhat extolling all the good things he did for Upper Egypt and the gods.

Mariette published the walls as plates 42–44 in his work on Karnak.[2] On 18 March 1881, the American Egyptologist Charles Edwin Wilbour took his copy of Mariette's book to the temple, comparing the plates to the reliefs, and annotating and correcting the drawings. Wilbour's collection of books, including this one, formed the core of the Brooklyn Museum's Wilbour Library of Egyptology; Wilbour's annotated plates are reproduced here as figs. 4.4, 4.6, and 4.8.

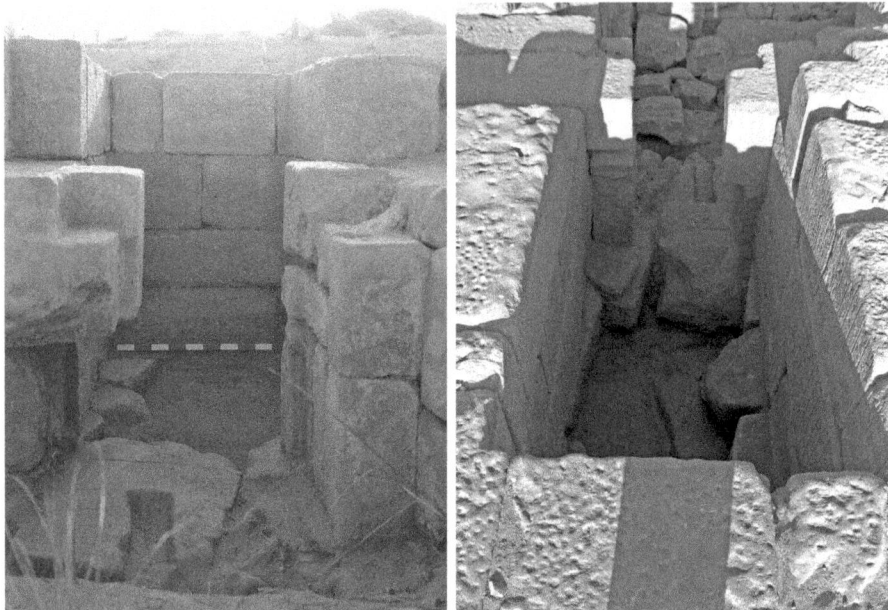

Fig. 4.1. (a) Antechamber and entrance to the Montuemhat Crypt; (b) view west of the crypt. Photographs by M. McKercher.

Wilbour saw signs that Mariette had not and crossed out signs that he could not confirm. Wilbour also corrected errors in Mariette's spacing of the hieroglyphs, deleting ones that did not exist (for example, B.4 after *im;* B.6 after *iw3.w*) or indicating how many signs might be missing (for example, B.51, 52).

Mariette and Wilbour were not alone in studying the crypt.[3] Carl Richard Lepsius made squeezes of the north and south walls that were the basis for Walter Wreszinski's publication.[4] Wreszinski made many of the same corrections as Wilbour had, but saw (or restored) more than either Wilbour or Mariette had noted. However, Wreszinski did not publish the rear wall.

The most significant and complete publication of the crypt was by Jean Leclant in his monumental work on Montuemhat.[5] Although the illustrations of the reliefs are squeezes, his photographs of the crypt demonstrate that he was able to study it in situ. He transcribes only what he was able to discern at the time, but includes the variant readings of Mariette, Wreszinski, and Dumichen, who earlier published a partial copy of the texts. For the rear wall, however, he relies on Mariette's drawing as the reliefs were no longer clear.

Jens Heise included the texts in his 2007 book on Late Period biographical inscriptions,[6] and Karl Jansen-Winkeln published the texts in 2009 as part of

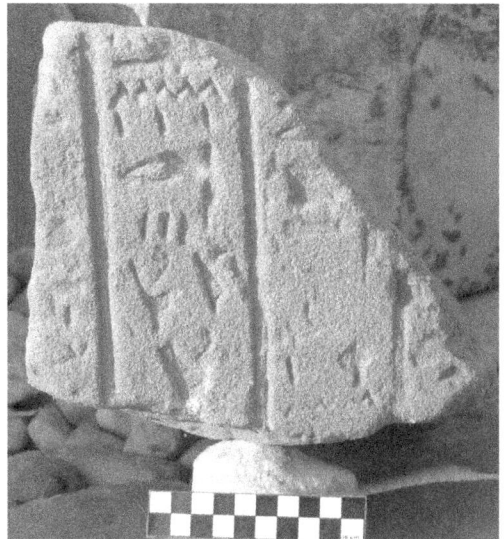
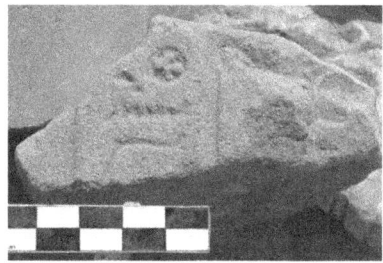
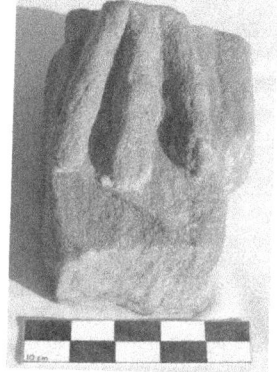

Fig. 4.2 (a–b) Two fragments of inscription, probably from the Montuemhat Crypt (7MWB.5 [left] and 7MWB.6 [top right]); (c) the foot of a possible vulture statue (17M.20). Photographs by M. McKercher.

his monumental *Inschriften der Spätzeit*.[7] In the same year, Robert Ritner published the inscriptions in transliteration and translation,[8] including signs that Wreszinski saw or restored but that were no longer visible by Leclant's time.

While the crypt has been widely studied for over one hundred years, photographs of the walls have never been published. Figs. 4.3, 4.5, 4.7, and 4.9 correct that omission. The numbering of the columns follows Leclant et al., rather than Mariette's drawing.

While excavating the area to the west in 1983, the Mut Expedition found two fragments of sandstone inscription that probably came from the crypt, although they do not join the existing texts (fig. 4.2a–b).[9] The larger block preserves parts of four columns of text, of which only the center two are clear. Column 2 mentions [*Mwt wrt nbt*] *Išrw*, while column 3 clearly shows three crowns. To us, this suggests that it may belong to a now-missing part of A.6–9 as A8 also shows three crowns. However, this is just a conjecture.

The smaller block shows only *niwt ns*. It can probably be restored as [*ḥȝty-ˁ n*] *niwt Ns*[*ptḥ*], which can only be Nesptah A. It probably comes from the north wall or the north door jamb.

THE MONTUEMHAT CRYPT IN THE MUT TEMPLE: A NEW LOOK   39

Door Jambs (fig. 4.3)

Mariette included these texts in his drawings of the north and south walls. Here they are shown separately as fig. 4.3. Curiously, Mariette did not draw the upper two blocks of the south jamb, nor did anyone else describe them. The top block has been erased, but a few signs are visible in the narrow center block. Both blocks are visible in Leclant's pl. LXVIc.

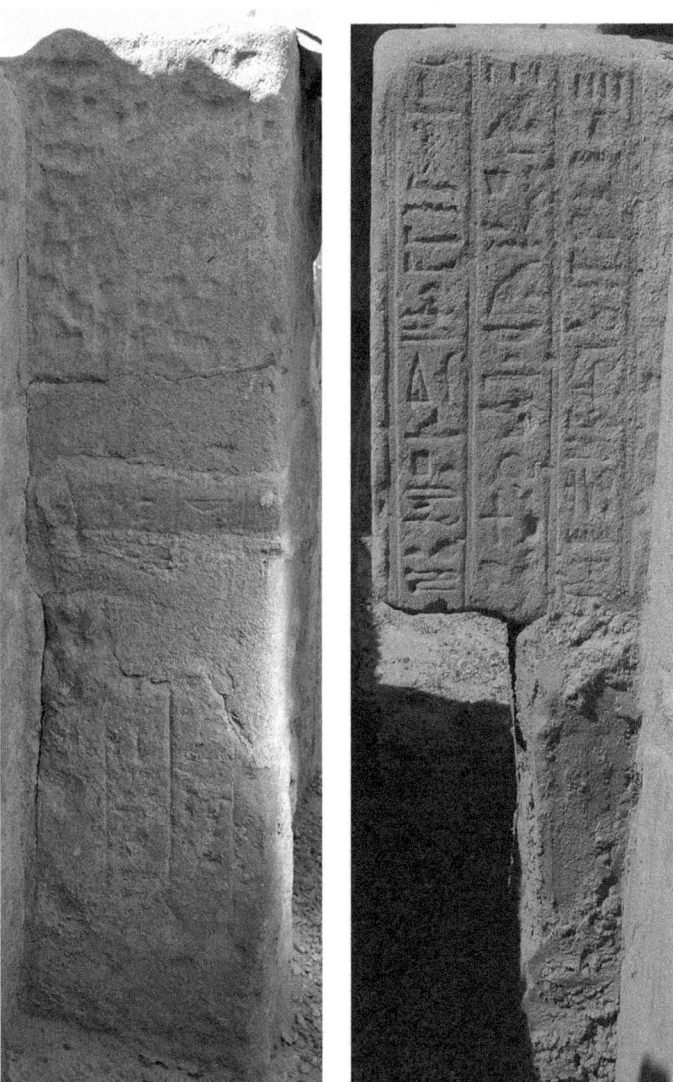

Fig. 4.3. Texts on the south (left) and north door jambs; columns A.1–3 and B.32–34, respectively. Photographs by M. McKercher.

East Wall (figs. 4.4, 4.5)

Above the offering scene are two full registers and part of a third depicting cultic objects. They may have been gifts to Mut by Montuemhat and his family that were once stored in the room, but they could also be part of the "Great Inventory" mentioned in A.10, which could have included treasures stored elsewhere in the temple. As Redford notes, "Great Inventories" were "a compilation of prescriptions governing the manufacture of divine statues, reliefs, cult paraphernalia, and the performance of rituals" on papyri kept in the temples.[10] However, cultic objects could also be shown on reliefs on naoi or in crypts or other chambers.[11]

Many of the images in our crypt labeled Mut show her in guises more common for other goddesses such as Hathor or Isis,[12] including the seated statue and the four menats in the upper complete register. This is not surprising given the syncretisms among deities by this time.[13] More surprising, perhaps, is the plaque or stela of the triad of Syro-Palestinian Reshep and Qudshu and Egyptian Onouris.[14] The lowest register shows a seated Sekhmet labeled as plural, perhaps referring to the large number of Sekhmet statues in the precinct. Of particular interest to us is the baboon with four strokes above its head. It may represent the four large baboon statues found in the Mut Temple by Benson and Gourlay,[15] restored by the Brooklyn Museum expedition, and removed to the National Museum of Egyptian Civilization by the Ministry of Antiquities in 2007 (fig. 4.4, inset).

Of the top register, only the lower portions of the figures remain. To the right are four birds, the first probably a mummified falcon (or falcon statue) as in the bottom register, the others vultures. Behind them are four standing and one seated statues. Curiously, in 1999 the Brooklyn Mut expedition found the front part of the foot of what was probably a vulture statue in the ruins of the Mut Temple's West Porch (fig. 4.2c).[16] Could this be the remains of one of the vultures shown on the east wall?

Wilbour noted that the reliefs were "nearly gone" in 1881; he was unable to read most of Mut's titles, Nesptah A's name, and Montuemhat's titles of "royal seal bearer" and "prophet." Since then, Mut's left hand, staff, and most of the offering table have disappeared. Only the feet of Taharqa and Nesptah A remain. The torsos of Montuemhat and his son are visible but Nesptah B's feet have been lost. The inscriptions are very faint: Mut's titulary is completely gone, Taharqa's cartouches are only just legible, and Nesptah B's name and that of his mother seem to have worn away entirely. In the register above the offering scene, the bottom of the right-hand block has broken away, robbing the scene of the lower parts of all the figures.

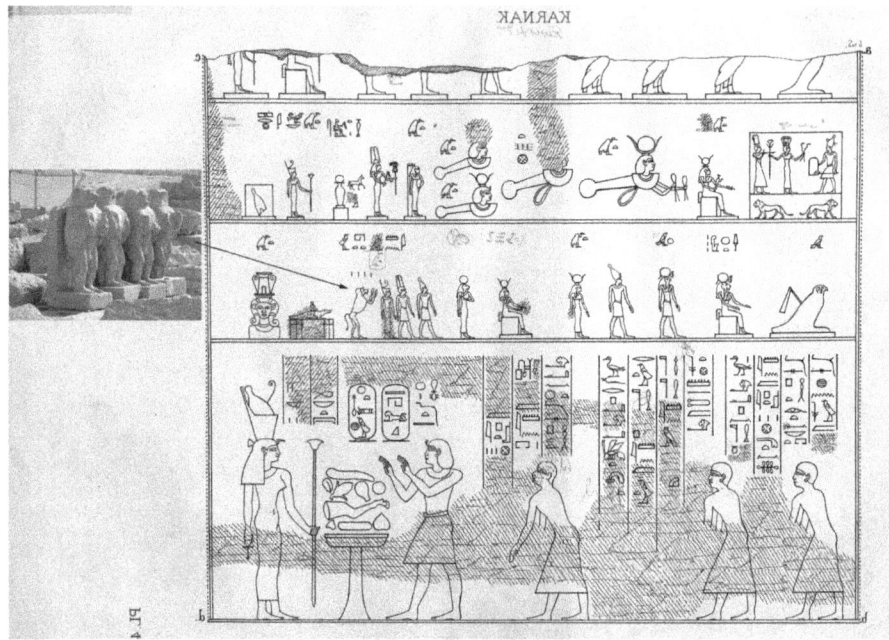

Fig. 4.4. Mariette's pl. 43 (east wall) with Wilbour's annotations; inset: the four baboon statues restored by the Brooklyn Museum expedition.

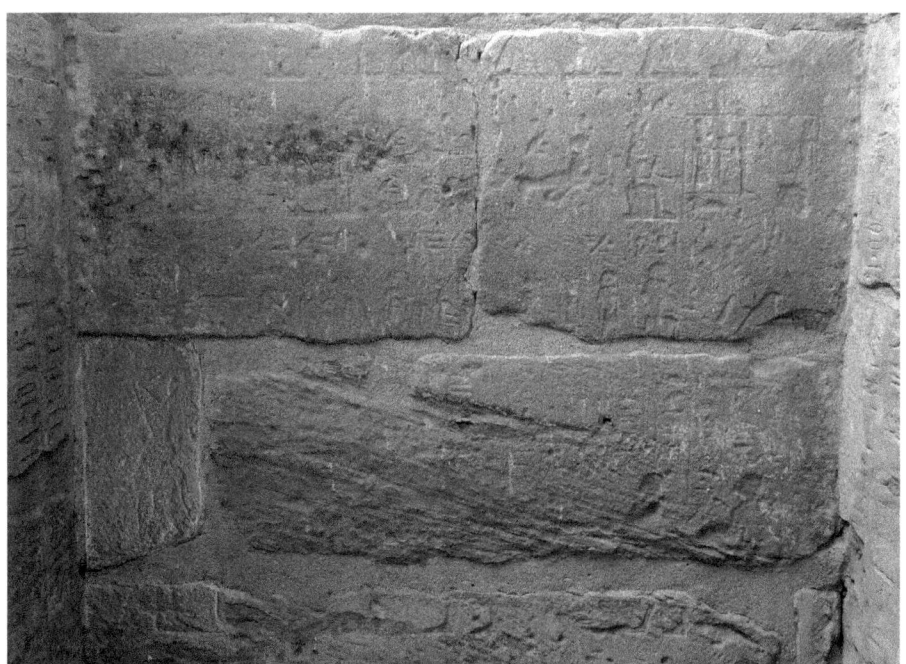

Fig. 4.5. East wall of the crypt. Photograph by M. McKercher.

Wilbour made relatively few suggestions for the back wall, but they are correct. In the lower register, the label for the seated goddess wearing a horned disk is clearly *Iw.s-ˁ3.s*, and the label above the three deities in front of the baboon is clearly *Imn Mwt*. The signs Wilbour saw above the shrine on the right in the second register and in front of the mummiform god in the upper register are faint but plausible, and most of the labels of the treasures can still be read.

North Wall (Text B; figs. 4.6, 4.7)

Here Montuemhat describes his many benefactions for Mut, Amun, Thebes, and Upper Egypt. As a reward, he requests a good life, a long old age, a proper burial, and that his heirs succeed him in his positions (B.25–29). He ends with a plea for funerary invocations and offerings (B.34).

Salt encrustations on the upper portions of the lowest course's eastern block now obscure several of the hieroglyphs in B.2–11. Breaks in the stone at the bottom of B.3–9 have eliminated several signs that were clear to Mariette, Wilbour, and Wreszinski, and others have been damaged. However, more is visible than Leclant indicated. The west half of the second course (B.28–31), already hard to read in Mariette's time, is now barely legible.

The most interesting lacuna is in B.12, where the wall's narrow second course is completely eroded. Neither Mariette nor Wilbour could read the signs between *ḥr* and *ii m rsy*. Wreszinski, however, restores *nb.i*,[17] and Ritner tentatively reads *ib nb.i*,[18] making the text "[my lord] who came from the south," seemingly a clear reference to a Kushite king.

South Wall (Text A; figs. 4.8, 4.9)

This text details Montuemhat's contributions to the cults of the gods from Elephantine to Abydos. He reinstated rituals, built barques and offering tables, repaired or rebuilt temples, and faced sacred lakes with stone, using only the finest materials: wood imported from Lebanon, gold, electrum, and precious stones.

Of most interest to the Mut Expedition is Wilbour's correction in the middle of A.12, describing a colonnade Montuemhat built for the Mut Temple. Wilbour read 2[3] columns rather than Mariette's 3[3]. There is now a large gap between the two blocks on which A.12 was inscribed, but close examination makes it clear that the text originally said "24 columns." The Brooklyn Museum Mut Expedition discovered two porches of twelve columns each in front of the Mut Temple. While they had been refurbished in the Ptolemaic Period, their Twenty-fifth Dynasty origin was clear, confirming Montuemhat's claim.[19]

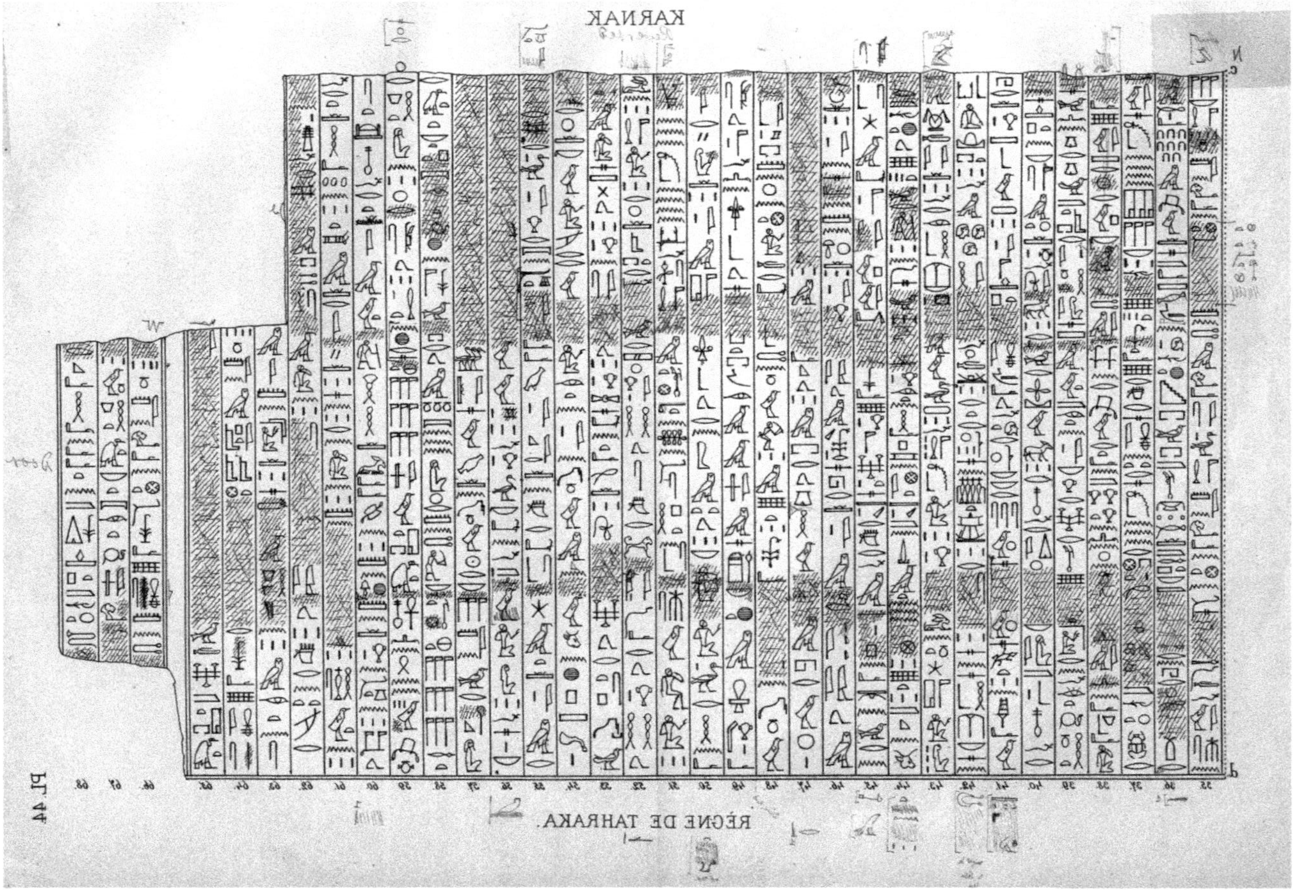

Fig. 4.6. Mariette's pl. 44 (north wall) with Wilbour's annotations.

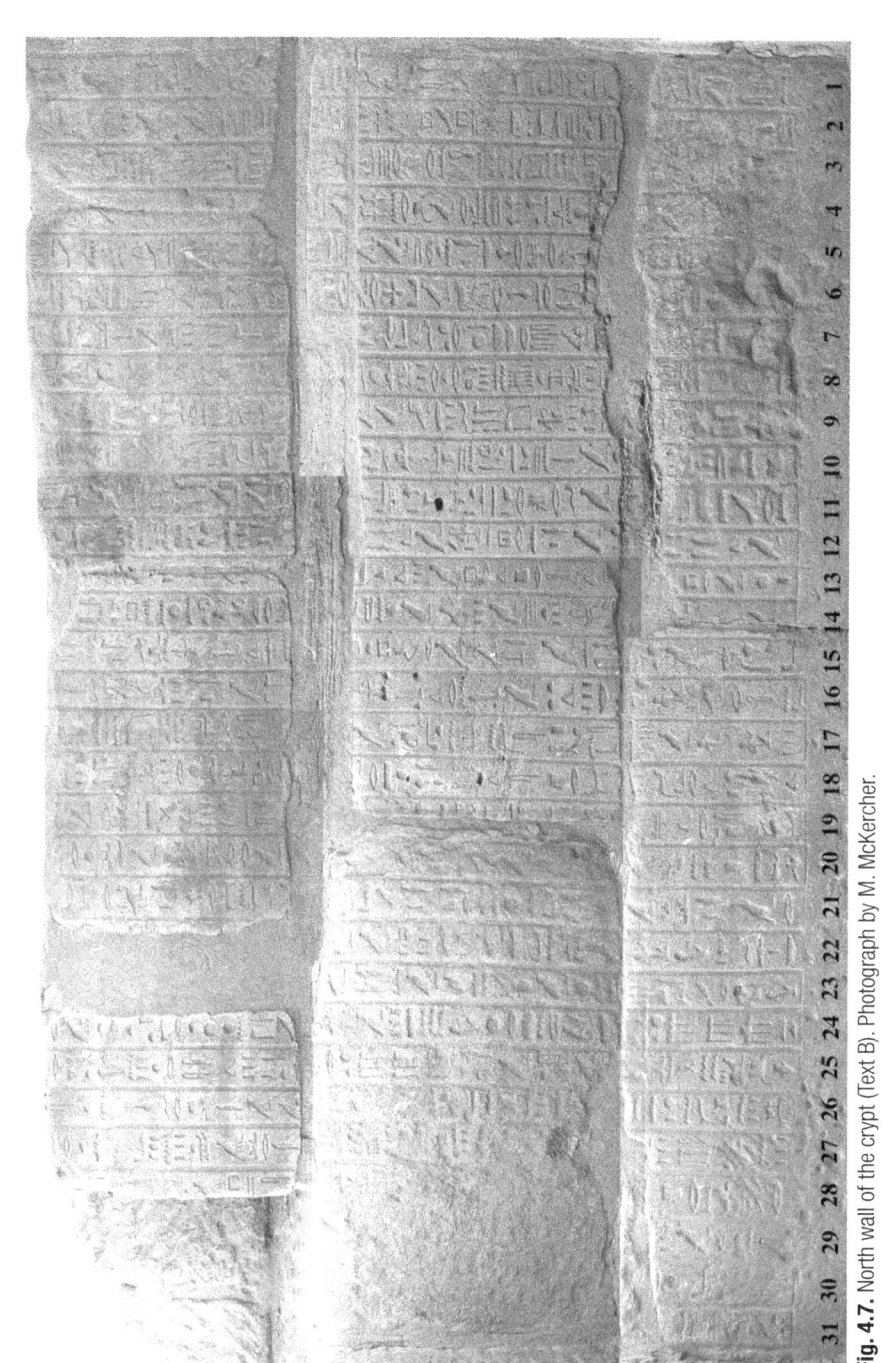

Fig. 4.7. North wall of the crypt (Text B). Photograph by M. McKercher.

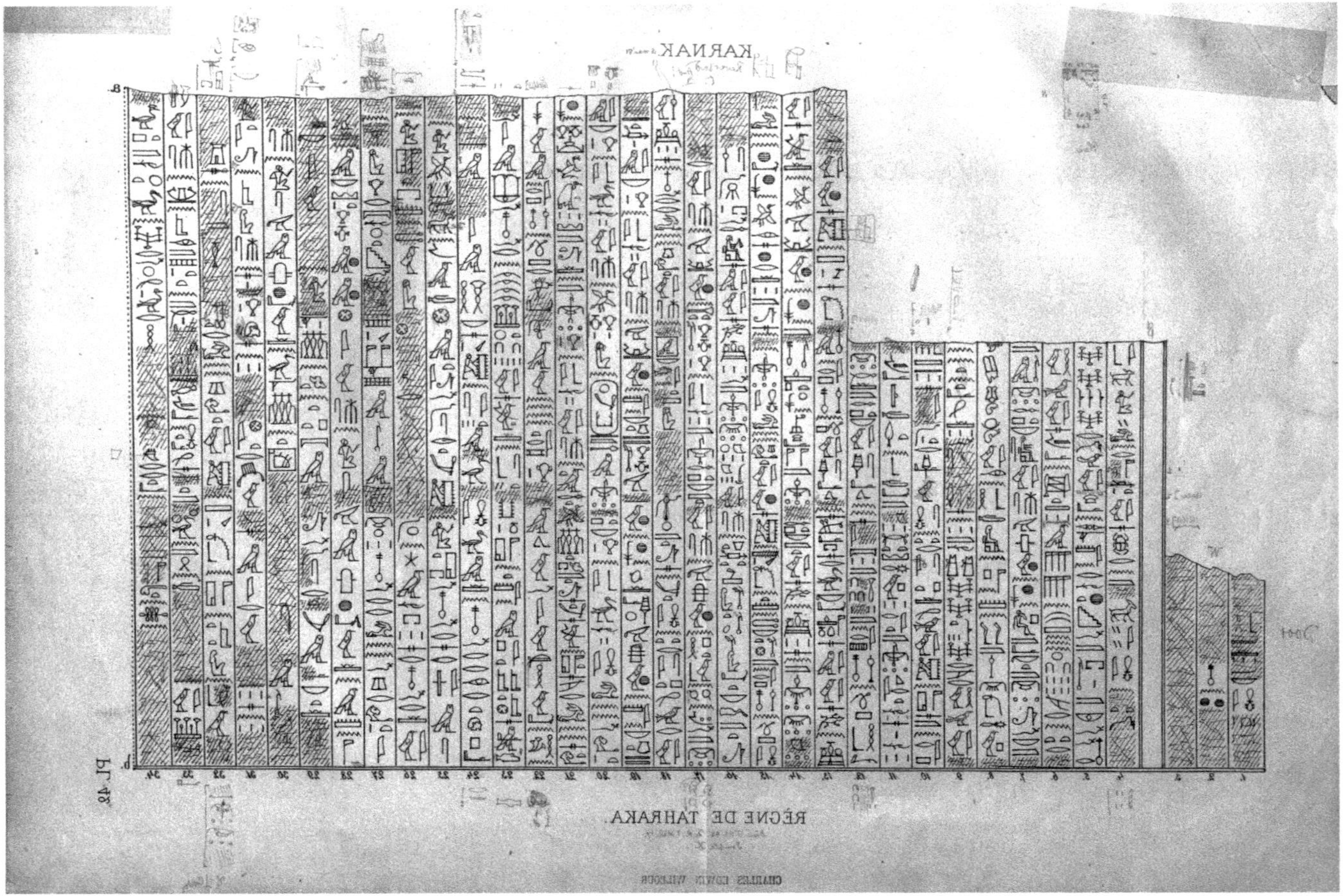

Fig. 4.8. Mariette's pl. 42 (south wall) with Wilbour's annotations.

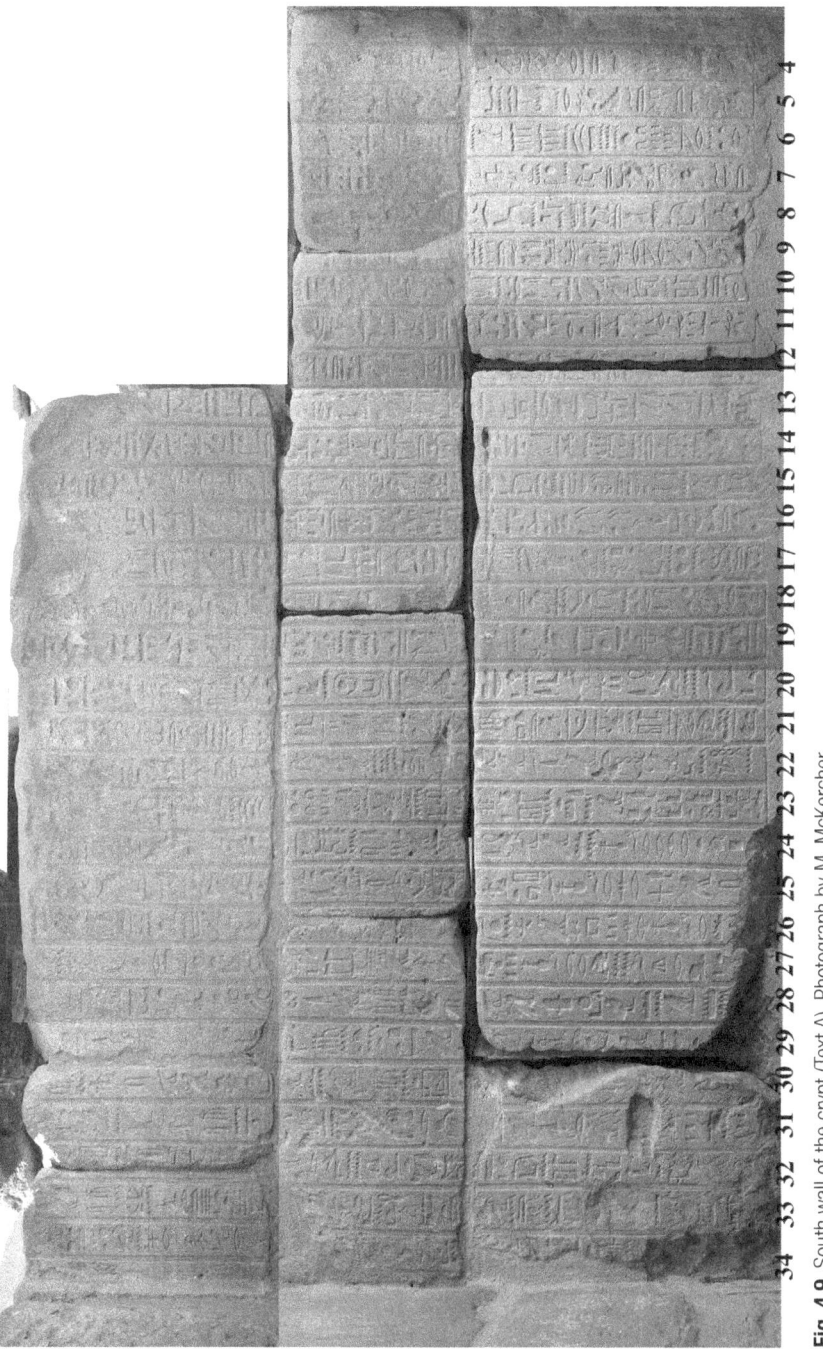

Fig. 4.9. South wall of the crypt (Text A). Photograph by M. McKercher.

The tops of the south wall's upper courses have suffered more wear than those of the north wall, and the bottom of the lowest course's center block has broken off, removing the lowest signs of A.24–29, with A.29 suffering the most damage.[20]

Dating

The east wall is surely earlier than the north and south walls as the inscriptions on the east wall indicate that Nesptah A is still alive, Montuemhat is not yet mayor of Thebes or governor of Upper Egypt, and Nesptah B is only a prophet of Amun and a phylarch. When the inscriptions on the north wall were carved, Nesptah A was dead, Montuemhat was mayor of Thebes and governor of Upper Egypt (B.1), and Nesptah B was inspector of prophets in Thebes as well as phylarch (B.17).

While the crypt may once have been a storeroom for temple treasures, that must have changed once Texts B and A were written, as stored furnishings would have obscured the texts. Given the request to make funerary invocations and offerings (B.34), the repurposing of the crypt as a funerary chapel or serdab containing a statue of Montuemhat is entirely possible.[21]

Montuemhat mentions generous inundations that made his city and the nomes prosperous (B.10). This may be a reference to the unusually high (and beneficial) floods of Taharqa's years 6–9.[22]

It is frequently argued that the references to the country being in upheaval (B.11), expelling rebels (B.14), purifying temples after some unfortunate event (B.3–4), rebuilding damaged temples (A.22, A.24), and so on must refer to the aftermath of the Assyrian sack of Thebes in 664–663 BCE.[23] It is possible, however, and as Leclant suggests,[24] that these descriptions belong to the tradition of boastful royal restoration texts known from the First Intermediate Period onward and have nothing to do with political reality.[25]

Egypt may not have been completely stable under Kushite rule until shortly before Taharqa's accession.[26] Relatively little building took place under Shabataka and Shabaka;[27] only under Taharqa do large-scale projects reappear.[28] Temples may have fallen into disrepair and not been rebuilt since Piankhi's time, especially given Egypt's involvement in wars in the Near East as late as 701 BCE; armies are expensive and consume resources that might otherwise be used for building projects.

In addition, the Assyrians are unlikely to be referred to as "rebels" but rather as enemies. If Text B is to be taken literally, then suppressing rebels could refer to Taharqa's reconquest of Memphis in 669 BCE. According to Dodson, when Ashurbanipal retook Lower Egypt in 667, he "reinstated his Delta vassals in their cities, at least some of whom had fled from a resurgent Taharqa."[29]

Given all this, we argue that it makes the most sense for the texts to have been inscribed between the inundations of Taharqa's years 6–9 (ca. 685 BCE) and the time just before the Assyrian invasion of 671 BCE, or perhaps as late as 667 BCE. In this period, the country was stable and prosperous and Montuemhat was in firm control of Upper Egypt, assisted by his son, Nesptah B, whom he was training to follow in his footsteps. Assyria's initial conquest of the Delta in 671 and the subsequent instability may have encouraged Montuemhat to leave a record of his many benefactions for his country and the gods, as well as a request for a long and happy life, with his sons succeeding him in his posts. That he placed these texts in a small, almost hidden chamber in the Mut Temple suggests that he did not want to annoy whoever was king by proclaiming his own king-like activities too publicly, although he repeated at least some of the crypt texts when he built the Contra-Temple, a small, inconspicuous building not accessible directly from the Mut Temple,[30] and on a number of statues made while he was still alive.[31]

If Ritner and Wreszinski are correct that B.12 can be read "[my lord] who came from the South," then it is unlikely that the texts were written later, when Psamtik I was king.

On a practical level, if the Assyrians did strip Thebes of its riches in 664–663 BCE, where would Montuemhat have found the resources after 664 BCE to build the barques, the offering tables, thrones, and so on, covered with precious metals and jewels, to import wood from Lebanon, and to quarry the stone to rebuild sacred lakes and temples? Trade would surely have been disrupted at least somewhat between 671 BCE and Psamtik I's accession (664 BCE) and perhaps even later. We argue that the work and its commemoration in the crypt are more likely the product of the middle years of Montuemhat's career, between ca. 685 BCE and 671 or 667 BCE, than the years between the Assyrians' arrival in 664 BCE and Montuemhat's death in ca. 648 BCE.[32]

Notes

1 PM II², page 258.
2 Mariette, *Karnak*. As I first pointed out in 1988 (Fazzini, *Egypt, Dynasty XXII–XXV*, 33), the plates as published show the reliefs and texts backward. This error was inadvertently repeated in my article on the cult at South Karnak in Gombert-Meurice and Payraudeau, *Servir les dieux*, 248. They are intentionally flipped here to show the texts and scenes in their proper orientation. Illustration courtesy of the Brooklyn Museum Libraries, the Wilbour Library of Egyptology, Special Collections.
3 For a summary of publications and commentaries, see Leclant, *Montouemhat*, 193–95; Jansen-Winkeln, *Inschriften der Spätzeit* 3, no. 142, 197–203; Spencer, "Sustaining Egyptian Culture?," 478–83; and Naunton, *Regime Change*, 21–24. It should be noted that when these publications refer to the history of the Twenty-fifth

Dynasty, all have Shabaka preceding Shabataka, as the chronological revisions by Bányai, Payraudeau, and Broekman (see n27) had not yet been published.
4   Wreszinski, "Inschriften des Monthemhat."
5   Leclant, *Montouemhat*, Doc. 44, 193–238; pls. LXVI–LXX. His pl. LXVIII omits the western end of the lowest course of the north wall (cols. 28–31), and he does not illustrate either of the door jambs.
6   Heise, *Erinnern und Gedenken*, 80–89.
7   Jansen-Winkeln, *Inschriften der Spätzeit* 3, 197–204.
8   Ritner, *Libyan Anarchy*, no. 166, 556–64.
9   Expedition nos. 7MWB.5 (h: 17 cm; w: 20.5 cm; d: 30.2 cm) and 7MWB.6 (h: 9.2 cm; w of inscribed surface: 13 cm; d: 18 cm).
10 Redford, *Royal Speech*, 94.
11 Redford, *Royal Speech*, 94.
12 For discussions of various aspects of Mut by the late Prof. Herman te Velde and Dr. Jacobus van Dijk, two valued members of the Brooklyn Museum Mut Expedition who were formerly associated with the Rijksuniversiteit Groningen, see te Velde, "Towards a Minimal Definition," "Mut," "The Cat as Sacred Animal," "Mut, the Eye of Re," "Mut and Other Egyptian Goddesses"; and van Dijk, "Over de tempel." The latter (in Dutch) is a useful source of information on Eye of Re cults and the form of Mut called Ash-sejemes ("She who listens to the one who calls her"), who bears the epithet "Mistress of young women" and was a patron of women seeking a partner and the birth of a child. It is hoped that an updated version of this article will be published in English. For discussions of the representations of Mut in the Montuemhat crypt, see also Wahlberg, *Goddess Cults*, 51n266, 53n274, 75, 269, 278, and tables 1–8, on iconography, attributes, and priestly titles associated with goddesses.
13 Baines, *Fecundity Figures*, 59.
14 Cf. Schulman, "Winged Reshep" and "Stela of Qudshu."
15 Benson and Gourlay, *Temple of Mut*, 75 and pl. IX.
16 Expedition no. 17M.20: h: 8.7 cm; w: 9.5 cm; d: 11.5 cm.
17 Wreszinski, "Inschriften des Monthemhat," 395, and Tafel 4.
18 Ritner, *Libyan Anarchy*, 559, 560.
19 Fazzini, "Some Comments on the Preserved Figural Decoration," 7–11.
20 This loss is also clear in Leclant, *Montouemhat*, pl. LXIX.
21 Fazzini, *Dynasty XXII–XXV*, 16; Fazzini, "Two Semi-Erased Kushite Cartouches," 96.
22 Morkot, *Black Pharaohs*, 231.
23 See Leclant, *Montouemhat*, 209, 266–68; and Spencer, "Sustaining Egyptian Culture?," 479. De Meulenaere's suggestion that Nesptah B inscribed the crypt after Montuemhat's death as an act of filial piety seems rather far-fetched (De Meulenaere, "Nesptah," 99–102).
24 For instance, Leclant, *Montouemhat*, 209. More recently, see Spencer, "Sustaining Egyptian Culture?," 479.
25 Naunton, *Regime Change*, 111, suggests that the relief on the rear wall, at least, was carved prior to 671 BCE.
26 Payraudeau, "Shabaqo-Shabataqo," 125–26.
27 We accept the reordering of Shabataka and Shabaka proposed by Bányai, "Ein Vorschlag zur Chronologie," Payraudeau, "Shabaqo-Shabataqo," and Broekman, "Order of Succession," "Genealogical Considerations," "Suggesting a New Chronology."

28 Dodson, *Afterglow of Empire*, 152, 159–60, 163.
29 Dodson, *Afterglow of Empire*, 167.
30 Fazzini and O'Rourke, "Mut Temple's Contra-Temple." The Montuemhat Crypt and the Contra-Temple are part of a trend, begun in the Third Intermediate Period, of private individuals building small chapels within temple precincts, including the Osiris chapels at Karnak and the chapels of the God's Wives of Amun at Medinet Habu. See, for example, Spencer, "Sustaining Egyptian Culture?," 453n45. The Mut Precinct contains the Nitocris Chapel in Temple A (Fazzini, "A Monument in the Precinct of Mut"), a magical healing chapel of Horwedja (Fazzini, "The Brooklyn Museum's 2010 Season," 13 and fig. 43), a *ḥwt-k3* for Nesptah B (unpublished), and the lintels for at least two more chapels naming Montuemhat (unpublished).
31 For example, Leclant, *Montouemhat*, Doc. 9, 58–64 (Berlin 17271) and Doc. 10, 65–78 (Cairo CG 646). Leclant points out (p. 15) that while the back pillar is the typical "Saite" formula (Leclant's quotation marks), this formula is known from the New Kingdom to the Ptolemaic Period, so need not reflect a Saite date for the statue. However, since Psamtik I essentially left Upper Egypt in Montuemhat's hands for years, the statues (which are more public than the crypt and Contra-Temple) may have been created in the early Twenty-sixth Dynasty. See also Spencer, "Sustaining Egyptian Culture?," 479–83.
32 Montuemhat's last known inscription dates to year 16 of Psamtik I (Leclant, *Montouemhat*, Doc. 43, 191–92).

Bibliography

Baines, John. *Fecundity Figures: Egyptian Personification and the Iconology of a Genre*. Warminster and Chicago: Aris & Phillips, 1985.

Bányai, Michael. "Ein Vorschlag zur Chronologie der 25. Dynastie in Ägypten." *JEH* 6 (2013): 46–129.

Benson, Margaret, and Janet Gourlay. *The Temple of Mut in Asher: An Account of the Excavation of the Temple and of the Religious Representations and Objects Found Therein, as Illustrating the History of Egypt and the Main Religious Ideas of the Egyptians*. London: J. Murray, 1899.

Broekman, Gerard. "Genealogical Considerations Regarding the Kings of the Twenty-fifth Dynasty in Egypt." *GM* 251 (2017): 13–20.

———. "The Order of Succession between Shabaka and Shabataka: A Different View on the Chronology of the Twenty-fifth Dynasty." *GM* 245 (2015): 17–31.

———. "Suggesting a New Chronology for the Kushite Twenty-fifth Dynasty and Considering the Consequences for the Preceding Libyan Period." In *A True Scribe of Abydos: Essays on First Millennium Egypt in Honour of Anthony Leahy*, edited by Claus Jurman, Bettina Bader, and David A. Aston, 39–52. OLA 265. Leuven: Peeters, 2017.

De Meulenaere, Herman. "Nesptah, fils et successeur de Montouemhat." *CdÉ* 83 (2008): 98–108.

Dodson, Aidan. *Afterglow of Empire: Egypt from the Fall of the New Kingdom to the Saite Renaissance*. Cairo: American University in Cairo Press, 2012.

Fazzini, Richard. "The Brooklyn Museum's 2010 Season of Fieldwork at the Precinct of the Goddess Mut at South Karnak." Brooklyn: Brooklyn Museum, 2010. www.brooklynmuseum.org//features/mut/mut_expedition_reports

———. *Egypt, Dynasty XXII–XXV*. Iconography of Religions 16, 10. Leiden: Brill, 1988.

———. "A Monument in the Precinct of Mut with the Name of the God's Wife Nitocris I." In *Artibus Aegypti: Studia in Honorem Bernardi V. Bothmer a Collegis, Amicis, Discipulis Conscripta*, edited by Herman de Meulenaere and Luc Limme, 51–62. Brussels: Musées royaux d'art et d'histoire, 1983.

———. "Some Comments on the Preserved Figural Decoration." In *The First Pylon of the Mut Temple, South Karnak: Architecture, Decoration, Inscriptions*, edited by Richard Fazzini and Jacobus van Dijk, 5–18. OLA 236. Leuven: Peeters, 2015.

———. "Two Semi-Erased Kushite Cartouches in the Precinct of Mut at South Karnak." In *Causing His Name to Live: Studies in Egyptian Epigraphy and History in Memory of William J. Murnane*, edited by Peter Brand and Louise Cooper, 95–102. Leiden and Boston: Brill, 2009.

———, and Paul F. O'Rourke. "Aspects of the Mut Temple's Contra-Temple at South Karnak Part I." In *Hommages offerts à Jean-Claude Goyon pour son 70ème anniversaire*, edited by Luc Gabolde, 139–50. BdÉ 143. Lyon: IFAO, 2008.

Gombert-Meurice, Florence, and Frédéric Payraudeau. *Servir les dieux d'Égypte: Divines adoratrices, chanteuses et prêtres d'Amon à Thèbes*. Paris: Somogy, 2018.

Heise, Jens. *Erinnern und Gedenken: Aspekte der biographischen Inschriften der ägyptischen Spätzeit*. Fribourg: Academic Press; Göttingen: Vandenhoeck & Ruprecht, 2007.

Jansen-Winkeln, Karl. *Inschriften der Spätzeit 3: Die 25. Dynastie*. Wiesbaden: Harrassowitz, 2009.

Leclant, Jean. *Montouemhat, quatrième prophète d'Amon, prince de la ville*. BdÉ 35. Cairo: IFAO, 1961.

Mariette, Auguste. *Karnak: Étude topographique et archéologique, avec un appendice comprenant les principaux textes hiéroglyphiques découverts ou recueillis pendant les fouilles exécutées à Karnak*. Leipzig: J.C. Hinrichs, 1875.

Morkot, Robert. *The Black Pharaohs: Egypt's Nubian Rulers*. London: Rubicon, 2000.

Naunton, Christopher. "Regime Change and the Administration of Thebes During the Twenty-fifth Dynasty." PhD diss., University of Wales, 2011. https://independent.academia.edu/ChristopherNaunton

Payraudeau, Frédéric. "Retour sur la succession Shabaqo–Shabataqo." *Nekhet* 1 (2014): 115–27.

Redford, Donald. "A Royal Speech from the Blocks of the 10th Pylon." *BES* 3 (1981): 87–102.

Ritner, Robert. *The Libyan Anarchy: Inscriptions from Egypt's Third Intermediate Period*. Atlanta, GA: Society of Biblical Literature, 2009.

Schulman, Alan. "A Stela of Qudshu from Memphis." *BES* 4 (1982): 81–91.

———. "The Winged Reshep." *JARCE* 16 (1979): 69–84.
Spencer, Neal. "Sustaining Egyptian Culture? Non-royal Initiatives in the Late Period Temple Building." In *Egypt in Transition: Social and Religious Development of Egypt in the First Millennium BCE, Proceedings of an International Conference, Prague, September 1–4, 2009*, edited by Ladislav Bareš, Filip Coppens, and Květa Smoláriková, 441–90. Prague: Czech Institute of Egyptology, Charles University of Prague, 2010.
te Velde, Herman. "The Cat as Sacred Animal of the Goddess Mut." In *Studies in Egyptian Religion Dedicated to Professor Jan Zandee*, edited by Heerma van Voss et al., 127–37. Leiden: Brill, 1982.
———. "Mut." *LÄ* 4, no. 2: cols. 246–48. Wiesbaden: Harrassowitz, 1980.
———. "Mut and Other Egyptian Goddesses." In *Ancient Egypt, the Aegean, and the Near East: Studies in Honour of Martha Rhoads Bell* 1, edited by Jacke Phillips et al., 455–62. San Antonio: Van Siclen Books, 1997.
———. "Mut, the Eye of Re." In *Akten des Vierten Internationalen Ägyptologenkongresses, München*, 3, edited by Sylvia Schoske, 395–403. Hamburg: Buske, 1988.
———. "Towards a Minimal Definition of the Goddess Mut." *JEOL* 26 (1979–80): 3–9.
van Dijk, Jacobus. "Over de tempel en de cultus van de Egyptische godin Moet." In *Onder Orchideeën: Nieuwe Oogst uit de Tuin der Geesteswetenschappen te Groningen*, edited by Jacobus van Dijk, 63–76. Groningen: Barkhuis, 2010.
Wahlberg, Nina. "Goddess Cults in Egypt between 1070 BC and 332 BC." PhD diss., University of Birmingham, 2002. https://www.scribd.com/doc/147221589/Goddess-Cults-in-Egypt
Wreszinski, Walter. "Die Inschriften des Monthemhat im Tempel der Mut: Mit vier Tafeln in Autographie." *Orientalistische Literaturzeitung* 13 (1910): 385–99.

2 Egyptian Afterlives in Antiquity

5 A Visit with the Egyptian Statues of the Alexandria Serapeum and Iseum Campense

Paul Edmund Stanwick

IN THE YEARS IMMEDIATELY FOLLOWING the Roman takeover of Egypt in 30 BCE, representatives of the emperor Augustus started changing the visual landscape of Alexandria. The lavish Caesareum temple, devoted to the cult of Egypt's new rulers, received two huge granite obelisks originally carved for Pharaoh Thutmose III and erected well over one thousand years earlier at Heliopolis, about two hundred kilometers southeast of Alexandria (Pliny, *Natural History* 36.69). Greek and Latin texts on a bronze crab that decorated one of the obelisks' new bases stated that the prefect Barbarus had dedicated the monoliths in honor of the emperor in 13–12 BCE.[1] The obelisks' position near the harbor made them an Alexandrian landmark until the nineteenth century, when one obelisk traveled to London and the other to New York.

Because we know almost nothing about the Caesareum archaeologically, we must rely on a description from the Alexandrian philosopher Philo. If we squint our eyes on a sunny day, so that they are almost shut, we can perhaps imagine the expansive complex with the obelisks, possibly gilded and gleaming like the temple's gold statues, presiding over an array of porticos, libraries, groves, and open courts (*Embassy to Gaius*, 151). We might ask a few questions: Why did the prefect dedicate "antique" obelisks rather than create new ones? Did his aides know the Egyptian meaning of the obelisks? What new ideas did they have? This chapter will consider these types of questions.

After annexing Egypt, the Romans extensively engaged with the former kingdom's material culture. They moved many objects from Egypt's temples, placing them in new contexts, both in the province of Egypt and abroad.

Romans also commissioned new objects, extending the use of the Egyptian style for their own purposes.

Rome's engagement with Egypt is a vast topic.[2] Here, we will address one specific aspect: how Egyptian objects—mostly statues, but we will consider other objects as well—acquired new meanings in Roman temple settings in the imperial era. We will examine this question by visiting two of the most important temples of the Roman Empire, the Alexandria Serapeum and the Iseum (et Serapeum) Campense of Rome. We cannot, of course, actually do this because both sanctuaries are mostly destroyed, but we will use available evidence to discern probable stories of devotees who interacted with the Egyptian statues at both temples.

To a modern Egyptologist's eyes, these two temples, with their classical elements and sculptures, seem like alien contexts for Egyptian objects. Yet, for the Romans, the combination was clearly both expected and meaningful.

A Bit of History

The Romans were not the first to send Egypt's objects abroad, nor to interpolate them into nonnative temple settings. Egyptian material already had a long history of travel because of war, trade, and diplomacy. Herodotos (2.182) tells us that Pharaoh Amasis of the Saite dynasty—famous for allowing Greeks to settle at the Delta site of Naukratis—offered Egyptian objects to temples of Rhodes, Samos, and Cyrene in the sixth century BCE.[3] Less than three hundred years later, engagement with the classical world deepened under the Ptolemies, Egypt's Greek Macedonian rulers, when Serapis and Isis temples started multiplying in Alexandria and abroad and were equipped with Egyptian statues and more. The god Serapis was promoted under the early Ptolemies and the Egyptian mother goddess Isis was adopted into the Greek milieu.[4]

Though the template for the Isiac cults originated in the predominantly Greek culture of Alexandria,[5] it also incorporated a strong native Egyptian voice. (Isiac collectively denotes Egyptian gods worshiped in the classical world.) Traders and itinerant priests who undertook treacherous Mediterranean travel initially spread the cults, attracting more and more believers. The cults not only morphed in response to new environments, but also addressed key spiritual needs. Isis, for example, became the patron of safe travel.

The island of Delos was a major ex-Egypt center for Isiac enthusiasm in the Ptolemaic era, as indicated by the remarkable number of related inscriptions[6] and Egyptian statues[7] found there. Traders from Italy and the eastern Mediterranean supported the island's Isiac shrines and priests, at least one of whom trained in Memphis.[8] Delos illustrates another reason for the growth of the Isiac cults. The newly wealthy could climb the social ladder by commissioning impressive temple dedications.

The Isiac cults continued to advance after Rome annexed Egypt. Existing temples were embellished and new ones established across the empire. The Romans, already familiar with Egypt through trade, religious, and political contacts, now had access to a vast supply of ready-made Egyptian "antiques" from the kingdom's past and the resources (materials and artisans) to commission new objects.

The annexation brought changes in patronage along with new ideas, new planners, and new devotees who then influenced the trajectory for Isiac temples in the succeeding centuries. In Alexandria, a resident civil administration headed by the prefect and a group of finance and trade officials replaced the Ptolemies.[9] In Rome, Isiac worship expanded and gained high-status devotees as the city's imperial history progressed.[10]

Alexandria and Rome

Both the Alexandria Serapeum and the Iseum Campense have significant imperial-era histories. Archaeological evidence indicates a major initial construction phase for the Alexandria Serapeum under Ptolemy III and a significant expansion under Roman rule.[11] For the Iseum Campense, archaeological and other evidence suggests an initial construction in the late republican or early imperial era, followed by enhancements and rebuilding.[12] Various emperors were direct or indirect sponsors for the two temples. There are hints about elite donors and planners. For example, Aphthonius wrote that twelve builders created the Serapeum's magnificence (*Progymnasmata*, 12).[13]

About twenty-five Egyptian statues were found at each temple.[14] My counts are conservative: they exclude statues "said to be from," such as those mistakenly attributed to the Serapeum after Jean-Jacques Rifaud brought them to Alexandria from Tanis in the

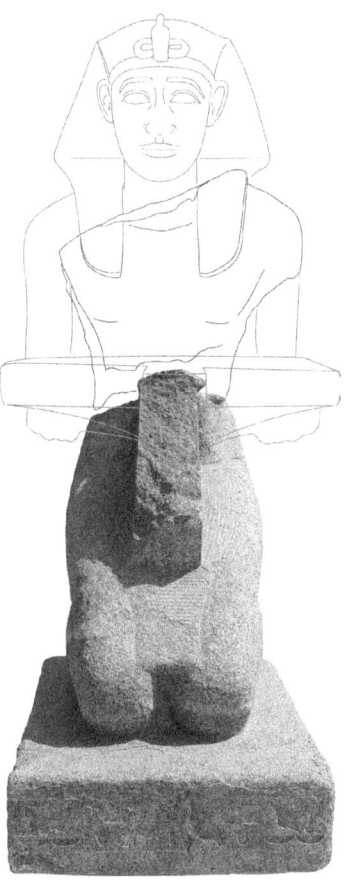

Fig. 5.1. Alexandria 20950. Kneeling Psamtik I with offering table. Granite. Found at Alexandria Serapeum. Originally from Heliopolis (?). Preserved height: 64 cm. Photograph and reconstruction by Simon Connor.

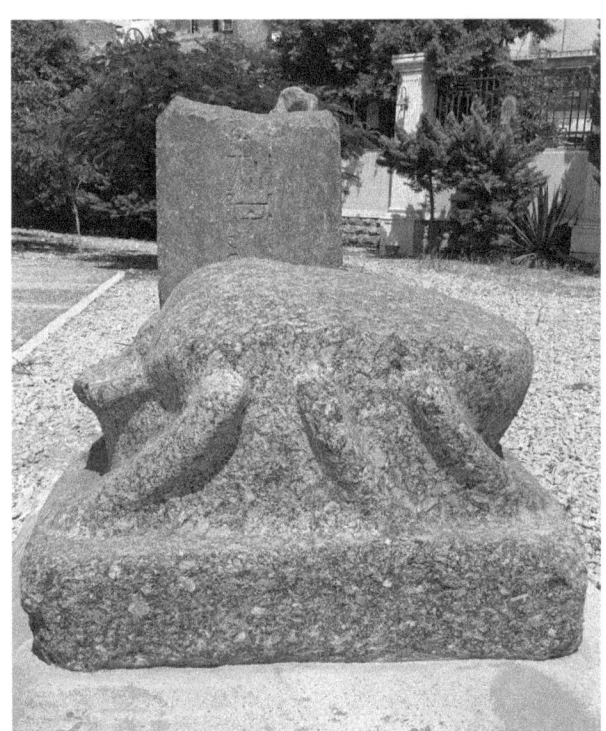

Fig. 5.2. Alexandria 352b. Scarab. New Kingdom. Granite. Found at Alexandria Serapeum. Originally from Heliopolis (?). Preserved height: 60 cm. Photograph above by Paul Stanwick; below by Ibrahim Mustafa.

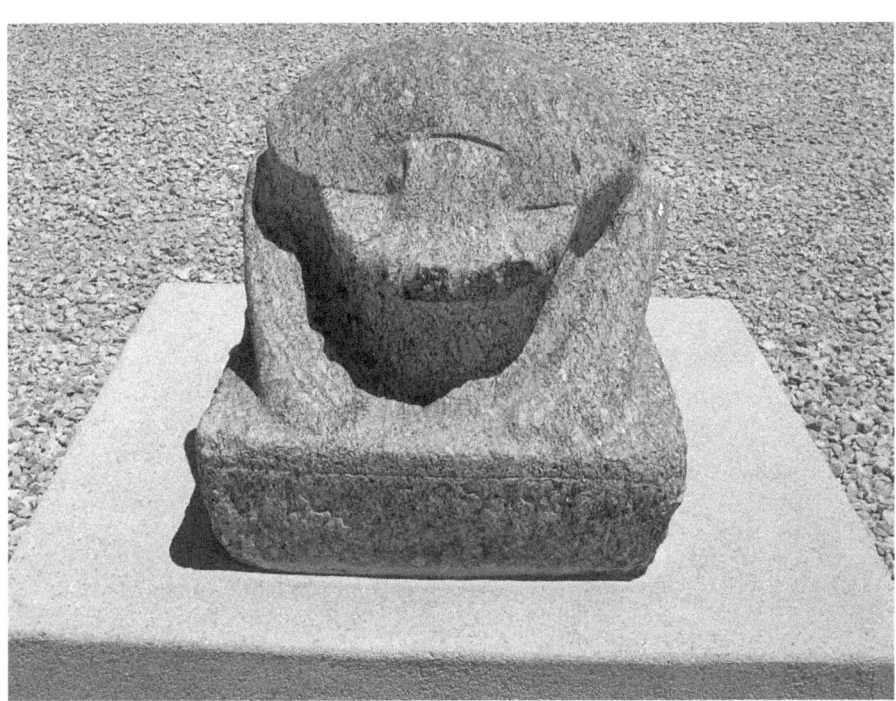

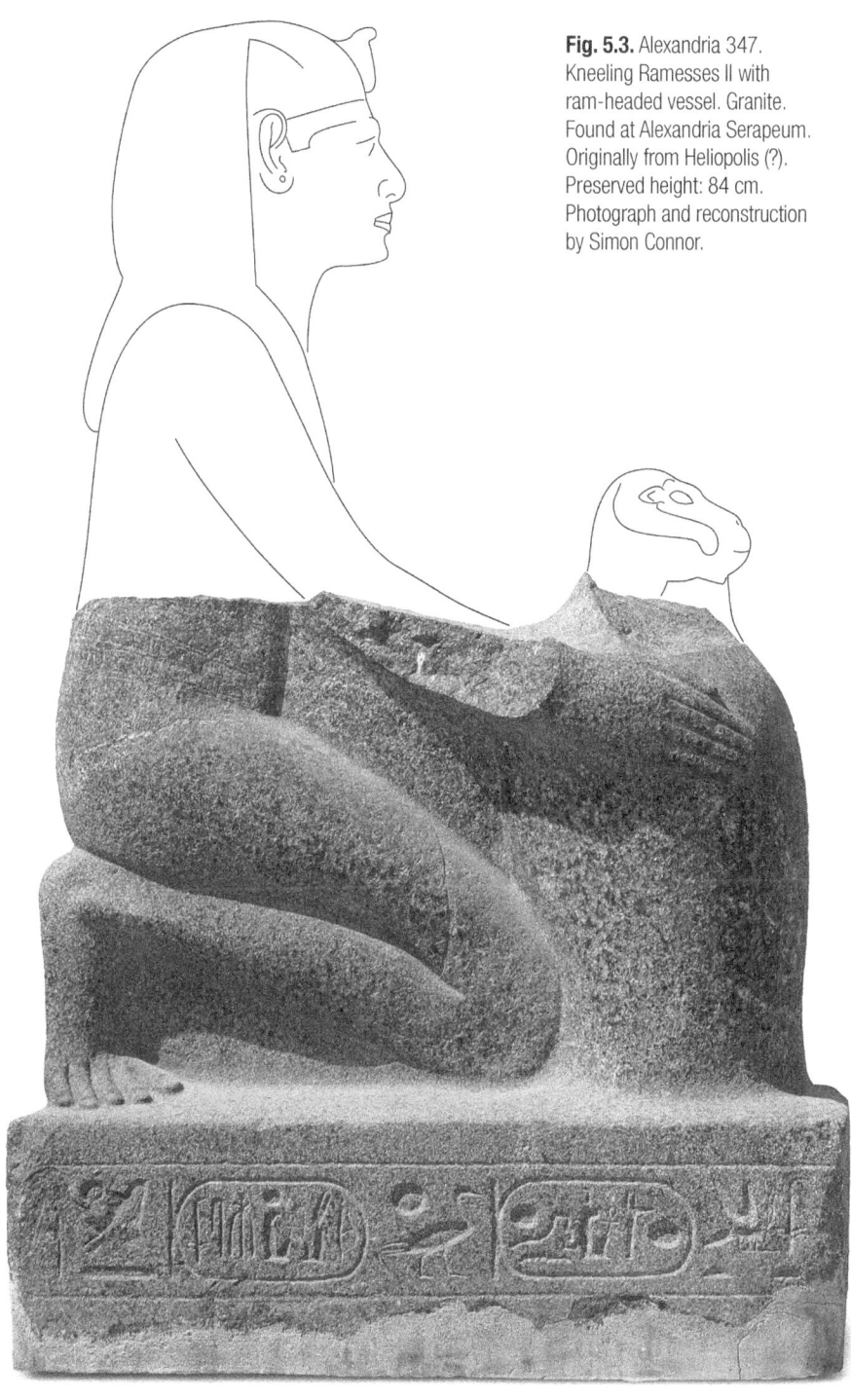

Fig. 5.3. Alexandria 347. Kneeling Ramesses II with ram-headed vessel. Granite. Found at Alexandria Serapeum. Originally from Heliopolis (?). Preserved height: 84 cm. Photograph and reconstruction by Simon Connor.

nineteenth century,[15] and art market purchases assigned to the Iseum Campense. These are two of the largest concentrations of Egyptian sculptures known from imperial-era Isiac temples.

Most are "antique" statues—of deities, sphinxes, and long-deceased pharaohs and nobles, some over a thousand years old and many with hieroglyphic texts—originally made for Egyptian temples in Heliopolis, Sais, and other sites (figs. 5.1–5.3). A few new commissions depict deities and sphinxes. Many "antiques" are cultically posed: kneeling with offering tables, bearing cult vessels, and holding naoi housing divinities. Many were originally over a meter high. Granite and other hard-stone materials are frequent. Apart from indications of ancient repairs (of uncertain date),[16] the "antiques" have not been altered. "Antiques" lack new dedicatory inscriptions for their new contexts; such texts perhaps appeared on separate bases or architectural features. Only one statue's inscription specifies its time of arrival: the Latin text on a newly commissioned, large-scale baboon from the Iseum Campense names officials from the time of Emperor Antoninus Pius.[17]

Archaeological evidence is insufficient to reconstruct the arrangement of the Egyptian sculptures or their immediate architectural context. The statues could have been either sheltered or alfresco, and juxtaposed with classical sculptures of deities and honorands, altars, and other dedicatory objects.

Egyptian Exotica and the Telephone Effect

Some modern scholarship describes Egyptian objects in Roman contexts as "Egyptianizing exotica," that is, as objects Romans recognized for their Egyptian style and decorative value, perhaps to make settings "look Egyptian." This perspective has many roots. To name a few: Egypt's portrayal as a dangerous and exotic "other" in some Latin literature; the inability of Romans to read hieroglyphs; and modern interpretations of how Romans decontextualized, appropriated, and commissioned Egyptian sculpture.[18] Particularly for Isiac sanctuaries, the challenges of reconstructing both the stories of people who frequented the temples and what can only have been very rich architectural and visual experiences have made it difficult to progress beyond the "make the place look Egyptian" label.

To get new perspectives, this chapter looks at a narrow slice of devotees who dedicated Egyptian statues and ritually interacted with them at the Alexandria Serapeum and Iseum Campense. How might these select devotees' beliefs and cult activities have informed their ideas about Egyptian statues?

From the outset, one should note that specialized knowledge about the meaning of Egyptian objects was available in Alexandria and Rome, and devotees may have sought such knowledge. Roman Alexandria's priests, intellectuals, and elites presumably played an important role in shaping Isiac cult practices and beliefs. Despite enormous information gaps, there are hints of the city's contribution. Apion was an Alexandrian-trained writer and sometime resident of Rome who wrote a famous book on Egypt.[19] Chaeremon was an Alexandrian philosopher-priest and tutor to the emperor Nero who wrote about Egypt and hieroglyphs.[20] Tiberius Claudius Balbillus was prefect of Egypt, head of the museum in Alexandria, high priest of Hermes (Thoth), astrologer, and friend of the emperor Claudius.[21] The Alexandria Serapeum was known for its library and its learned priests, some of whom may have been hieroglyph specialists.[22] Greek translations of Egyptian religious texts were available in Egypt, among them a lengthy manual about the ideal temple called the *Book of the Temple*.[23]

In the broader Roman world, there was a demand for knowledge about Egyptian religion and wisdom. Greek writers and thinkers of the Second Sophistic, as well as contemporary Latin writers, helped answer this demand. Notably, Plutarch's *De Iside et Osiride*, an account of the myths of Isis and Osiris, related Egyptian gods to comparable Greek deities. The philosopher Herodes Atticus commissioned an elaborate Isiac sanctuary in Marathon, Greece, replete with marble Egyptian statues.[24] The Sophist Philostratus describes a famous "antique"—the Memnon colossus (Egyptian statue of Amenhotep III)—as a cultic actor: the statue sings and appears to rise up in worship when struck by sunlight (*Vita Apollonii* 6.4).

With such diverse voices, we should not expect Isiac devotees' ideas about Egyptian objects to be fully "accurate" from the perspective of a native Egyptian priest (or a modern Egyptologist). One basic reason is the "telephone effect," in which stories are altered or garbled as they are retold along a chain of people. Knowledge would have passed through multiple filters and tongues from its original Egyptian sources, most probably via Alexandria. People in this chain also likely modified ideas through incomplete knowledge or to make the ideas more attractive or comprehensible in the wider Roman world. Further, Romans clearly came up with their own ideas about Egyptian objects.

Relational versus Material Entanglement

What ideas might the Romans have had? Some hints are available from appropriations of Greek "antique" statuary under Roman rule.[25] Greek portrait statues were reassigned to new individuals without necessarily altering the statues. Romans genericized: a statue of a specific athlete became a generic symbol of athleticism. Inscriptions were renewed, changed, or added. Prestige provenances and sculptors were desirable. New concepts about Greek "antiques" meant rearrangement in their existing sanctuaries or movement to faraway locations. Some "antiques" remained untouched. To be clear, however, this was a change in audience but not a complete shift in meaning. New Roman viewers to some extent understood the original meanings of Greek "antiques" but added fresh ideas that made the "antiques" relevant to new circumstances. This can be termed "relational entanglement," in which one culture assigns new meanings to an object appropriated from another culture without changing the object's materiality.[26]

Sparked by Greek ideas, Romans also commissioned new classical statuary with new meanings based on their own worldview.[27] This can be called "material entanglement,"[28] which is what happened when Egyptian ideas were integrated into Roman practices and systems of meaning. A newly commissioned Apis bull is an example from the Alexandria Serapeum:[29] the statue's Greek text, which addresses Serapis and prays for the emperor's safety, integrates the Egyptian dark stone and subject into a prevalent Roman ritual prayer practice.[30]

Temple Dedications

How might devotees have engaged with Egyptian objects in the Alexandria Serapeum and Iseum Campense? To answer this question, it is important to consider that most if not all temple objects, including the Egyptian ones, were dedications from specific individuals with specific purposes relative to specific deities. Dedications of temple architecture, equipment, and statuary demonstrated a dedicant–deity relationship and acknowledged a received (or hoped-for) blessing resulting from divine intervention. For an emperor or other devotees, these blessings included the right to rule, good health, safe travel, and others. In short, they are all the things that enable a good life.[31]

Dedicatory information from the Alexandria Serapeum and Iseum Campense confirms this general picture. The hieroglyphic inscription on an obelisk possibly commissioned for the Iseum Campense extols the emperor Domitian's relationship with the Isiac gods and includes a wish for his good health.[32] The Greek inscription on the aforementioned Alexandria Serapeum Apis statue wishes health and wellbeing for the emperor Hadrian.[33] Titus Aurelius Egatheus, a freed slave of the emperor Antoninus Pius, consecrated a gift at the Iseum Campense, perhaps seeking a better life.[34]

Returning to the Caesareum obelisks, what was the dedicatory intent? Perhaps they declared Augustus' divinely granted right to rule and victory over opponents, just as their hieroglyphic texts declared for Thutmose III[35] and the usurping Ramesses II.[36] Planners might have chosen to use Heliopolitan obelisks (rather than make new ones) to associate Augustus with Re, Egypt's supreme sun god who resided in Heliopolis. Two other "antique" obelisks that the Roman conqueror took to Rome had new Latin inscriptions that acknowledged his victory over Egypt and thanked Sol, a Roman sun god.[37] Were the Caesareum obelisks a similar "thank you" to Re?

Likewise, dedicators of the "antique" Egyptian statues at the Alexandria Serapeum and Iseum Campense were declaring their relationship with the Isiac gods. The dedicators perhaps saw the "antique" figures—presenting offerings and holding cult equipment—as a means to engage the Isiac gods, just as the statues originally engaged the gods in ancient Egyptian temples. The statues' capacity as cultic actors was the reason for their appropriation, rather than their specific identities as long-dead kings and nobles. Maybe whoever moved the "antiques" to their new temples was laying claim to the statues' power as divine intermediaries.

Mystery Cults

A group of individuals who may have had a special relationship with the Egyptian statues of the Alexandria Serapeum and Iseum Campense are the initiates of the Isiac mystery cults.[38] Guided by divine inspiration and hope for a happy life, some Isiac devotees were initiated via secret and dramatic rituals overseen by Greek- and Latin-speaking priests. These Isiac mysteries originated in the Hellenistic era and flourished in imperial times.

Metamorphoses is a second-century CE Latin novel by Apuleius whose final book recounts the initiation of a man named Lucius.[39] The comedic tale is an amazing testament to the longevity of selected ancient Egyptian ideas within the imperial-era Isiac mysteries. The stages of initiation partly mimic what is known about the training of ancient Egyptian priests and the cult ceremonies resemble ancient Egyptian ones. Initiates had responsibility for secret instruments, books with sacred writings, and animate divine statues.[40] Some claimed the ability to read hieroglyphs. The Christian writer Rufinus mentions priests, hidden shrines, and secret rites at the Alexandria Serapeum, suggesting mystery cults were present (*Historiae ecclesiasticae* 11.23),[41] and *Metamorphoses* (11.26) notes that Lucius spends part of his initiation at the Iseum Campense.[42]

The progressively staged initiation provided an experience in the mysteries of Isis and Osiris.[43] Upon successful completion, some initiates regularly performed cult activities. The reward was a happy life. Lucius morphed into an ass after an ill-advised encounter with a magic ointment (*Metamorphoses*, 3.24–25). More bad things followed. Then, through the ministrations of Isis and initiation to her mysteries, he returned to human form, practiced law, made plenty of money, and devotedly attended Isis (his version of happiness).

Isis for Everyone

Noninitiates had many ways to encounter the Isiac gods and their statuary. Processions with ornate divine images were part of the public face of the Isiac cults for the people of Alexandria and Rome. In *Metamorphoses* (11.10–17), priests bearing golden Isiac statues and emblems in procession preside over the *Navigium Isidis*, an annual public festival intended to bless the upcoming seagoing season.[44] The Alexandria Serapeum and Iseum Campense probably had similar sacred statues in gold, bronze, and wood, possibly including "antiques" taken from Egyptian temples, though none are preserved. As described in *Metamorphoses* (11.17), the precious statues were usually kept hidden in the inner sanctum of temples. We can get an impression of the statues' appearance in reliefs on granite columns from the Iseum Campense, which show priests holding divine statues that are partly derived from ancient Egyptian iconography.[45]

People visited Isiac temples to seek the gods' solutions to their life problems. Some, like Clitophon in Achilles Tatius' second-century CE novel, went to the Alexandria Serapeum to pray for an end to their troubles (*Leucippe and Clitophon*, 5.2). Some also left dedications, possibly near a relevant statue.[46] Others sought divination, which was perhaps practiced in a statue-rich setting at the Alexandria Serapeum[47] and Iseum Campense.[48] A small shrine preserved at a Roman fortlet at Dios in Egypt provides a modest example of how this could work: an Egyptian and several classical statues (including Serapis) created a sacral setting for visitors seeking oracular advice.[49]

Selected Egyptian statues at the Alexandria Serapeum and Iseum Campense perhaps marked doorways to shrines reserved for particular rituals. A cameo shows three Egyptian statues—an Isis figure, falcon, and sphinx—beside an entrance to a shrine housing the Osiris Hydreios figure of the Isiac cults.[50] For initiates, such statues could signify what they had gained: Plutarch suggests that shrine-fronting sphinxes symbolized enigmatic wisdom (*De Iside et Osiride* 9[354C]).[51]

Why "Antiques"?

"Antiques" are more prevalent at the Alexandria Serapeum and Iseum Campense than newly commissioned Egyptian statues. This preference—particularly at high-status temples with patrons who could afford many types of dedications—suggests devotees had beliefs about the value of "antiques." Provenance from a sacred site was perhaps important: an imperial-era Isis aretology from Kyme in Turkey claimed to be copied from a stele at the famous Ptah temple in Memphis.[52] Hieroglyphs were powerful: in *Metamorphoses* (11.22), hieroglyphs are an inscrutable script that protects the mystery cult's secrets.

"Antiques" had substance worth preserving: more than 250 years after a cultic water clock (clepsydra) was inscribed in hieroglyphs for Philip Arrhidaeus, someone added Julian calendar months in Latin to facilitate the clock's continued use.[53] Granite was a suitable divine offering: the hieroglyphic text on the aforementioned Domitian obelisk named granite as appropriate for the Egyptian god Re-Horakhty.[54]

Who selected "antiques" for the Alexandria Serapeum and Iseum Campense? "Antique" dedications have the hallmarks of wealth and status, given the effort involved in moving heavy, large objects and the high rank needed to have the authority to take objects from Egyptian temples.[55] Officials also would need to approve the installation of significant dedications at such important Isiac temples in Alexandria and Rome. Dealers could have fulfilled requests for desired objects. Officials acting on behalf of the emperor may have acquired "antiques" (or commissioned new sculptures) in conjunction with a new or renovated construction. Over time, devotees may have acquired "antique" dedications when visiting Egyptian temples while on official business, or during the sacral travel that was a feature of the Roman world,[56] and, according to *Metamorphoses* (11.26), potentially part of an initiation. Dedicators could have been initiated or uninitiated devotees. For the Alexandria Serapeum, Egyptian statues from the site's Ptolemaic era could have been put to new uses.

Besides suitable provenances, hieroglyphic texts, and materials, the most obvious selection criterion for "antiques" was relevance to the myths of Isis and Osiris. Perhaps it helped if the statue displayed affinities with Roman rituals and myths that might attract new audiences. An encounter with the divine, perhaps through a dream, could have inspired choices: the Greek text on a sphinx, possibly a newly commissioned Egyptian-style example, declared that Serapis had commanded a priest to make the dedication.[57] Native priests or guides at ancient Egyptian temples—like the one who accompanied Germanicus at Thebes (Tacitus, *Annals* 2.60)[58]—could have aided "antique" selection.

Here are some hypothetical dedicatory narratives, using sculptures from the two temples and ideas discussed so far. To accompany new construction at the Iseum Campense, an emperor dedicates gold and bronze divine statues and emblems[59] and sphinxes. While visiting Heliopolis to see its wonders, a high official looks for an appropriate dedication he has vowed to the Isiac gods of the Alexandria Serapeum. He selects a kneeling statue (fig. 5.1) because it is impressive, made of red-black granite, and extends a food offering (explained by a guide) that is suitably similar to Roman acts of offering.[60] An initiate-in-progress from Rome travels to Isis' temple at Behbeit al-Hagar in Egypt and, aided by native priests, selects a relief depicting Isis' husband Osiris and son Horus; he has the wherewithal to transport the hugely heavy, 1.3 m × 1.6 m × 0.4 m, granite block by land and sea to the Iseum Campense.[61] In thanks for a successful seagoing season, a wealthy trader acquires a red-black granite sculpture of a Hathor cow suckling a pharaoh for the Iseum Campense because it mimics the sacred mother-cow effigy of the Isis cults (*Metamorphoses* 11.11; *De Iside et Osiride* 39[366E]), and recalls Roman imagery of the she-wolf suckling Romulus and Remus.[62] The city of Alexandria renovates a shrine at the Serapeum. Two colossal pink-granite sphinxes, preserved from the site's Ptolemaic era, are rededicated at the entrance.[63]

The "antiques" and their object biographies could have fulfilled several roles. They could have enhanced the Isiac cult and initiation experience. The statues could have provided an alternative to sacral travel, especially for those unable to do so. Finally, the "antiques" could have memorialized the special relationship between the dedicators and the Isiac gods. The effort required to acquire the "antiques" expressed devotion. The statues' venerable provenances, hieroglyphic texts, and granite material provided status and visibility to the dedicators' requests for divine blessings and set them apart from nearby classical-style marble and bronze dedications.

The Importance of Ritual

It is not surprising that the Roman dedicators of the Egyptian statues at the Alexandria Serapeum and Iseum Campense chose many "antiques" in ritual poses. Romans tightly linked rituals—vows, offerings, rites, and prayers—with statue dedications at temples.[64] Roman classical marble statues and reliefs display rituals, such as offerings and processions, that are easily equated with those of the Egyptian "antiques." Just as Plutarch linked classical and Egyptian myths, Isiac experts could have compared cross-cultural ritual gestures displayed in sculptures to seek deeper knowledge. Classical texts portray Egypt as a source of ritual expertise.[65]

One can suggest how Egyptian statues could play parts in Isiac rituals. Initial dedication would involve prayers. The statues could define physical spaces for specific rites: a marble relief from Ariccia depicts a large, Egyptian statue-filled portico before which Isiac devotees dance and play rhythmic instruments.[66] The statues could be ritual tools: might the Alexandria Serapeum's giant "antique" scarab (fig. 5.2),[67] have been a part of the Osiris mystery initiations? Winged scarabs often appear on Imperial-era Osiris Hydreios sculptures.[68] Like the vocal and tactile activities depicted in *Metamorphoses*, one could envisage addressing and touching Egyptian "antiques" and reading (symbolically rather than literally?) their inscriptions. An Alexandria Serapeum "antique" ceramic *shabti* seems particularly appropriate for vocal and tactile rituals because of its small size, hieroglyphic texts, and Osiris-mummy shape.[69]

"Antiques" from the Alexandria Serapeum and Iseum Campense are ideal cult actors eternally repeating sacred actions. They invite viewers to participate and emulate. Many "antiques" have attributes and poses associated with Isiac rites. Heads are shaved and bodies wear linen garments[70] in the manner of *Metamorphoses*' devotees (11.10). The statues' kneeling poses are emulated "live" by Isiac devotees in a painted cult scene from Herculaneum.[71] An Alexandria Serapeum statue holds a ram-headed vessel (fig. 5.3),[72] similar to the Osiris Hydreios vessel clasped by Isiac priests, such as those in reliefs from the Iseum Campense.[73] "Antique" figures of priests holding divine statues evoke both the Isiac public processions and the cult's secret rites.[74] Ritually posed statues were important for demonstrating ongoing piety: few hieroglyph-covered "antiques" are associated with the Isis temple at Beneventum but there are multiple newly commissioned statues of figures that kneel, hold cult instruments, and wear linen garments.[75]

Just as Roman classical statues and reliefs created lasting public monuments to ritual activity, so too the Egyptian "antiques" enabled their dedicators to prominently commemorate and enable their enduring sacred service, and in a visual vocabulary pleasing to the Isiac gods.

A Baboon for Lucius?

Baboon statues are a frequent feature of the Isiac cults. Many examples come from Rome and multiple such figures appear in the aforementioned Ariccia relief depicting an Isiac sanctuary.[76] The baboons are mostly new commissions, sometimes of large scale and over a meter high. In a few cases, the statue base prominently displays the donor's name.[77]

These are curious circumstances, especially because the baboon was not a common sight in Italy. The baboon represents the Egyptian god Thoth. In his guise as the Greek god Hermes, Thoth taught Isis and co-invented hieroglyphs, according to the Isis aretology from Kyme.[78] Clement of Alexandria describes Hermes as the author of priestly books of knowledge (*Stromata* 6.4).[79]

Might some of the baboon statues have celebrated a successful mystery cult initiation and high priestly station? The baboon could be a "thank you" dedication to the Isiac gods for the blessings and wisdom gained from an initiation under the guidance of Thoth/Hermes. The aforementioned Iseum Campense baboon was a lavish new commission, recognized as such because of its huge size, resemblance to "antique" models, and elaborate Greek/Latin dedication that even featured the sculptors' names.[80] Two Greek-inscribed marble statues of draped males from Roman Alexandria have baboons at their sides, which may identify the men as initiates. One statue has a Greek dedication, perhaps to a doctor.[81] The other holds a scroll and a caduceus,[82] just like the caduceus described as being carried by an Isiac priest in a procession in *Metamorphoses* (11.10) and held by a priest in a painting from Pompeii's Isis temple.[83] The caduceus was an attribute of Hermes.

Isiac devotees of *Metamorphoses* beheld Lucius—the new initiate!—as the temple curtains parted at daybreak and revealed him standing before the statue of Isis after his first initiation in Cenchreae, Greece (11.24). Baboons were famous in ancient Egyptian lore for greeting the rising sun. If we squint our eyes almost shut in the dawn light, would we see devotees witnessing Lucius dedicate a giant baboon statue in Rome after he completes two more initiation stages and ascends the priestly ranks?

Finis

This chapter has theorized how the Egyptian statues at the Alexandria Serapeum and Iseum Campense enabled their select group of Isiac dedicators to elevate their relationship with the divine, seek and acknowledge blessings, and memorialize ritual service. Naturally, other types of audiences could have had very different interactions with Egyptian statues at the two temples and other places, and these are beyond the scope of this chapter. A Roman matron barely acquainted with Egypt might scratch her head in puzzlement while strolling by a Sekhmet statue in Rome. Or a Roman intellectual could see a smiling Egyptian sculpture as a beautiful addition to his villa and a springboard for musings on the Daedalic style. Or a wealthy Alexandrian merchant might seek "antique" sphinxes to preside over a tomb entrance. Or a retired trader might acquire "antiques" as a prop for tales about "the good old days" he spent in Alexandria, and the time he narrowly escaped the jaws of a crocodile. Or a Roman who . . .

Perhaps if we try squinting our eyes almost shut once more, we might see . . .

Notes

1. Metropolitan Museum of Art 81.2.2; *IAlexImp* (= Kayser, *Recueil des inscriptions*) 2; Pfeiffer, "Imperial Cult," 86–87.
2. See bibliography of Gasparini and Veymiers, *Individuals and Materials*.
3. Villing, "Greeks in Egypt," 75.
4. Bricault, "Traveling Gods."
5. Gallo, "Se l'Egitto dei romani è la costa Alessandrina."
6. *RICIS* (= Bricault, *Recueil des inscriptions*) 202/0101-0438.
7. Marcadé, "Statuettes hellénistiques."

8   Moyer, *Egypt and the Limits of Hellenism*, 157–61.
9   Jördens, "Government, Taxation, and Law."
10 Malaise, "La diffusion des cultes égyptiens," 1629–48.
11 McKenzie, *Architecture of Alexandria*, 53–55, 195–203.
12 Bülow Clausen, "Flavian Isea," 125–44; Lembke, "Iseum Campense and Its Social, Religious and Political Impact."
13 McKenzie, *Architecture of Alexandria*, 201.
14 Tkaczow, *Topography*, 68–70, 338 (Site 15); Lembke, *Iseum Campense*, 221–43.
15 Bruwier, Claes, and Quertinmont, *Description de l'Égypte*, 95–99.
16 Also, royal names were removed from an Amasis sphinx from the Iseum Campense (Rome Capitolini MC 35), a possible *damnatio memoriae* after the king's death; Müskens, *Egypt beyond Representation*, 246–47[117].
17 Vatican Egizio inv. 22833[34]; *RICIS* 501/0123; Müskens, *Egypt beyond Representation*, 270–71[129]; Swetnam-Burland, "Material Evidence," 600–603.
18 Vout, "Embracing Egypt," 189; Kleibl, *Iseion*, 169; Bülow Clausen, "Flavian Isea," 14–15; Lembke, "Iseum Campense and Its Social, Religious and Political Impact," 39; Mol, "Roman Cyborgs!," 73–74.
19 van der Horst, *Japheth*, 207–21.
20 Capponi, "Reflections," 75–76.
21 Capponi, "Reflections," 71–74.
22 McKenzie, *Architecture of Alexandria*, 198–203.
23 Quack, "Translating the Realities of Cult."
24 Mazurek, "Middle Platonic Isis."
25 Keesling, *Early Greek Portraiture*, 182–216; Neudecker, "Greek Sanctuaries."
26 Stockhammer, "From Hybridity to Entanglement."
27 Kousser, "Adapting Greek Art."
28 Stockhammer, "From Hybridity to Entanglement."
29 Alexandria Graeco-Roman Museum 351; *IAlexImp* 48; Tkaczow, *Topography*, 245–46[161].
30 Christodoulou, "Serapis, Isis, and the Emperor," 169–73.
31 Naerebout, "Sanctuary, Monument," 55.
32 Lembke, *Iseum Campense*, 210–12; Müskens, *Egypt beyond Representation*, 190–191[089].
33 *IAlexImp* 48.
34 *RICIS* 501/0119.
35 Raue, *Heliopolis*, 298–301.
36 Kitchen, *Ramesside Inscriptions* 2, 297–301 (183A–B).
37 Swetnam-Burland, *Egypt in Italy*, 100–103.
38 Bommas, *Heiligtum und Mysterium*; Bowden, *Mystery Cults*, 156–80; Bremmer, *Initiation*, 110–41.
39 Benson, *Apuleius' Invisible Ass*.
40 Benson, *Apuleius' Invisible Ass*, 202–205.
41 McKenzie, *Architecture of Alexandria*, 202.
42 Lembke, "Iseum Campense and Its Social, Religious and Political Impact," 32.
43 Bowden, *Mystery Cults*, 166–68, 177.
44 Pfeiffer, "Comments on the Egyptian Background."

45 Lembke, *Iseum Campense*, 186–88.
46 Alexandria Graeco-Roman Museum 65; *IAlexImp* 66; Gasparini, "Listening Stones," 562–63, fig. 3a.
47 Renberg, *Where Dreams May Come*, 379–86.
48 Renberg, "Dreams and Other Divine Communications," 661–62.
49 Cuvigny, "Shrine in the *Praesidium* of Dios."
50 Munich Münzsammlung A.2412; Magni, "Cammeo."
51 Herrmann and van den Hoek, "The Sphinx."
52 *RICIS* 302/0204.
53 British Museum 1873,0812.1 (EA938); Winter, *Zeitzeichen*, 407–408.
54 Müskens, *Egypt beyond Representation*, 338n442.
55 Lembke, "Iseum Campense and Its Social, Religious and Political Impact," 35.
56 Rutherford, "Travel and Pilgrimage," 703–704.
57 Lembke, *Iseum Campense*, 144 (C13); *RICIS* 501/0153.
58 Klotz, *Caesar in the City of Amun*, 21–25.
59 As depicted in reliefs from the Iseum Campense. Lembke, *Iseum Campense*, 186–88.
60 Alexandria Graeco-Roman Museum 20950 + British Museum EA600; Perdu, *Recueil des inscriptions*, 95–99[17A].
61 Rome MNR 52045; Müskens, *Egypt beyond Representation*, 160–61[074].
62 Florence 5419; Müskens, *Egypt beyond Representation*, 162–63[075].
63 Tkaczow, *Topography*, 188–89[11].
64 McCarty, "Religious Dedications."
65 Dieleman, *Priests, Tongues, and Rites*, 239.
66 Rome MNR 77255; Veymiers, "Relief with Isiac Ceremony."
67 Alexandria Graeco-Roman Museum 352b; Tkaczow, *Topography*, 235[129].
68 Vatican Egizio inv. 22852[39]; Roullet, *Egyptian and Egyptianizing Monuments*, 99[146].
69 Alexandria Graeco-Roman Museum P5931; Rowe, "Two Royal Funerary Figurines," 37; Malaise, *Pour une terminologie*, 17–19.
70 Rome MNR 112108, 362623; Müskens, *Egypt beyond Representation*, 214–15[101], 226–27[107].
71 Naples 8919; Moormann, "Ministers of Isiac Cults," 368–69.
72 Alexandria Graeco-Roman Museum 347; Raue, *Heliopolis*, 359.
73 Lembke, *Iseum Campense*, 45, pls. 6.1–2.
74 Malaise, "Statues égyptiennes naophores"; for example, Alexandria Graeco-Roman Museum 17533, 17534; Tkaczow, *Topography*, 188[9].
75 Bocciero, *Il culto di Iside*, 41–43[14–16], 48–49[24], 52–55[33–34].
76 Veymiers, "Relief with Isiac Ceremony."
77 Examples from Rome/Ostia: Roullet, *Egyptian and Egyptianizing Monuments*, 125–26[243–51]; *RICIS* 503/1108 (misidentified as kneeling figure); Müskens, *Egypt beyond Representation*, 152–55[070–071], 234–35[111; misidentified as prostrate figure], 270–71[129].
78 *RICIS* 302/0204.
79 Fowden, *Egyptian Hermes*, 58–59.
80 *RICIS* 501/0123.
81 Turin Antichità 269; *IAlexImp* 44; Barberis and Gastaldi, "Gruppo statuario"; Renberg, *Where Dreams May Come*, 381–82; Arachne 30581.

82 Vienna I 273; *IAlexImp* 78; Arachne 22647.
83 Naples 9558; Pearson, "Io Arriving in Egypt."

Bibliography

Arachne = iDAI.objects arachne of the German Archaeological Institute (DAI) and the Archaeological Institute of the University of Cologne. https://arachne.dainst.org/

Barberis, Valentina, and Enrica Culasso Gastaldi. "Gruppo statuario di Pappos Theognostos." In *I Greci a Torino: Storie di collezionismo epigrafico*, edited by Enrica Culasso Gastaldi and Gabriella Pantò, 46–49. Turin: Museo di Antichità di Torino, 2014.

Benson, Geoffrey C. *Apuleius' Invisible Ass: Encounters with the Unseen in the* Metamorphoses. Cambridge and New York: Cambridge University Press, 2019.

Bocciero, Luisa, et al. *Il culto di Iside a Benevento*. Milan: Electa, 2017.

Bommas, Martin. *Heiligtum und Mysterium: Griechenland und seine ägyptischen Gottheiten*. Mainz: Philipp von Zabern, 2005.

Bowden, Hugh. *Mystery Cults of the Ancient World*. London: Thames & Hudson, 2010.

Bremmer, Jan N. *Initiation into the Mysteries of the Ancient World*. Berlin: De Gruyter, 2014.

Bricault, Laurent. *Recueil des inscriptions concernant les cults isiaques (RICIS)*. 3 vols. Paris: De Boccard, 2005.

———. "Traveling Gods: The Cults of Isis in the Roman Empire." In *Beyond the Nile: Egypt and the Classical World*, edited by Jeffrey Spier, Timothy Potts, and Sara E. Cole, 224–29. Los Angeles: Paul Getty Museum, 2018.

Bruwier, Marie-Cécile, Wouter Claes, and Arnaud Quertinmont. *"La description de l'Egypte" de Jean-Jacques Rifaud (1813–1826)*. Brussels: Editions Safran, 2014.

Bülow Clausen, Kristine. "The Flavian Isea in Beneventum and Rome: The Appropriation of Egyptian and Egyptianising Art in Imperial Beneventum and Rome." PhD diss., Københavns Universitet, Det Humanistiske Fakultet, 2015. https://research.ku.dk/search/?pure=en/publications/the-flavian-isea-in-beneventum-and-rome(8f03656b-d3d6-4d16-8a69-b605cd67d061).html

Capponi, Livia. "Reflections on the Author, Context, and Audience of the So-called Apotheosis of Poppaea (P.Oxy. LXXVII 5105)." *Quaderni di Storia* 86 (2017): 63–79.

Christodoulou, Perikles. "Serapis, Isis, and the Emperor." In *Romanising Oriental Gods? Religious Transformations in the Balkan Provinces in the Roman Period*, edited by Aleksandra Nikoloska and Sander Müskens, 167–211. Skopje: Skopje Macedonian Academy of Sciences and Arts; Leiden: University of Leiden, 2015.

Cuvigny, Hélène. "The Shrine in the *Praesidium* of Dios (Eastern Desert of Egypt): Graffiti and Oracles in Context." *Chiron* 40 (2010): 245–99.

Dieleman, Jacco. *Priests, Tongues, and Rites: The London-Leiden Magical Manuscripts and Translation in Egyptian Ritual (100–300 CE)*. Leiden and Boston: Brill, 2005.

Fowden, Garth. *The Egyptian Hermes: A Historical Approach to the Late Pagan Mind*. Princeton, NJ: Princeton University Press, 1986.

Gallo, Paolo. "Se l'Egitto dei romani è la costa Alessandrina." In *Il Nilo a Pompei: Visioni d'Egitto nel mondo romano*, edited by Federico Poole, 63–69. Modena: Franco Cosimo Panini, 2016.

Gasparini, Valentino. "Listening Stones: Cultural Appropriation, Resonance, and Memory in the Isiac Cults." In *Vestigia: Miscellanea di studi storico-religiosi in onore di Filippo Coarelli nel suo 80° anniversario*, edited by Valentino Gasparini, 555–74. Stuttgart: Franz Steiner, 2016.

Gasparini, Valentino, and Richard Veymiers, eds. *Individuals and Materials in the Greco-Roman Cults of Isis: Agents, Images, and Practices*. 2 vols. Leiden and Boston: Brill, 2018.

Herrmann, John J., and Annewies van den Hoek. "The Sphinx: An Egyptian Theological Symbol in Plutarch and Clement of Alexandria." In *Pottery, Pavements, and Paradise: Iconographic and Textual Studies on Late Antiquity*, edited by Annewies van den Hoek and John J. Herrmann, 149–74. Leiden and Boston: Brill, 2013.

Jördens, Andrea. "Government, Taxation, and Law." In *The Oxford Handbook of Roman Egypt*, edited by Christina Riggs, 56–67. Oxford and New York: Oxford University Press, 2012.

Kayser, François. *Recueil des inscriptions grecques et latines (non funéraires) d'Alexandrie impériale (1er–IIIe s. apr. J.-C.)*. Cairo: IFAO, 1994.

Keesling, Catherine M. *Early Greek Portraiture: Monuments and Histories*. Cambridge and New York: Cambridge University Press, 2017.

Kitchen, Kenneth A. *Ramesside Inscriptions: Translated and Annotated. Translations II: Ramesses II, Royal Inscriptions*. Oxford and Cambridge, MA: Wiley Blackwell, 1996.

Kleibl, Kathrin. *Iseion: Raumgestaltung und Kultpraxis in den Heiligtümern gräco-ägyptischer Götter im Mittelmeerraum*. Worms: Wernersche Verlagsgesellschaft, 2009.

Klotz, David. *Caesar in the City of Amun: Egyptian Temple Construction and Theology in Roman Thebes*. Turnhout: Brepols, 2012.

Kousser, Rachel. "Adapting Greek Art." In *A Companion to Roman Art*, edited by Barbara Borg, 114–29. Chichester, UK: Wiley Blackwell, 2015.

Lembke, Katja. "The Iseum Campense and Its Social, Religious, and Political Impact." In *The Iseum Campense from the Roman Empire to the Modern Age: Temple—Monument—Lieu de mémoire*, edited by Miguel J. Versluys, Kristine Bülow Clausen, and Giuseppina C. Vittozzi, 29–40. Rome: Edizioni Quasar, 2018.

———. *Das Iseum Campense in Rom: Studien über den Isiskult unter Domitian*. Heidelberg: Archäologie und Geschichte, 1994.

Magni, Alessandra. "Cammeo." In *Iside: Il mito il mistero la magia*, edited by Ermanno Arslan, 255, IV.273. Milan: Electa, 1997.

Malaise, Michel. "La diffusion des cultes égyptiens dans les provinces européennes de l'Empire romain." In *Aufstieg und Niedergang der römischen Welt*, part 2, edited by Wolfgang Haase, 17, no. 3, 1615–91. Berlin and New York: De Gruyter, 1984.

———. *Pour une terminologie et une analyse des cultes isiaques*. Brussels: Académie Royale de Belgique, 2005.

———. "Statues égyptiennes naophores et cultes isiaques." *BSEG* 26 (2004): 63–80.

Marcadé, Jean. "À propos des statuettes hellénistiques en aragonite du Musée de Délos." *BCH* 76 (1952): 96–135.

Mazurek, Lindsey A. "The Middle Platonic Isis: Text and Image in the Sanctuary of the Egyptian Gods at Herodes Atticus' Marathon Villa." *AJA* 122, no. 4 (2018): 611–44.

McCarty, Matthew M. "Religious Dedications." In *The Oxford Handbook of Roman Sculpture*, edited by Elise A. Friedland, Melanie Grunow Sobocinski, and Elaine K. Gazda, 358–73. Oxford and New York: Oxford University Press, 2015.

McKenzie, Judith Sheila. *The Architecture of Alexandria and Egypt, c. 300 BC to AD 700*. New Haven and London: Yale University Press, 2007.

Mol, Eva. "Roman Cyborgs! On Significant Otherness, Material Absence, and Virtual Presence in the Archaeology of Roman Religion." *EJA* 23, no. 1 (2020): 64–81.

Moormann, Eric M. "Ministers of Isiac Cults in Roman Wall Painting." In *Individuals and Materials in the Greco-Roman Cults of Isis: Agents, Images, and Practices*, 2 vols., edited by Valentino Gasparini and Richard Veymiers, 366–83. Leiden and Boston: Brill, 2018.

Moyer, Ian S. *Egypt and the Limits of Hellenism*. Cambridge: Cambridge University Press, 2011.

Müskens, Sander. *Egypt beyond Representation: Materials and Materiality of Aegyptiaca Romana*. Leiden: Leiden University Press, 2017. https://openaccess.leidenuniv.nl/handle/1887/46693

Naerebout, Frederick G. "Sanctuary, Monument, lieu de mémoire? The Iseum Campense, Memory and Religious Life." In *The Iseum Campense from the Roman Empire to the Modern Age: Temple—Monument—Lieu de mémoire*, edited by Miguel J. Versluys, Kristine Bülow Clausen, and Giuseppina C. Vittozzi, 41–57. Rome: Edizioni Quasar, 2018.

Neudecker, Richard. "Greek Sanctuaries in Roman Times: Rearranging, Transporting, and Renaming Artworks." In *Restaging Greek Artworks in Roman Times*, edited by Gianfranco Adornato et al., 147–71. Milan: LED-Edizioni Universitarie di Lettere Economia Diritto, 2018.

Pearson, Stephanie. "Io Arriving in Egypt." In *Beyond the Nile: Egypt and the Classical World*, edited by Jeffrey Spier, Timothy Potts, and Sara E. Cole, 255. Los Angeles: J. Paul Getty Museum, 2018.

Perdu, Olivier. *Recueil des inscriptions royales saïtes I: Psammétique Ier*. Paris: Collège de France and Cybèle, 2002.

Pfeiffer, Stefan. "Comments on the Egyptian Background of the Priests' Procession during the *Navigium Isidis*." In *Individuals and Materials in the Greco-Roman Cults of Isis: Agents, Images, and Practices*, 2 vols., edited by Valentino Gasparini and Richard Veymiers, 672–89. Leiden and Boston: Brill, 2018.

———. "The Imperial Cult in Egypt." In *The Oxford Handbook of Roman Egypt*, edited by Christina Riggs, 83–100. Oxford and New York: Oxford University Press, 2012.

Quack, Joachim Friedrich. "Translating the Realities of Cult: The Case of the *Book of the Temple.*" In *Greco-Egyptian Interactions: Literature, Translation, and Culture, 500 BCE–300 CE*, edited by Ian Rutherford, 267–86. Oxford and New York: Oxford University Press, 2016.

Raue, Dietrich. *Heliopolis und das Haus des Re: Eine Prosopographie und ein Toponym im Neuen Reich*. Berlin: Achet-Verlag, 1999.

Renberg, Gil H. "Dreams and Other Divine Communications from the Isiac Gods in the Greek and Latin Epigraphical Record." In *Individuals and Materials in the Greco-Roman Cults of Isis: Agents, Images, and Practices*, 2 vols., edited by Valentino Gasparini and Richard Veymiers, 649–71. Leiden and Boston: Brill, 2018.

———. *Where Dreams May Come: Incubation Sanctuaries in the Greco-Roman World*. 2 vols. Leiden and Boston: Brill, 2017.

Roullet, Anne. *The Egyptian and Egyptianizing Monuments of Imperial Rome*. Leiden: Brill, 1972.

Rowe, Alan. "Two Royal Funerary Figurines Recently Found at Kôm El-Shuqafa and the Serapeum." *BSRAA* 36 (1943–44): 33–37.

Rutherford, Ian C. "Travel and Pilgrimage." In *The Oxford Handbook of Roman Egypt*, edited by Christina Riggs, 701–16. Oxford and New York: Oxford University Press, 2012.

Stockhammer, Philipp W. "From Hybridity to Entanglement, From Essentialism to Practice." *Archaeological Review from Cambridge* 28 (2013): 11–28.

Swetnam-Burland, Molly. *Egypt in Italy: Visions of Egypt in Roman Imperial Culture*. Cambridge and New York: Cambridge University Press, 2015.

———. "Material Evidence and the Isiac Cults: Art and Experience in the Sanctuary." In *Individuals and Materials in the Greco-Roman Cults of Isis: Agents, Images, and Practices*, 2 vols., edited by Valentino Gasparini and Richard Veymiers, 584–608. Leiden and Boston: Brill, 2018.

Tkaczow, Barbara. *The Topography of Ancient Alexandria: An Archaeological Map*. Translated by Iwona Zych. Warsaw: Centre d'archéologie méditerranéenne de l'Académie polonaise des sciences, 1993.

van der Horst, Pieter Willem. *Japheth in the Tents of Shem: Studies on Jewish Hellenism in Antiquity*. Leuven: Peeters, 2002.

Veymiers, Richard. "Relief with Isiac Ceremony (the Ariccia Relief)." In *Beyond the Nile: Egypt and the Classical World*, edited by Jeffrey Spier, Timothy Potts, and Sara E. Cole, 269–70. Los Angeles: J. Paul Getty Museum, 2018.

Villing, Alexandra. "The Greeks in Egypt: Renewed Contact in the Iron Age." In *Beyond the Nile: Egypt and the Classical World*, edited by Jeffrey Spier, Timothy Potts, and Sara E. Cole, 73–81. Los Angeles: J. Paul Getty Museum, 2018.

Vout, Caroline. "Embracing Egypt." In *Rome the Cosmopolis*, edited by Catherine Edwards and Greg Woolf, 177–202. Cambridge and New York: Cambridge University Press, 2003.

Winter, Eva. *Zeitzeichen: Zur Entwicklung und Verwendung antiker Zeitmesser*. 2 vols. Berlin and Boston: De Gruyter, 2013.

6 The Various Lives of Statues in the City of the Sun

Simon Connor

Introduction

It is both a pleasure and an honor to dedicate this chapter to Edward Bleiberg, with whom I have had so many enjoyable discussions about Egyptian sculpture. The first time was in 2012, when I came to study Middle Kingdom material in the Brooklyn Museum for my PhD. More recently, our interests were joined when, working on iconoclasm in the framework of a fellowship at the Metropolitan Museum of Art, I again met Edward. He was then curating an exhibition on a similar subject for the Pulitzer Arts Foundation in St. Louis.[1]

Heliopolis is probably one of the best sites to approach the topic of iconoclasm—or, more precisely, the mutilations carried out on ancient Egyptian material, and the various ways that such practices may be understood. The city's rich repertoire not only illustrates the great creativity of pharaonic artists, but also offers ways to approach the manner in which the ancient monuments were perceived throughout the different phases of Egyptian history.

The site of ancient Heliopolis now lies in the northeastern part of modern Cairo. The extension of the ancient city and necropolis is in large part covered by the neighborhoods of Ain Shams and Matariya, while the remaining part of the urban area within the temenos is more and more threatened by the construction of new buildings. On the northern half of the city's precinct enclosure wall are the ruins of 'Arab al-Hisn, the western part of which is currently being excavated by Cairo University, while the southern half of Heliopolis has been the object of investigations by the Egyptian–German mission in recent years.

Since Heliopolis is no longer a landscape composed of standing walls, reliefs, columns, and statues, like Tanis and Karnak, it is quite difficult to reconstruct the appearance that it may have originally had. Nevertheless, the large repertoire that can be gathered from Alexandria and Old Cairo provides a first glimpse of the monumentality and originality of Heliopolis' sculptural program. An overview will be completed with the study of material found in Matariya at the beginning of the twentieth century and now housed in various museums, as well as with the corpus that continues to come out from the ground in the framework of the excavations led by the mission currently working in the field.[2]

Heliopolis in Alexandria

If the monumental architecture of the ancient city is now lost, we may look at other sites in Egypt that provide glimpses of its original appearance. Alexandria is one of the most important sites where one can look for Heliopolis outside of Heliopolis. The ruins of Alexandria delivered a rich pharaonic repertoire, found both in the archaeology of the city, particularly in the area of the Serapeum, and under the sea. A large part of this material includes inscriptions that designate Heliopolis as the materials' original location, as can be assumed from the dedications to Atum-lord-of-Iunu, Re-Horakhty, and the Baw of Iunu, or "*Ba* spirits of Heliopolis."[3] This large repertoire clearly predates the foundation of Alexandria and was brought there at some point in Egyptian history, perhaps as early as the Ptolemaic Period, or perhaps later, during Roman times.[4] Dating the (gradual?) dismantlement of Heliopolis in order to decorate Alexandria is still difficult. It is possible that some of the Heliopolitan material found in Alexandria would have passed through other sites, as the movement of monuments to new royal residences and construction sites was already a well-established practice.

The reason for the presence of pharaonica in Alexandria is perhaps less political than we would like to imagine. It is important to note that the pharaonic statues installed in the city do not seem to have been subject to reappropriation or usurpation by the Ptolemies or by Roman emperors. They may have had a cultic, but most probably a decorative, role in the public spaces, as well as in the temples dedicated to Egyptian deities. Temples like the Serapeum of Alexandria may therefore have had an ornamental program similar to those of the Iseums of Rome, Benevento, and even Pompeii, with ancient Egyptian artifacts, already seen as antiquities, creating an orientalizing atmosphere of religious space.

None of the statues known to me show any trace of changes to their inscriptions or physiognomy in order to transform the original representations of a

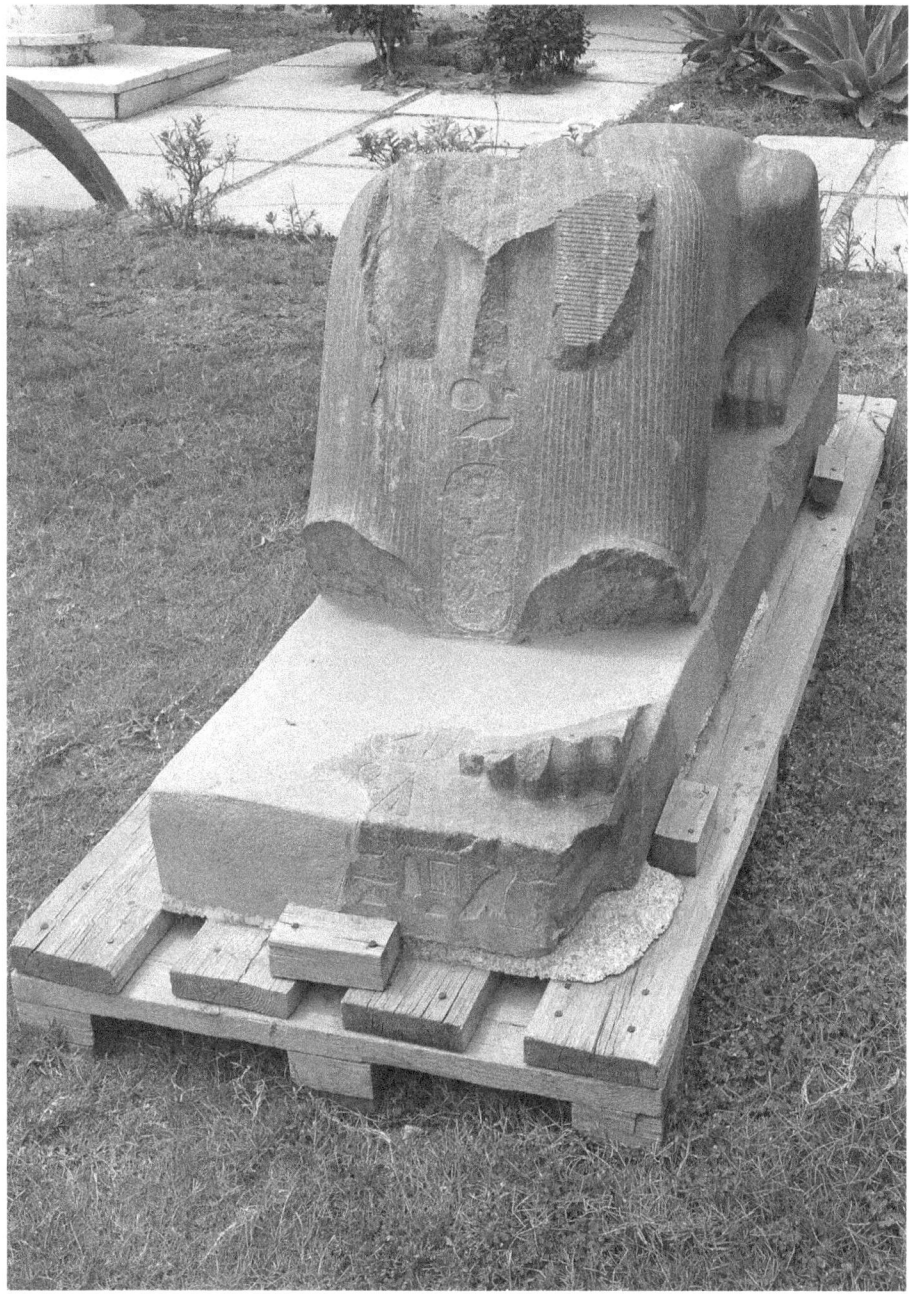

Fig. 6.1. Sphinx of Amenemhat IV (Alexandria NM 361). Quartzite. H. 73; W. 56; D. 187 cm. Photograph by Simon Connor.

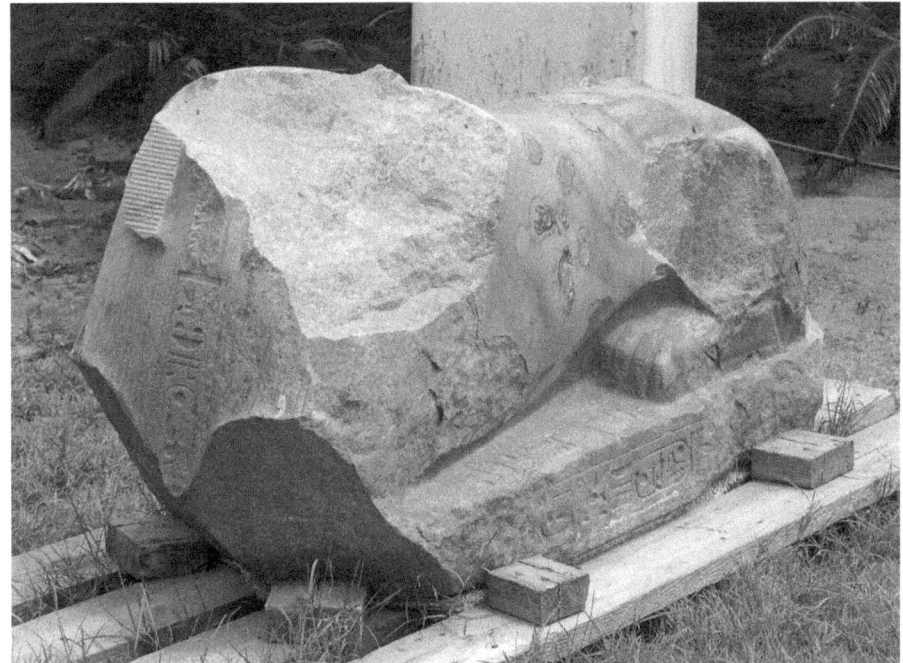

Fig. 6.2. Middle Kingdom (?) sphinx inscribed for Ramesses II (Alexandria NM 363). Quartzite. H. 62; W. 57; D. 140 cm. Photograph by Simon Connor.

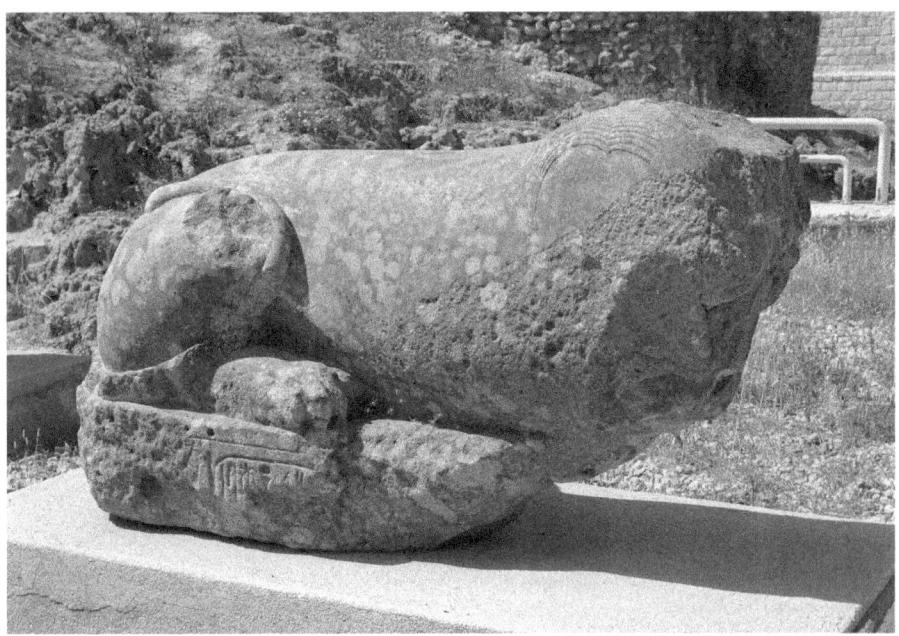

Fig. 6.3. Middle Kingdom (?) sphinx inscribed for Ramesses II (Alexandria, Serapeum 158). Quartzite. H. 68; W. 50; D. 122 cm. Photograph by Simon Connor.

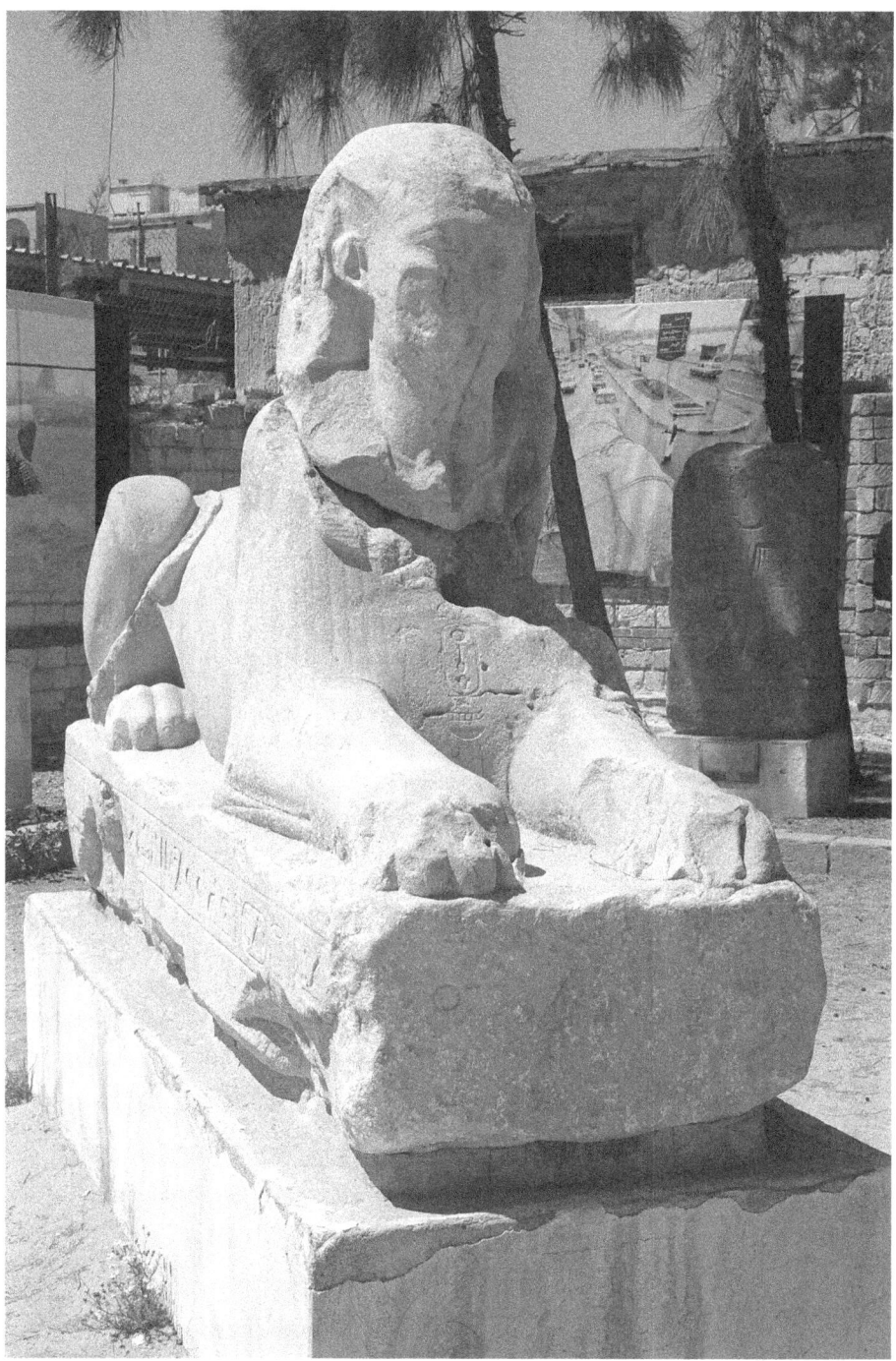

Fig. 6.4. Sphinx of Psamtik II found in submarine excavations close to the lighthouse's ruins. Alexandria, Kom al-Dikka 101. Quartzite. H. 130; W. 90; D. 310 cm. Photograph by Simon Connor.

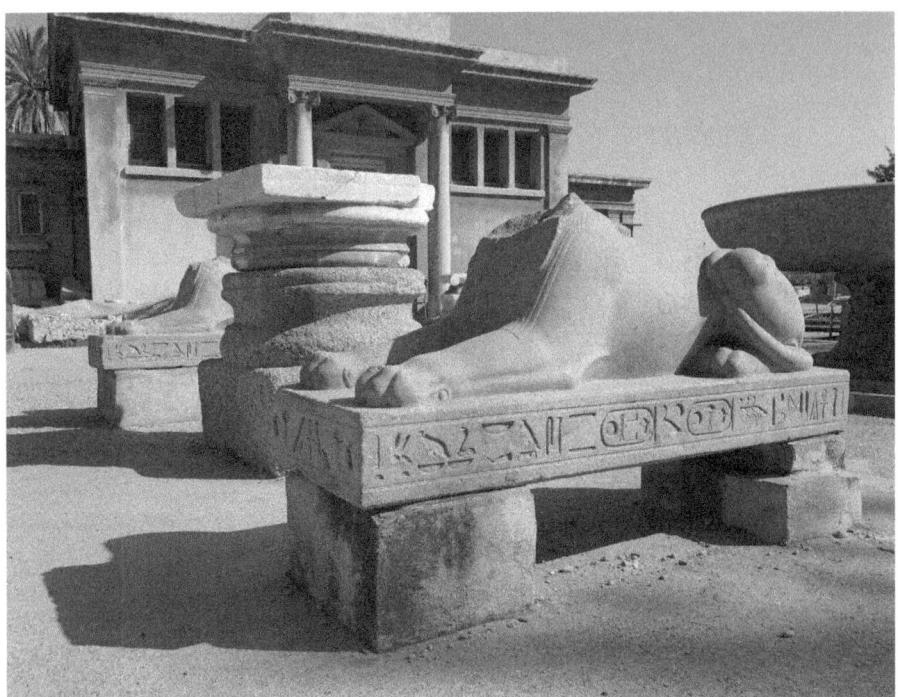

Fig. 6.5. Sphinxes of Apries, "beloved of the Baw of Heliopolis," found in Alexandria, on the southern slope of the Serapeum. Today in Alexandria, Kom al-Shugafa, 90 (H. 60; W. 46; D. 149 cm) and 91 (H. 60; W. 46; D. 156). Quartzite. Photograph by Simon Connor.

pharaoh into a Ptolemy or a Roman emperor. There might be one exception, which is perhaps more likely to be understood as a restoration than as a reidentification: the sphinx in London, British Museum EA 58892, carved in anorthositic gneiss. This sphinx represents Amenemhat IV as "beloved of Atum, lord of Heliopolis," according to the inscription finely carved between its front legs.

However, the oval face shows Ptolemaic features, with long and rounded cheeks, a small mouth, slanting eyes placed high, a low forehead, and oblique eyebrows, which is not at all the appearance of a Late Middle Kingdom figure. The shape of the hieroglyphic signs is characteristic of the Late Middle Kingdom, and there is no reason to believe that it is a Ptolemaic statue of Amenemhat IV. The sphinx's profile, as well as a close examination of the *nemes*, shows that the king was originally represented as a "mane sphinx" (a typical shape of the late Twelfth Dynasty). Without any intention of changing the identity of the king, only its front part was recut, for a yet unknown reason. Whether it was for repair or to change the sphinx's shape for aesthetic reasons in an attempt to "fit" into a decorative program is unknown. The sphinx was found in Beirut in 1926 in the foundations of a building.[5] Various hypotheses have proposed interpretations of the presence of Egyptian statues in the Near East; they go beyond the scope of this chapter.[6] They could have been sent to the northeastern courts at different moments of history and for a vast range of motives. Since the British Museum sphinx bears the style of the Ptolemies it is likely that it did not leave Egyptian territory before the Greco-Roman period. Its dedication to the *baw* of Heliopolis suggests that the statue was moved from the City of the Sun to Alexandria, before ending up in Beirut.

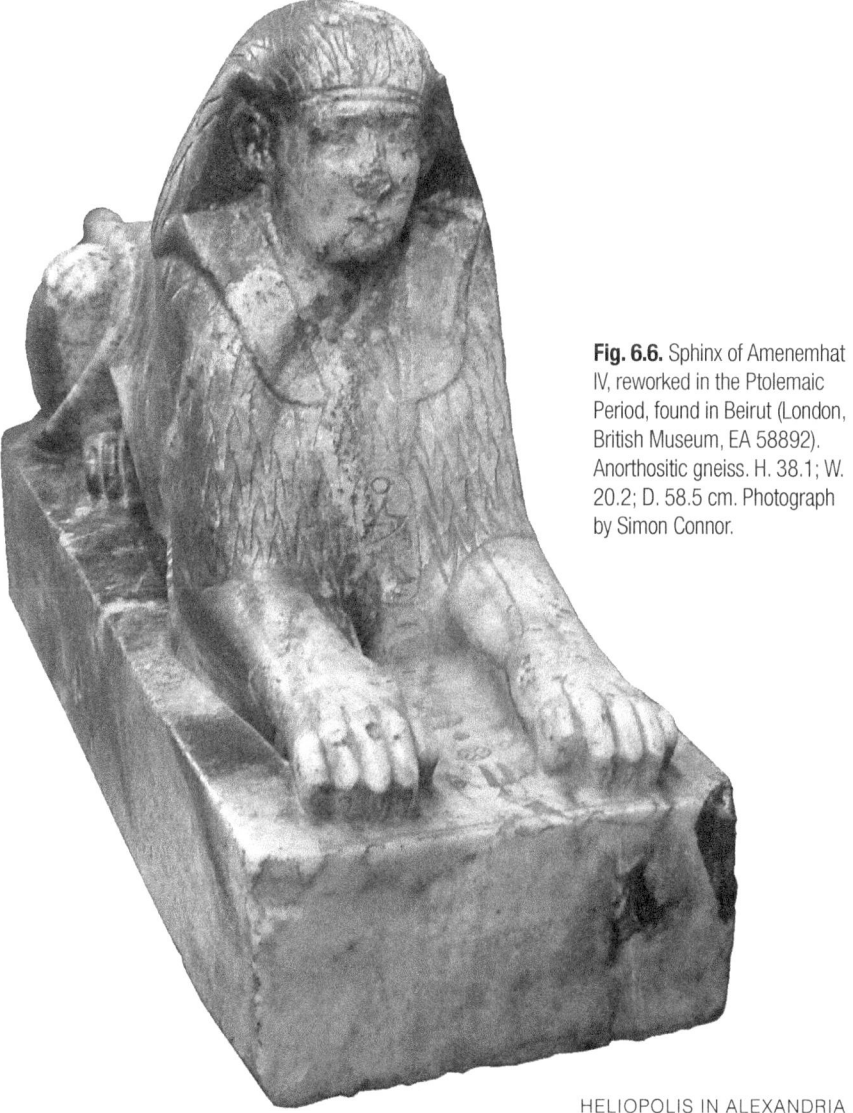

Fig. 6.6. Sphinx of Amenemhat IV, reworked in the Ptolemaic Period, found in Beirut (London, British Museum, EA 58892). Anorthositic gneiss. H. 38.1; W. 20.2; D. 58.5 cm. Photograph by Simon Connor.

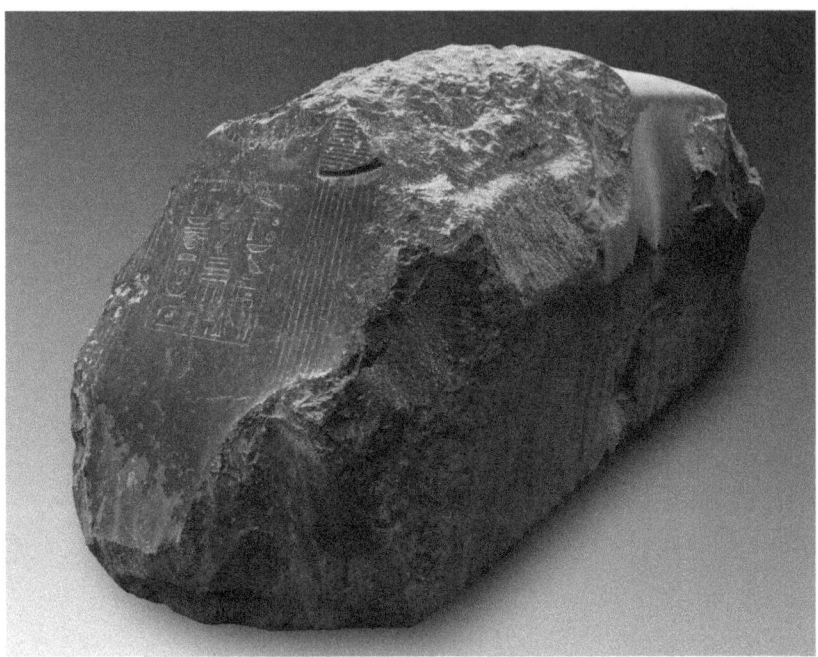

Fig. 6.7. Sphinx of Senwosret II found reused in the Mottahar mosque's masonry. Cairo JE 37796. Graywacke. H. 47; D. 162 cm. Photograph by Simon Connor.

Heliopolis in Cairo

Another place that delivers a lot of Heliopolitan material is Old Cairo. In the Middle Ages and in modern times, the ruins of ancient Heliopolis lay less than ten kilometers northeast of the city of al-Qahira. From there, roads and even a canal provided easy access to Matariya's field of ruins that emerged from the lake that had formed inside the ancient precinct.

What the Alexandrians had left visible was gradually taken by the builders and inhabitants of medieval Cairo to build their palaces, mosques, and city walls. Architraves, thresholds, pillars, columns, and statues were massively reused in the masonry of new buildings, and one can still see them today when walking in Sharia Moaz and its surroundings.[7]

Among other statues found reused in the masonry of buildings, one may mention a graywacke sphinx of Senwosret II, dedicated to the "*baw* of Heliopolis, lords of the great house," which was once part of the walls of the Mottahar mosque and registered in the Egyptian Museum in Cairo in 1905 (fig. 6.7).[8] Headless and deprived of its paws, the sphinx's hard-stone body has been reduced to a parallelepiped, ideal for a lintel or threshold.

The Ruins of Heliopolis

A large number of Heliopolitan statues can be found outside of Heliopolis itself. Alexandria and Old Cairo are only the two main destinations presented here, but several monuments also seem to have been relocated, already in the pharaonic period, perhaps to Tanis,[9] while other statues may have reached Rome, like the numerous obelisks now adorning the city, either directly from Heliopolis or perhaps indirectly, after a few centuries in Alexandria.

Despite this massive reuse and moving of monuments, either again as proper statues transferred into a new context or more often(?) as building material for new constructions, a large amount of sculptural material remained abandoned or intentionally buried in Matariya and had to wait for several centuries before being rediscovered.

Joseph Hekekyan first explored some parts of the site in 1851. The geologist and explorer mentions in his reports several monuments, including a monumental sphinx with the cartouche of Ramesses III, probably the same one that was found some 717 meters west of the obelisk, in connection with a gate.[10] The fate of this sphinx is unknown: did it go to some collection or magazine? Or did it remain where it was found and does it still need to be relocated and re-excavated? It is not impossible that a claw once belonging to a gigantic sphinx in quartzite, recently found during the excavations of Suq al-Khamis, is in fact a fragment of the missing sphinx.

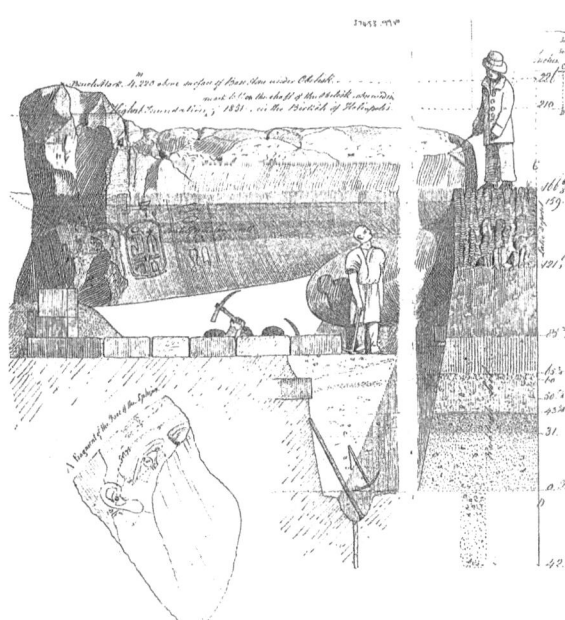

Fig. 6.8. Sphinx of Ramesses III found during Hekekyan's excavations (1851). After Jeffreys, "Hekekyan at Heliopolis," 166, fig. 7.

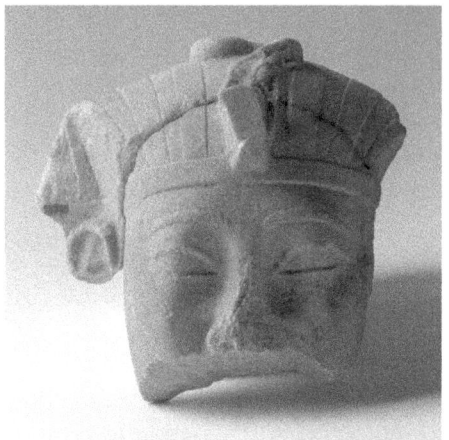
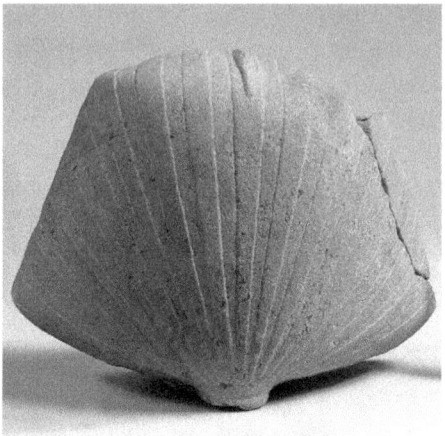

Fig. 6.9. Head of a Twenty-sixth Dynasty king, Turin S. 2699. Quartzite. H. 16; W. 15.5; D. 16.7 cm. Photograph by Pino Dell'Aquila © Museo Egizio

Fig. 6.10. Back of a head of a Twenty-sixth Dynasty king (?), Turin S. 2696+2701. H. 20.5; W. 15; D. 25.5 cm. Quartzite. Photograph courtesy of Museo Egizio.

Ernesto Schiaparelli (1903–1906)

In 1903, new excavations took place in Matariya, under the direction of Ernesto Schiaparelli, director of the Museo Egizio, Turin. In the southeast area of Matariya, the team notably found a large quantity of statuary, now in Turin. This material is extremely fragmentary and was probably found in small "cachettes" or deposits containing temple material, what Schiaparelli called *bucca*. These were built inside the masonry of what we interpret today as a large embankment wall from the reign of Thutmose III (previously misunderstood as a Hyksos fortress or "high sand" by early twentieth-century excavators).[11] Ugliano's and Dietze's recent research suggests the interpretation of these *bucche*, or cachettes, as being intended for the ritual burial of fragments of reliefs, statues, and cult objects that were damaged during a massive destruction of the city's monuments, perhaps at the beginning of the first millennium BCE (precise dating under study).[12] From among these pockets of statues and relief fragments found by Schiaparelli, one may mention several quartzite heads of a Twenty-sixth Dynasty king (inv. S. 2699, S. 2702/1-2, S. 2696+2701) (figs. 6.9, 6.10); a head of a New Kingdom king (probably an early portrait of Ramesses II, inv. S. 2700) (fig. 6.11); and two small sphinxes, one of pink quartzite representing Thutmose III (S. 2673) (fig. 6.12), the other one, of graywacke, bearing the name of Sheshonq I (S. 2677) (fig. 6.13), both perhaps elements from processional boats or cultic objects. As pointed out by Ugliano and Dietze, the recent excavations in the Army Camp sector in the southeast part of Matariya, which is in the vicinity of the areas excavated by Schiaparelli, shed light on material very similar to that found in 1904. Another serpentinite sphinx of similar dimensions, with the name of Merenptah, was found in the Army Camp sector in 2017, also close to where Schiaparelli dug 113 years earlier. It is a sphinx with human hands, holding an altar topped with a scarab (fig. 6.14). A fourth similar sphinx, with the name of Merenre, of unknown provenance but likely to be from Heliopolis based on its inscription, may belong to the same category of statuettes that decorated ritual objects.[13]

The largest of the pieces found by Schiaparelli is an enormous paw of a sphinx, today on display in the Museo Egizio's Gallery of Kings (figs. 6.15, 6.16). The sphinx to which it once belonged must have measured around 5.5 m high and some 10 m long.[14]

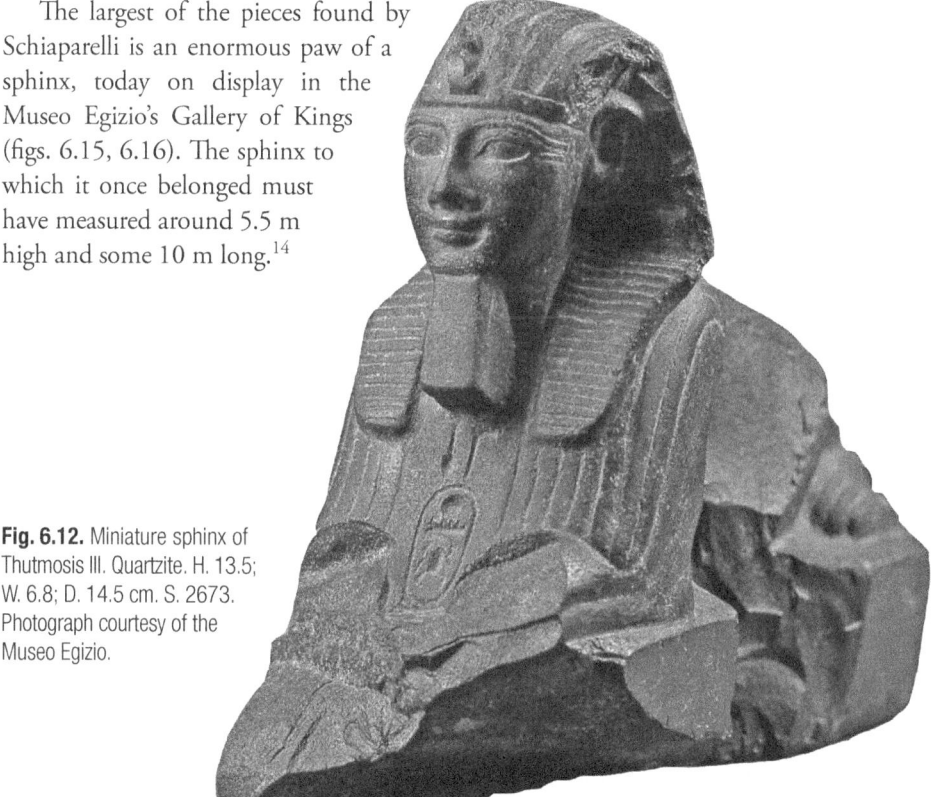

Fig. 6.11. Head of an early Nineteenth Dynasty king, Turin S. 2700. Quartzite. H. 25.5; W. 11.5; D. 24 cm. Photograph by Pino Dell'Aquila, courtesy of the Museo Egizio.

Fig. 6.12. Miniature sphinx of Thutmosis III. Quartzite. H. 13.5; W. 6.8; D. 14.5 cm. S. 2673. Photograph courtesy of the Museo Egizio.

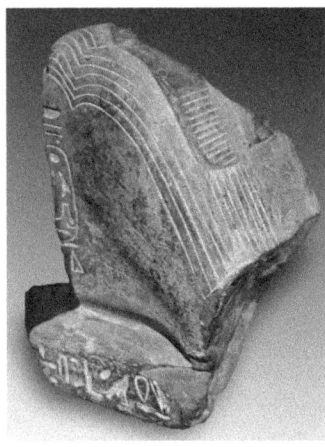
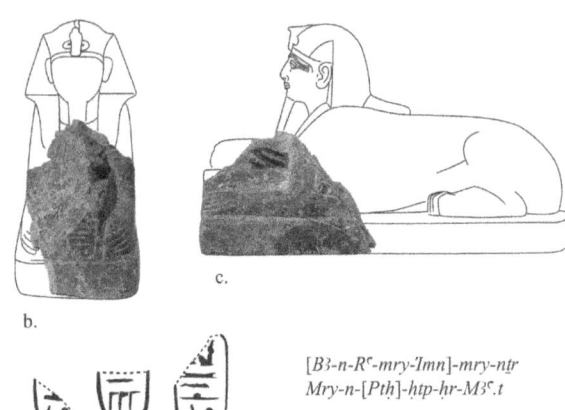

Fig. 6.13. Miniature sphinx of Sheshonq I. Graywacke. Turin S. 2677. Photograph by Simon Connor.

Fig. 6.14. Miniature human-handed sphinx of Merenptah, presenting an altar with a scarab. Serpentinite. Matariya, sector 232 (April 2017). H. 7.3; W. 6.5; D. 10.9 cm (originally ca. 13.5 × 6.5 × 22.5 cm). Photographs and drawings by Simon Connor.

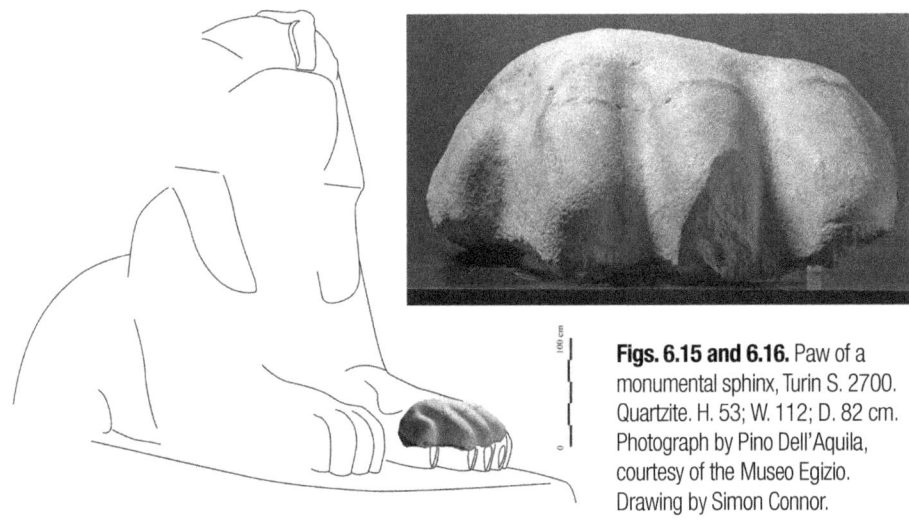

Figs. 6.15 and 6.16. Paw of a monumental sphinx, Turin S. 2700. Quartzite. H. 53; W. 112; D. 82 cm. Photograph by Pino Dell'Aquila, courtesy of the Museo Egizio. Drawing by Simon Connor.

W.M. Flinders Petrie (1912)

A few years later, Petrie came in his turn to Matariya and also excavated in the proximity of Senwosret I's obelisk. Among other objects, he mentions three heads of statues found "near the obelisk" (fig. 6.17). During the division of finds, the Egyptian Research Account (ERA) and the British School of Archaeology in Egypt gave a Late Period or early Ptolemaic Period graywacke face to the

Metropolitan Museum of Art, in return for the contribution of the museum to the excavations.[15] The location of the limestone royal head that Petrie found is currently unknown.[16] According to its stylistic features, it is datable to the Thutmoside Period. The almond-shaped eyes, triangular shape of the face, pointy chin, and somewhat feline expression are reminiscent of Hatshepsut's statues from Deir al-Bahari, but the only published photograph does not allow a precise dating. The third head of a king, the nose and lower part of the face of which are missing, was also of unknown location until recently (fig. 6.18).[17] An investigation carried out by the author in the Museum August Kestner in Hanover proved once more that exploring museum storerooms can be an important source of exciting revelations. From the head's discovery to its acquisition by the museum, the piece's provenance had been lost. Previously part of the private collection of the Egyptologist Friedrich Wilhelm von Bissing, the head was sold, together with other objects of the same collection, to the Museum August Kestner (then known as the Kestner-Museum) in 1935. It is unlikely that von Bissing would have financed Petrie's excavations, but he bought numerous objects at the Egyptian Museum's "salon de vente," where pieces considered as secondary were often sold.[18] Would the head found in Matariya have reached the Egyptian Museum before being sold and acquired by von Bissing? It is a possibility. Thanks to Petrie's photograph, we can now ascertain that the head today in Hanover is not only genuine but that it comes from an archaeological context.

Its stylistic features, with prominent cheekbones and arched eyebrows, the absence of makeup lines for the eyebrows and eyes, the heavy upper eyelids, the oversized ears, and the square jaw, are all in favor of a late Middle Kingdom date—more specifically, the Thirteenth Dynasty.[19] The stone is unusual: a variety of grayish stone with purple inclusions, similar to serpentinite, was frequently used in late Middle Kingdom sculpture, but usually for much smaller statues. The deep projection of the back part of the Hanover head speaks in favor of it being a sphinx that would have measured some 170 cm to 180 cm long. It is perhaps more likely that the stone is a variety of granodiorite, which was much more common in statues of this size. The stone's unusual appearance might be the result of a fire. Many of the stone objects recently found close to the obelisk in Heliopolis in the area of the "high sand" or Hyksos fort, now reconsidered as an embankment of the mid-Eighteenth Dynasty, indeed show traces of burning. Although the burial or abandonment of these objects is still difficult to date with precision, there seems to have been a large-scale destruction by fire. Either before or after this fire, the front and upper part of the head were cut, perhaps even sawn, apparently in order to transform the head into a block.

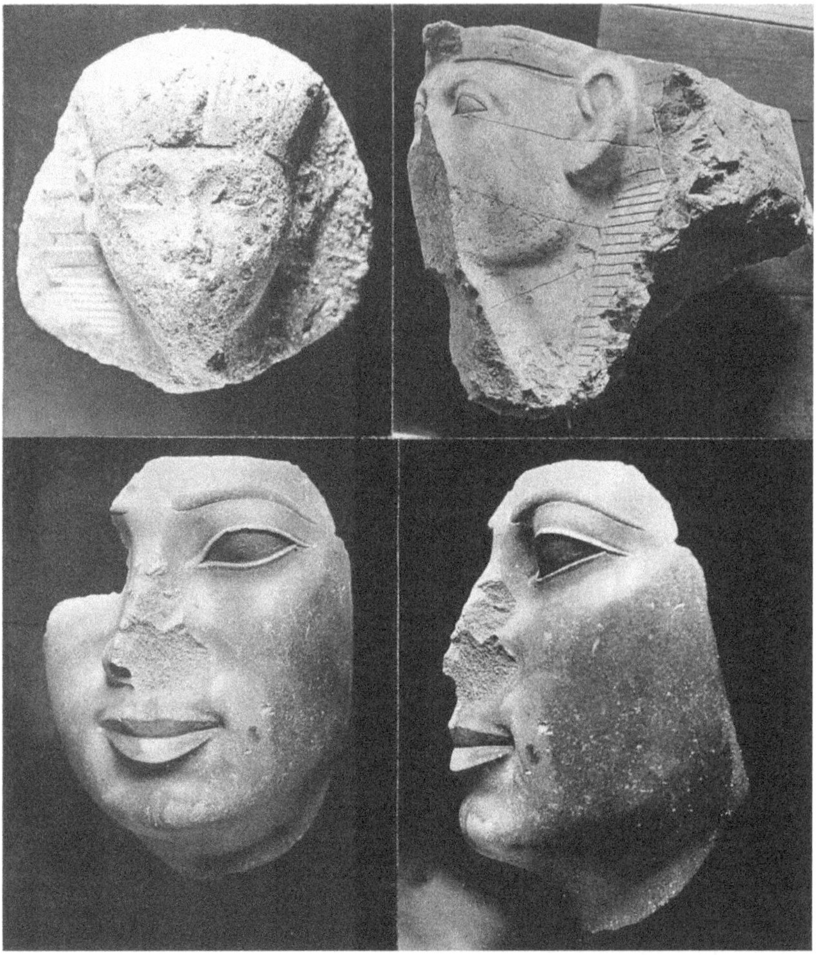

Fig. 6.17. Three heads of statues found near the obelisk (Petrie and Mackay, Heliopolis, pl. 6).

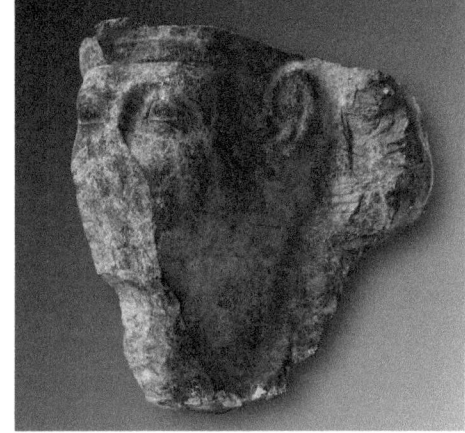

Fig. 6.18. Head of a sphinx in burnt (?) granodiorite (?), Hanover 1935.200.128. H. 25.6; W. 29.7; D. 31 cm. Photograph by Simon Connor.

So Many Sphinxes

A large proportion of the Alexandrian statues of Heliopolitan origin are sphinxes, including several of the statues found by Schiaparelli, as well as the Hanover head. Hekekyan's sphinx and the enormous paw in Turin show that monumental sphinxes, similar to the one found in Mit Rahina (today in Memphis' open-air museum), were set up in some parts of the city, probably guarding passages or flanking processional ways. Sphinxes of various sizes seem to have been an important part of the sculptural program in Heliopolis. Hekekyan's plan mentions an "alley of sphinxes" in the middle of the archaeological area. It is difficult to ascertain whether or not such an alley was still visible in the nineteenth century or if this was an interpretation of the few remains. Several fragments (mostly front paws) of granite and quartzite sphinxes were indeed found in various spots during the most recent seasons of excavation (figs. 6.19, 6.20).[20] Many of them belonged to statues of particularly large size: from the fragments preserved, one can reconstruct sphinxes of approximately 270 cm, 420 cm, and 580 cm in length, while two quartzite claws seem to belong to even larger statues.

Among the numerous sphinxes attributable to Heliopolis, one group is particularly notable: a series of quartzite statues, all of approximately the same dimensions, originally 150 cm to 200 cm long and around 90 cm to 120 cm high, made and completed by numerous kings over more than a thousand years.[21] The oldest sphinx of this series, found in Old Cairo, shows the cartouche of Pepi I Meryre (Cairo CG 541) (fig. 6.21), while the most recent ones, today in Alexandria, show the cartouches of Apries (Kom al-Shugafa 90 and 91) and Psamtik II (Kom al-Dikka 101 and Serapeum 04). Most of the sphinxes belonging to this group date to the late Middle Kingdom, with the cartouches of Senwosret III (Kom al-Dikka 99), Amenemhat IV (Alexandria NM 361, Cairo CG 388, Giza 17, Abu Qir), and even the obscure Amenemhat V Sekhemkare (second king of the Thirteenth Dynasty, so far only known from another statue found in Heqaib's sanctuary in Elephantine) (fig. 6.22).[22]

Some of these Middle Kingdom sphinxes were reused and reinscribed by Ramesses II (Alexandria NM 363, as well as probably Serapeum 158). The same king also ordered the production of new sphinxes for himself, still clearly for the same series, as attested by a sphinx with human arms holding an offering table, found reused as a threshold for a postern in a northern medieval wall of Cairo, close to Bab al-Nasr (fig. 6.23).[23] Until 2019, all the sphinxes belonging to that series of statues were found in secondary contexts: Alexandria, Abu Qir, Giza, Medieval Cairo. Only their dedication to Atum, Re-Horakhty, or the Baw of Iunu indicate their origin. In September 2019, a fragment of a

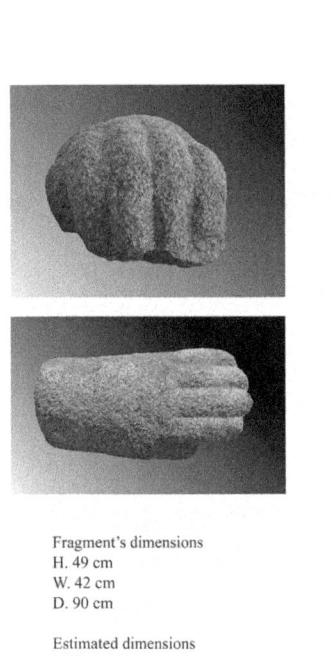
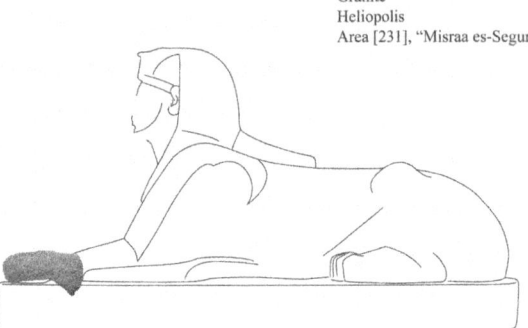
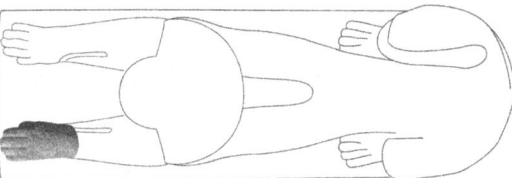

Sphinx Nb. 3
Granite
Heliopolis
Area [231], "Misraa es-Segun"

Fragment's dimensions
H. 49 cm
W. 42 cm
D. 90 cm

Estimated dimensions
of the sphinx
H. 310 cm
W. 180 cm
D. 580 cm

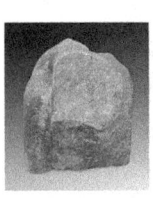
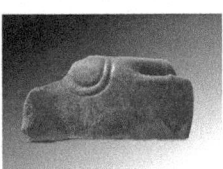
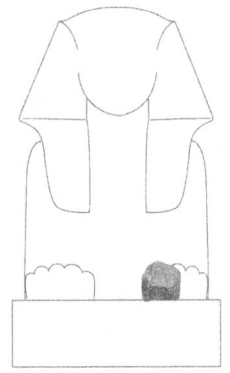

Sphinx Nb. 5
Quartzite
Heliopolis
Area [231], "Misraa es-Segun"

Fragment's dimensions
H. 27 cm
W. 29 cm
D. 54 cm

Estimated dimensions
of the sphinx
H. 250 cm
W. 150 cm
D. 420 cm

Figs. 6.19 and 6.20. Two of numerous fragments of sphinxes found in Matariya during recent excavations. Photographs and drawings by Simon Connor.

quartzite sphinx, clearly from the same series (same format and stone), probably dating to the Middle Kingdom (by comparison with the sphinxes of Senwosret III, Amenemhat IV, and Amenemhat V), confirmed that the city of Heliopolis must have been the original location for this series of quartzite sphinxes. This fragment from the left shoulder of a sphinx and lappet of the *nemes* (fig. 6.24) was found within a thick dump layer of the Nineteenth Dynasty, against the western face of an enclosure wall, probably belonging to one of the New Kingdom temples, in the heart of ancient Heliopolis.[24] This series of quartzite sphinxes testifies to a tradition of adding, reign after reign, new items to a pre-existing series of statues, thus producing a very homogeneous group, step by step, over more than a thousand years.

Almost all the sphinxes attributable to ancient Heliopolis were found headless, and many lack their front paws. Several single front paws appeared during recent excavations, as mentioned earlier. A possible reason is their

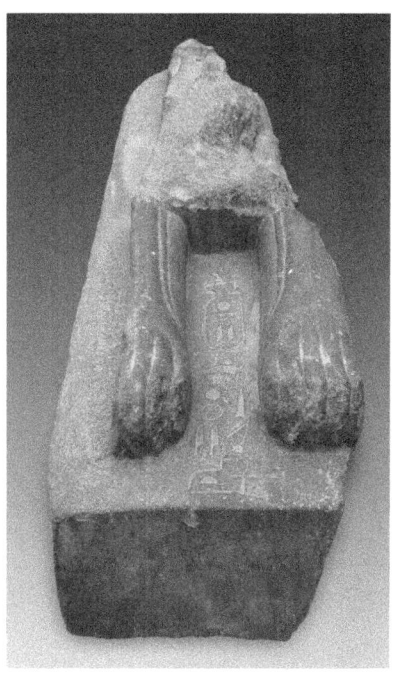

Fig. 6.21. Sphinx of (Pepi I) Meryre "beloved of the *baw* of Heliopolis," found in Haret al-Rum (1891). Cairo CG 541. Quartzite. D. 215 cm. Photograph by Simon Connor.

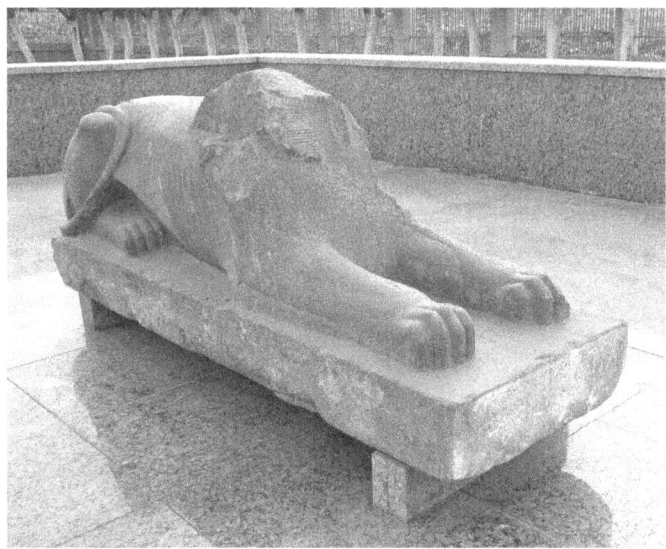

Fig. 6.22. Sphinx of Amenemhat V Sekhemkare "beloved of Re-Horakhty," from Bab al-Nasr. Quartzite. H. 68; W. 50; D. 156 cm. Photograph by Simon Connor.

reuse as masonry blocks: a decapitated sphinx provides a particularly suitable parallelepiped block reusable for thresholds and lintels, as attested by the two sphinxes from the Bab al-Nasr area (Amenemhat V and Ramesses II).

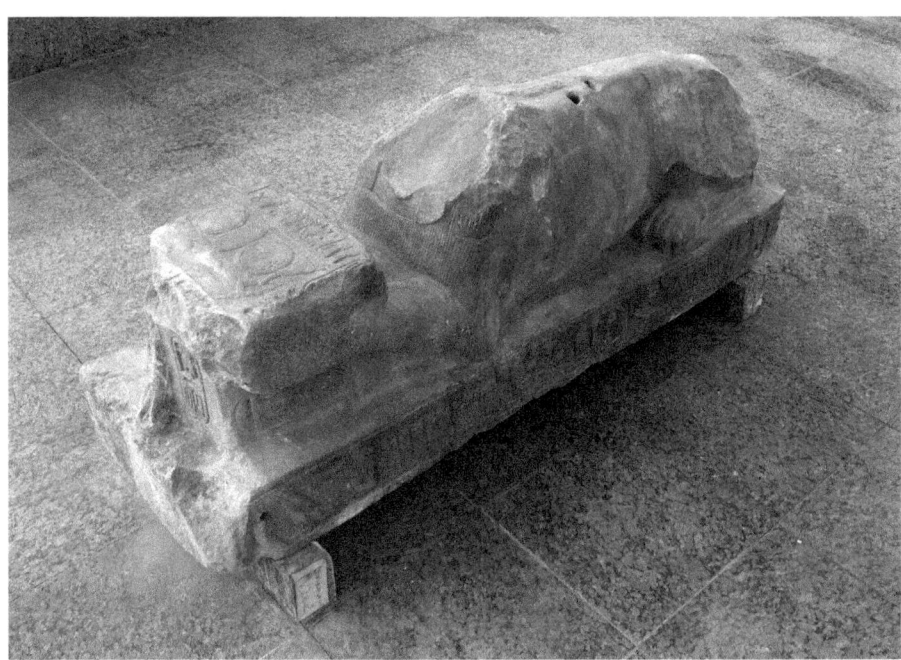

Fig. 6.23. Sphinx of Ramesses II, from Bab al-Nasr. Quartzite. H. 54; W. 51; D. 157 cm. Photograph by Simon Connor.

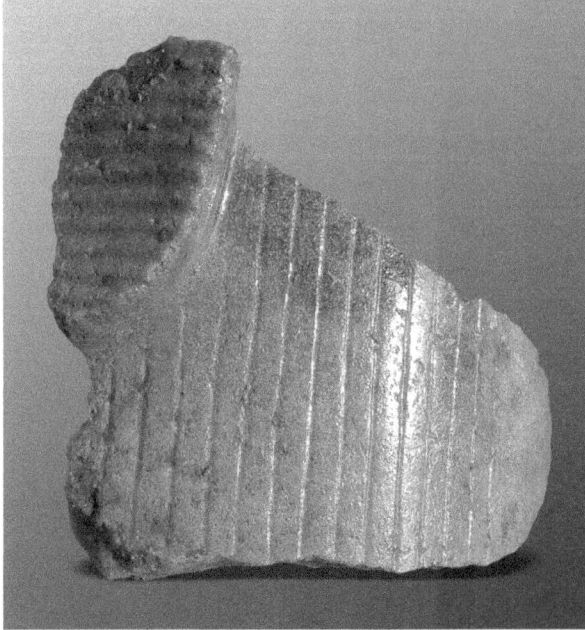

Fig. 6.24. Fragment of a quartzite sphinx found in Matariya, area 251, in a Ramesside dump layer (Egyptian–German mission, September 2019). H. 13.4; W. 9.3; D. 15.5 cm. Photograph by Simon Connor.

Recent Excavations (Egyptian–German Mission)

Since 2012 the Egyptian–German mission of Heliopolis (directed by Aiman Ashmawy and Dietrich Raue)[25] has discovered in Matariya a number of statue fragments; most are still under study. A few of them are presented in this chapter, offering sources for reflection on the reuse and destruction of statues.

The southeastern area of the site, area 232[26] (Army Camp sector), yielded a large number of statue fragments, most of them from what seems to be the equivalent of Schiaparelli's *bucche*; that is, caches of sacred material within the mud-brick masonry of the embankment. Buried together with damaged elements of reliefs, these small statue fragments, dating from the Middle Kingdom, New Kingdom, and Late Period, show traces of burning, which would explain the ritual burial following the destruction of parts of the city by fire. Area 221 to the west yielded a large number of quartzite and granite blocks with the names of Ramesses II and Merenptah, as well as quartzite and basalt blocks inscribed for Nectanebo I.[27] Not enough remains for a plan of the temple to which the blocks belonged, but the blocks seem to indicate a large-size temple. Among them, several fragments of sphinxes came to light—paws, claws, and headless bodies—while two large Ramesside heads may have belonged to a pair of monumental sphinxes (ca. 250 cm high and 470 cm long) (figs. 6.25, 6.26, 6.27). One of these heads is sufficiently well preserved to show that its upper part was cut horizontally and was meant to wear a separately sculpted crown, like the monumental sphinxes of Amenhotep III today in St. Petersburg, among many other examples.[28]

These various fragments show several traces of serrated cuts. These teeth-like, regular cuts are the result of using hard-metal chisels. Such tools are not attested, as far as we know, before the mid-first millennium BCE, which provides us a probable, though unfortunately not very precise, *terminus post quem* for the dismantling of these statues. Such marks are very common on granite blocks and statues all over Egypt. They can also be observed on most other granite monuments found in Matariya, and should most likely be linked to a large-scale reuse of blocks at a point of Egyptian history when the ancient city had lost its influence and was transformed into a proper quarry, perhaps as early as the Greco-Roman period.

Two large fragments of an important statue of a prostrate Merenptah come from the same area (figs. 6.28 and 6.29). The angle of his arms suggests that the king was presenting a rather tall object, either a stela or an altar. The statue must have measured some 260 cm in height and reached almost 4 m in length, which makes it by far the largest attested statue of this type.[29]

Still farther to the west (sector 248), among the remains of the temple of Amun and Mut built by Ramesses II (450 m west of the obelisk), several other

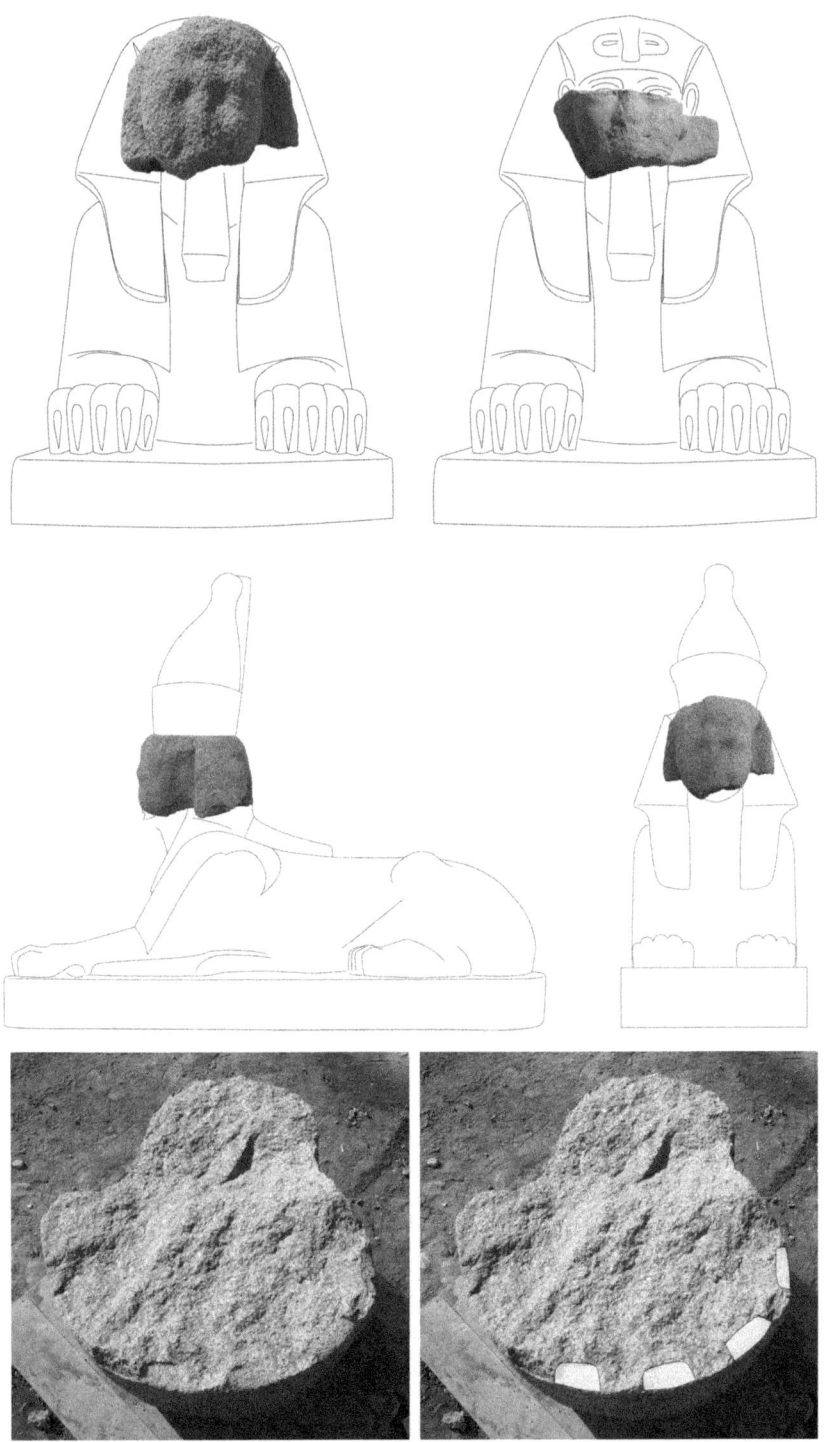

Figs. 6.25–6.27. Fragments of sphinxes found in Matariya during the recent seasons of excavations. Photographs and drawings by Simon Connor.

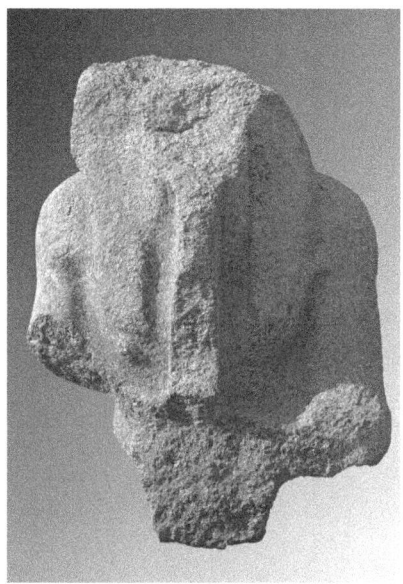
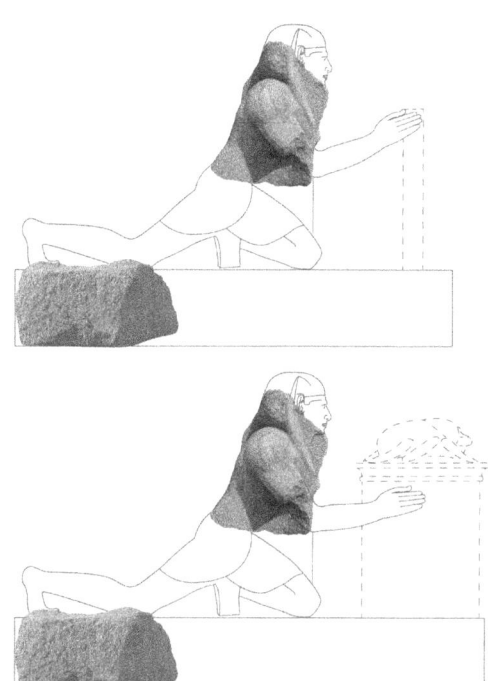

Figs. 6.28–6.29. Prostrate statue of Merenptah. Photographs and drawings by Simon Connor.

elements of sculpture were found. These include the lower part of a seated statue of Ramesses VI (fig. 6.30), and a fragment of the Upper Egyptian crown from a quartzite colossal statue, surmounted by a protruding element above the bulb of the crown (figs. 6.31, 6.32). A possible interpretation for this element could be a scarab, which is attested above the *nemes* headdress and on the wig of other statues.[30] However, in this case it would not have been visible from the ground. The protrusion is most likely the remains of a solar disc. If the fragment belonged to a standing statue, as has been suggested by Ashmawy, it must have reached some 8 meters in height.

Among other significant finds, the same area yielded a torso of a male deity (figs. 6.33, 6.34). At first glance, it looks like a female figure due to the tripartite wig and the slightly prominent breasts, but the latter has to be understood as a stylistic feature inherited from the post-Amarna period. This figure likely dates to the early Nineteenth Dynasty. The tripartite wig and the remaining parts of the neck speak in favor of a deity with a human face. Considering the provenance, we may suggest seeing here a depiction of Khepri, with a scarab on the wig; Atum, with a double crown; or Nehebkau, of whom another, larger statue in sandstone was found in Matariya in 1985.[31] A remarkable

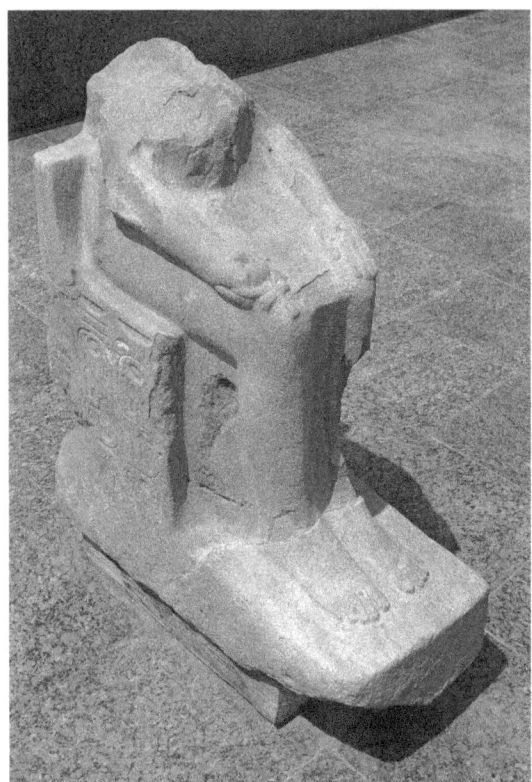

Fig. 6.30. Lower part of a statue of Ramesses VI. Quartzite. Photograph by Simon Connor.

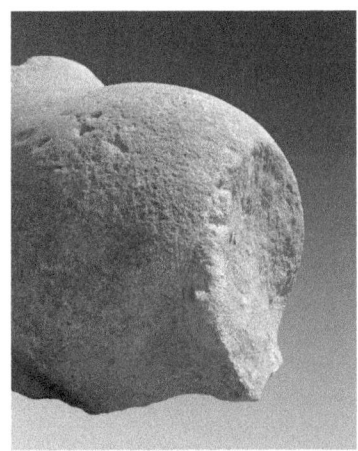

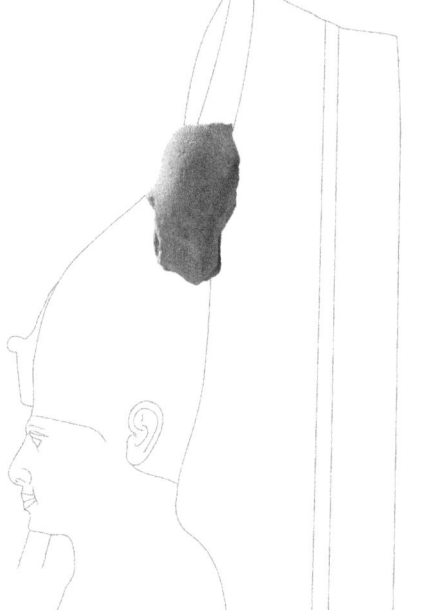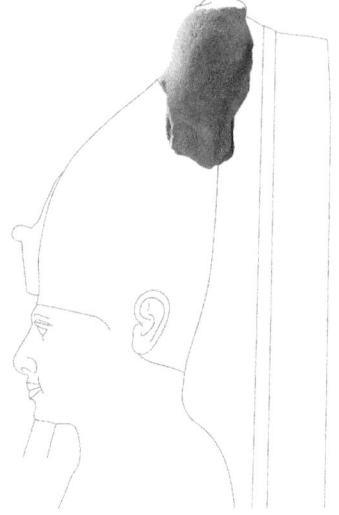

Figs. 6.31 and 6.32. Upper part of an Upper Egypt crown from a colossal statue. Quartzite. H. 67; W. 45; D. 41 cm. Photographs and drawings by Simon Connor.

Figs. 6.33 and 6.34. Torso of a male deity. Quartzite. Photographs and drawing by Simon Connor.

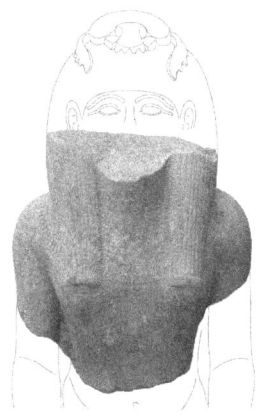
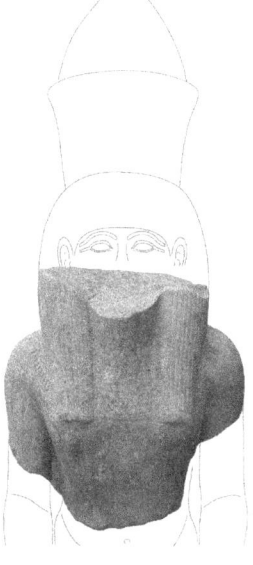
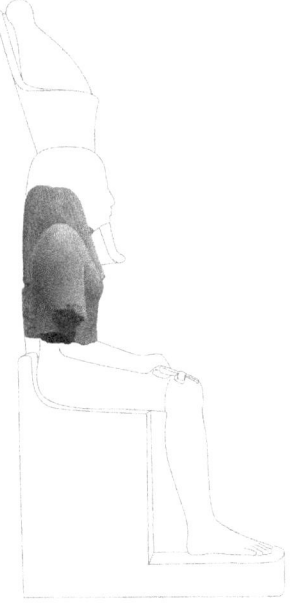

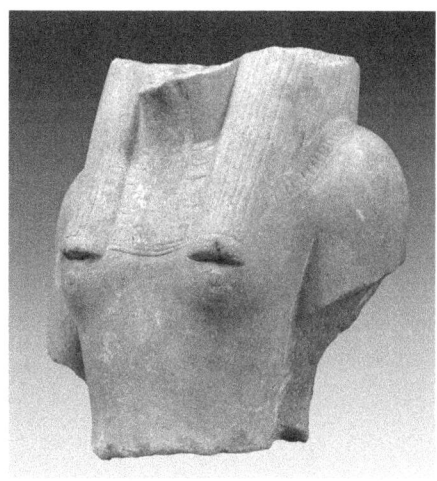

feature is the careful removal of the beard, which a raking light allows to see quite clearly. The beard was not simply broken or smashed but clearly erased from the surface of the statue. This phenomenon was not rare in Egyptian statuary. Noses and uraei were also common targets of defacing, either during brutal and wild destruction of monuments, or in the framework of more targeted, perhaps ritual, deactivations of images. False beards are similarly an almost systematic focus for depredators, perhaps so as to dispossess the figure of a protective element, or even of its male strength or capacity.[32]

Several other outstanding pieces of statuary were found in the western part of the site (sector 200, Suq al-Khamis), probably in the area where Hekekyan found a monumental sphinx in 1851. A temple built by Ramesses II stood there. Only a few limestone blocks from it remain, but a path made of basalt blocks, as well as a series of bases for colossal statues, were still found in situ. Several standing and seated granite statues of Ramesses II were once erected in

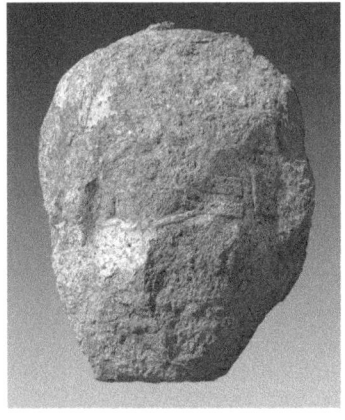
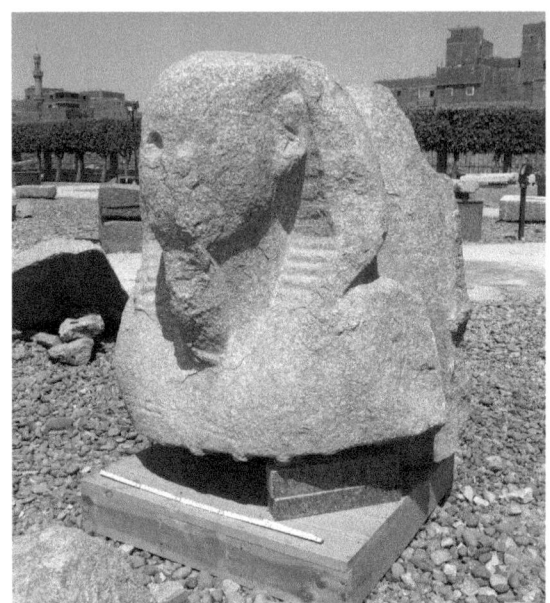

Figs. 6.35 and 6.36. Head and bust of two of the granite colossi of the early Twelfth Dynasty, reused by Ramesses II. Original height: ca. 550 cm. Photographs by Simon Connor.

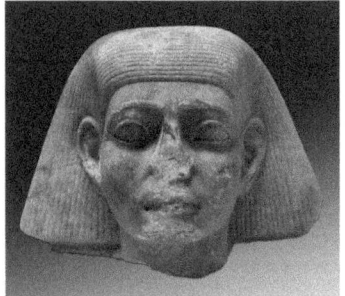

Fig. 6.37. Head of a private official, early Twelfth Dynasty. Quartzite. H. 16.6; W. 23.3; D. 15 cm. Photograph by Simon Connor.

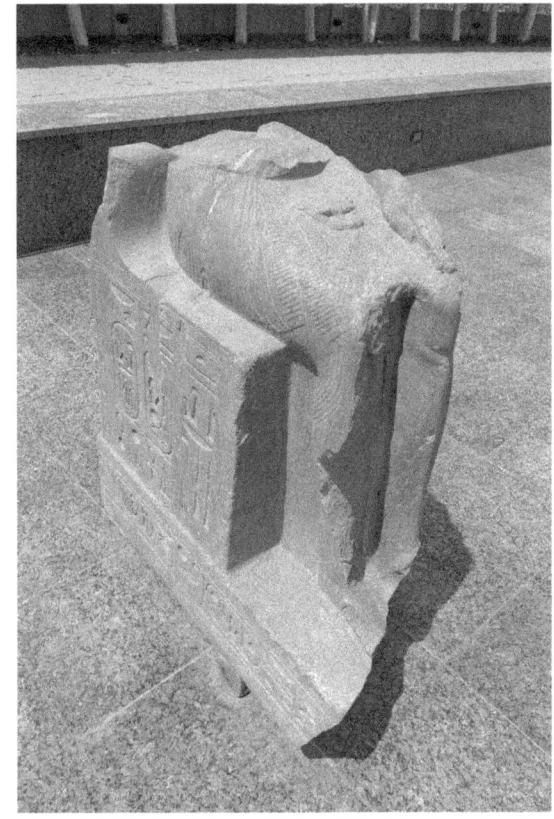

Fig. 6.38. Life-size statue of Ramesses II found in Matariya (now in Matariya open-air museum). Quartzite. H. 120.5; W. 54; D. 67 cm. Photograph by Simon Connor.

front of the pylon.[33] They were dismantled and cut into blocks at some point in Egyptian history (at the earliest, during the second half of the first millennium BCE, but most probably later, in the Greco-Roman period and perhaps also as late as the Islamic period).[34] Enough of them is preserved to recognize that at least some of these 550-cm-high statues were reused early Middle Kingdom statues. The broad face with square jaw and chin, large horizontal mouth, rounded cheeks, thick horizontal makeup lines, and low forehead, as well as the long undulating uraeus tail pointing toward the top of the *nemes* headdress, are all stylistic features characteristic of the first half of the Twelfth Dynasty.[35]

At least six of these statues were seated. The back of the seated statues is not the usual narrow back pillar, but a real slab similar to the large standing colossi with white crowns found in Memphis and Tanis. In this case, however, since all statues wear a *nemes*, the slab may have been rounded at the top rather than rectangular.

The reuse of early Middle Kingdom granite colossi by Ramesses II (figs. 6.35, 6.36) is well attested, particularly in the nearby city of Memphis and in the Eastern Delta.[36] Do these colossi support the presence of a Middle Kingdom temple in this region of Heliopolis? Not necessarily, since Ramesside reuse of statues often involved transportation, sometimes over long distances.[37] These statues may have been originally connected with the (main?) temple of the sun god, closer to the obelisk of Senwosret I. Nevertheless, a head from a quartzite statue of fine quality, belonging to a private individual of the same period (fig. 6.37), was found in the same context and may further attest to the presence of a Middle Kingdom sanctuary in this area of the city. Such a statue, a bit smaller than life size, is exceptional since, as far as we know, few private individuals were commemorated by hard-stone statues of such large dimensions in the first half of the Twelfth Dynasty. The statue's material, quartzite, rarely used for nonroyal figures in this period, and its quality make it a really extraordinary piece.

Ramesses II did not just install reused statues in the Suq al-Khamis temple. The lower part of a very finely carved life-size statue in quartzite, depicting the king with a priestly garment,[38] is clearly an "authentic" Ramesside statue (fig. 6.38). The left hand lay on the knee, while the right hand most probably held the *heqa* scepter. This links the statue to a quite homogeneous series erected by Ramesses in various temples of Egypt: in Karnak (Turin cat. 1380 and Cairo CG 42140); Memphis (Mit Rahina open-air museum); Bubastis (open-air museum); probably another statue from Heliopolis (today in Alexandria, on display at the Serapeum);[39] as well as other unidentified sites (Paris, Louvre E 27455).[40] This series, produced for numerous sites, shows a remarkable variety of dimensions and materials (granite, granodiorite, graywacke, alabaster, and,

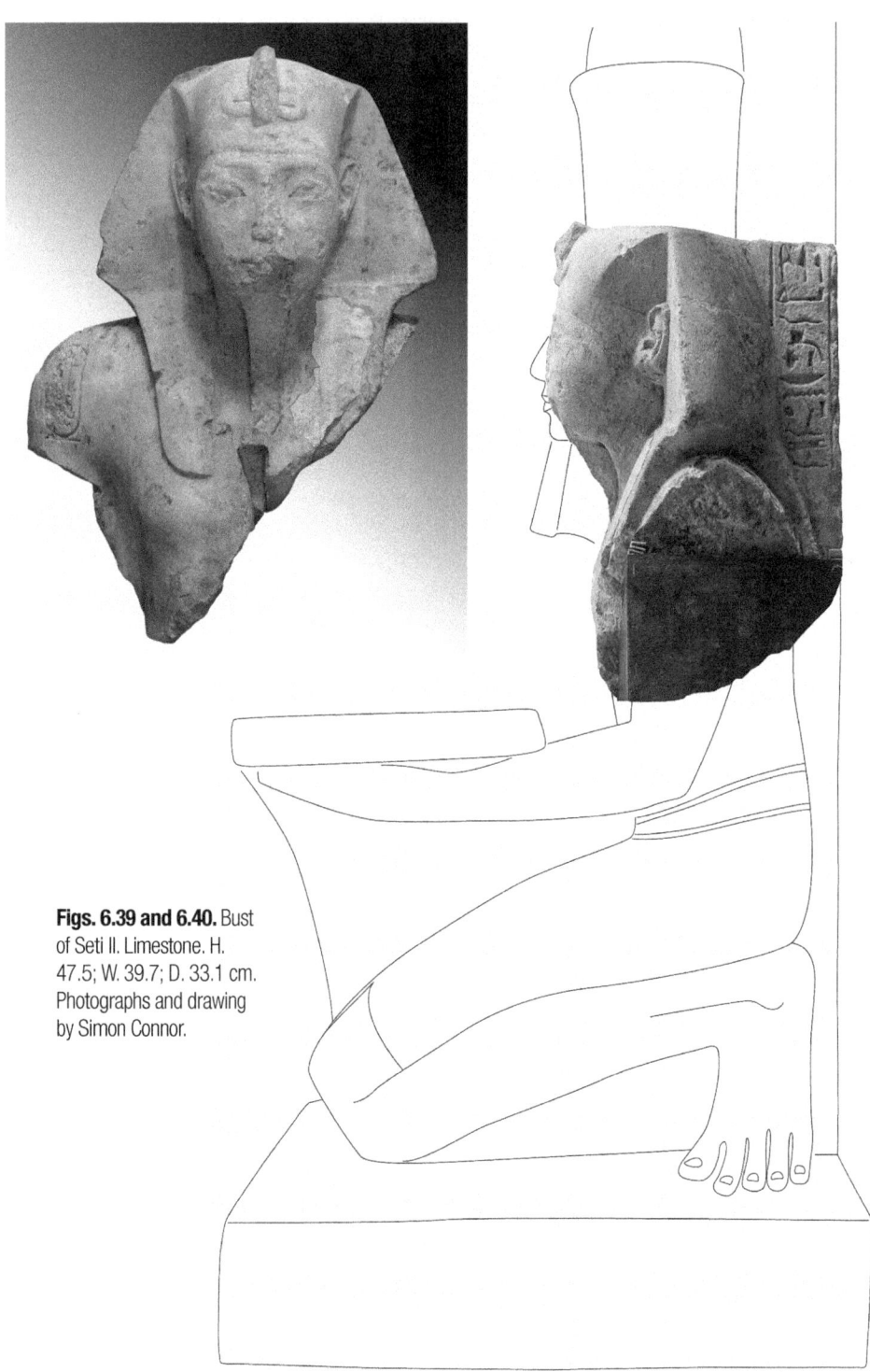

Figs. 6.39 and 6.40. Bust of Seti II. Limestone. H. 47.5; W. 39.7; D. 33.1 cm. Photographs and drawing by Simon Connor.

in the case of the Heliopolitan statue, quartzite), while following a consistent type (seated with an arm raised and holding a scepter, wearing an elaborate garment) and produced in the same very fine quality.

A limestone bust of King Seti II found in the same sector in 2017 (figs. 6.39, 6.40) gives rise to further questions. As with the Nineteenth Dynasty god's statue mentioned above, the beard on this statue was also carefully removed, as were the nose and the uraeus. A bit smaller than life size, this statue originally showed the king in a kneeling position, as indicated by the inclination of the neck and back tail of the *nemes*, compared to the back pillar. Offering statues seem to have been quite appreciated by Seti II, who commissioned several others, either kneeling or seated, for Karnak and Heliopolis, while all the standing statues seem to have been of the "standard-bearer" type. All may have played a role in the processions of Amun's bark during religious festivals. This recently found limestone bust was once surmounted by a separately sculpted element, perhaps a crown that was fixed by a tenon; the mortise is still visible on the upper part of the head. Another mortise visible on this bust is more difficult to explain. It is in the middle of the chest, almost vertical but slightly inclined. Is this the trace of an (aesthetically inept) ancient repair of the statue? Or was it intended to affix this bust to another block, in the case of a reuse in masonry?

Although the (quite damaged) features seem, at first glance, reminiscent of the late Eighteenth Dynasty, there is no reason to believe that it is a usurped statue. Not only does the statue type fit within Seti II's repertoire, but the elongated oval of the face, the almond-shaped eyes with marked upper eyelids, the large horizontal mouth, and smooth cheeks, as well as the generally neutral expression, appear on other representations of this king (see London, British Museum, EA 26).

A New Landmark for Late Period Statuary

The discovery of Seti II's bust went largely unnoticed due to the interest produced by the spectacular colossus of Psamtik I, found just one day later (figs. 6.41, 6.42, 6.43, 6.44). This statue is most remarkable for its extraordinary dimensions, quality, and typology.[41] Between the bases of two of the above-mentioned granite statues in Suq al-Khamis, a larger platform, made of limestone blocks cased with quartzite slabs, once supported another colossus in front of Ramesses II's pylon. After the limestone pylon had been totally dismantled, this quartzite colossus was pulled into pieces that were buried on both sides of the pedestal: the torso and head in front of it, and several thousand other pieces behind it. Interestingly, the upper part of the statue (from

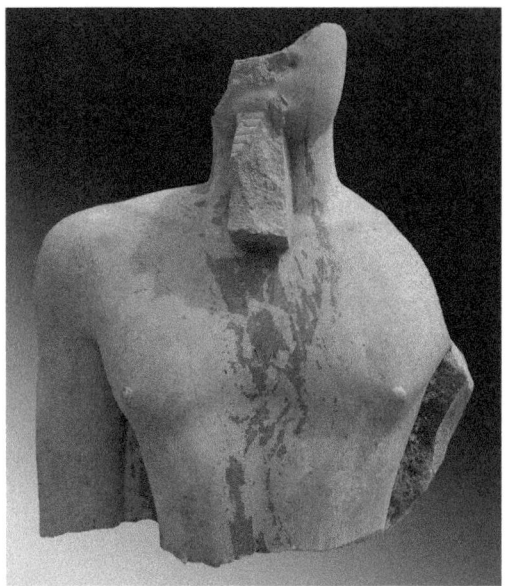
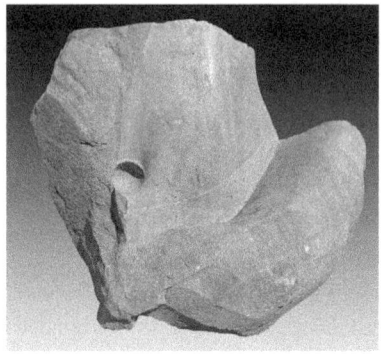

Figs. 6.41–6.44. Fragments of Psamtik I's colossal statue, including the torso, face, abdomen, and left hand, and rounded top of the back slab. Quartzite. H. orig. 11 m. Photographs by Simon Connor.

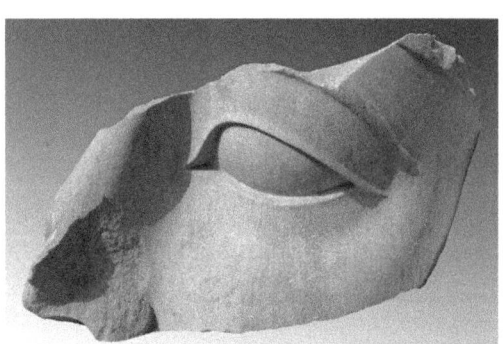
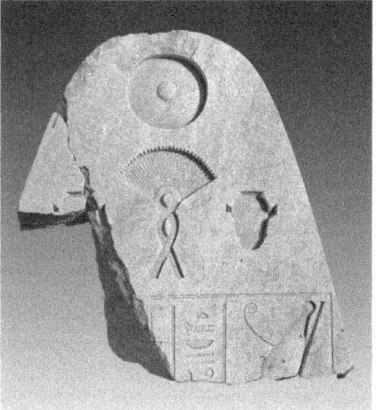

the top of the crown to the thighs) was broken into large fragments, while the legs and base of the statue were reduced to tiny chips and possibly burnt. The destruction of the statue is difficult to date[42] but the purpose was neither a *damnatio memoriae* (the king's names are entirely preserved on the back slab) nor a reuse of blocks for another purpose (although reassembling the puzzle will require years of work, virtually every part of the statue seems to be present). An accident cannot be totally discounted as the possible cause of the collapse, although destroying an eleven-meter quartzite statue, apparently by fire, would require an impressive amount of energy. The date is also questionable, as is the succession of events. Had the pylon already totally disappeared when the statue collapsed? Were the statue's fragments buried later? Or were the dismantling of the pylon and the burial of the statue(s)' fragments (including perhaps the Middle Kingdom granite statues reused by Ramesses II) all part of the same action of reusing and burying material following the temple's destruction by fire?

A detailed stylistic analysis will appear soon in the publication of recent excavations.[43] It is important to note that this colossus bears no trace of reuse or modification of the features. The inscriptions are also entirely original. It is not a reused statue from an earlier period, even if some stylistic elements point to different phases of Egyptian art history. Considered individually, the massive musculature, square shoulders, narrow waist, absence of uraeus on the white crown, shape of the temporal lappets, and other elements could point to a contradictory dating (early Twelfth Dynasty, Amenhotep III, or Ramesses II). Nevertheless, their combination allows us to identify the elements as probably intentional "archaisms" and ascertain that the statue is indeed contemporary to the back pillar's inscription. The elongated proportions of the torso (which can be virtually reconstructed from various fragments) and, more than anything else, the preserved facial features, leave no doubt concerning the Twenty-sixth Dynasty dating. Psamtik I, perhaps willing to pay homage to Ramesses II, but also to compare himself to his six-hundred-year-old great predecessor, placed a new standing statue (or probably a pair, though this remains unknown as the other half of the pylon is now under modern buildings), in a luminous variety of quartzite, more than twice as big as the Ramesside colossi that surrounded it. The dimensions would indeed have fitted more with an early Twelfth Dynasty or Ramesside statue. However, the lack of known Twenty-sixth Dynasty colossi does not prove that colossi were not produced at this later time.[44] So far unique, the Matariya colossus of Psamtik I can be considered a new landmark for the study of Late Period sculpture. It should be noted that while the size and proportions of the statue may be interpreted as archaism, the position of the right hand, apparently flat under the navel, is so far unattested.

The back slab itself, perhaps inspired by Middle Kingdom examples, is neither a rectangle, nor a round-topped stela, nor an obelisk, but an unusual mix of all of these. It is tempting to see it as evoking the Benben stone—an interpretation supported by the solar disc of Psamtik's throne name, conveniently placed at the top of the inscription on the back slab.

Conclusion

Once one of the largest and most important urban and cultic centers of Egypt,

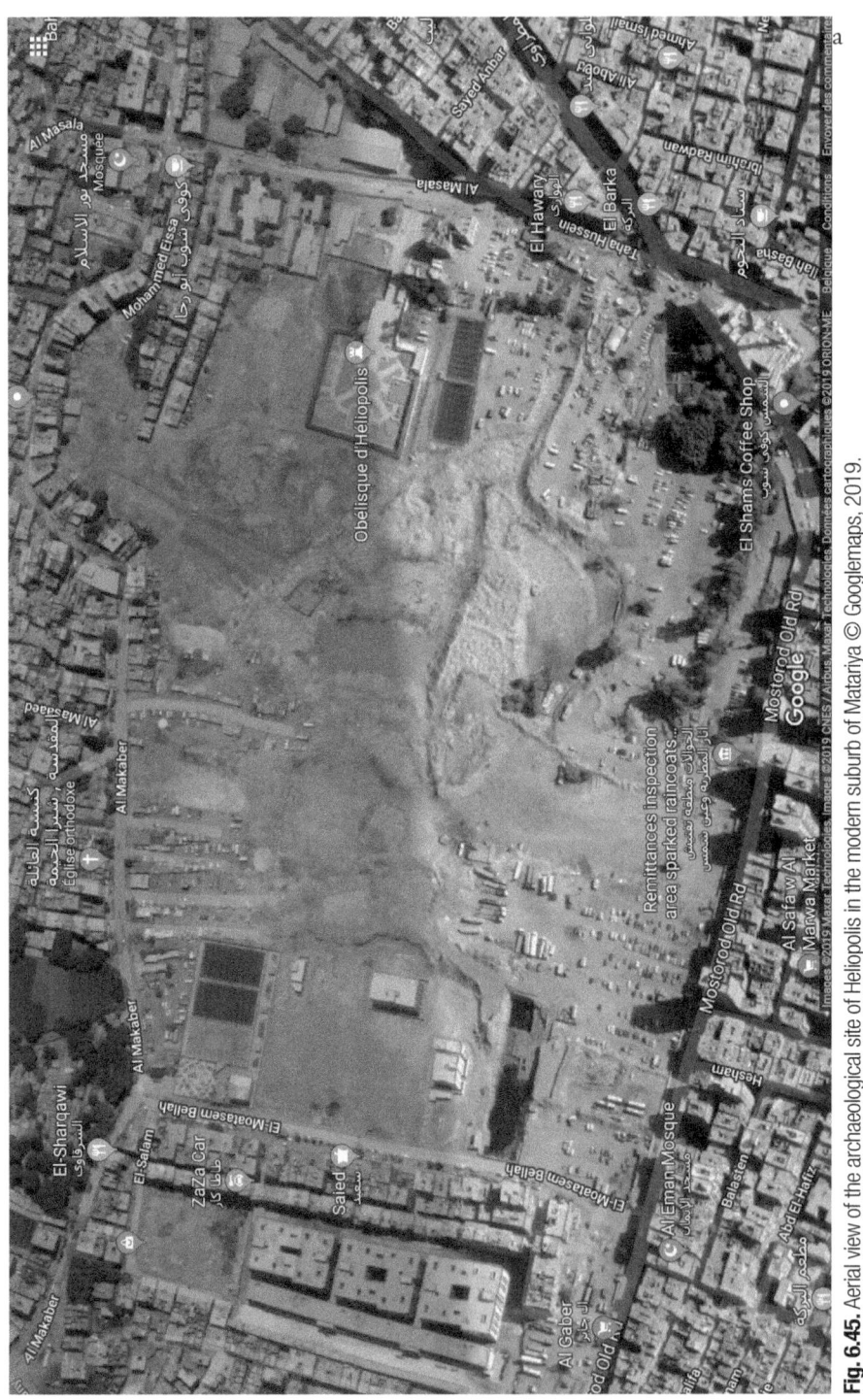

Fig. 6.45. Aerial view of the archaeological site of Heliopolis in the modern suburb of Matariya © Googlemaps, 2019.

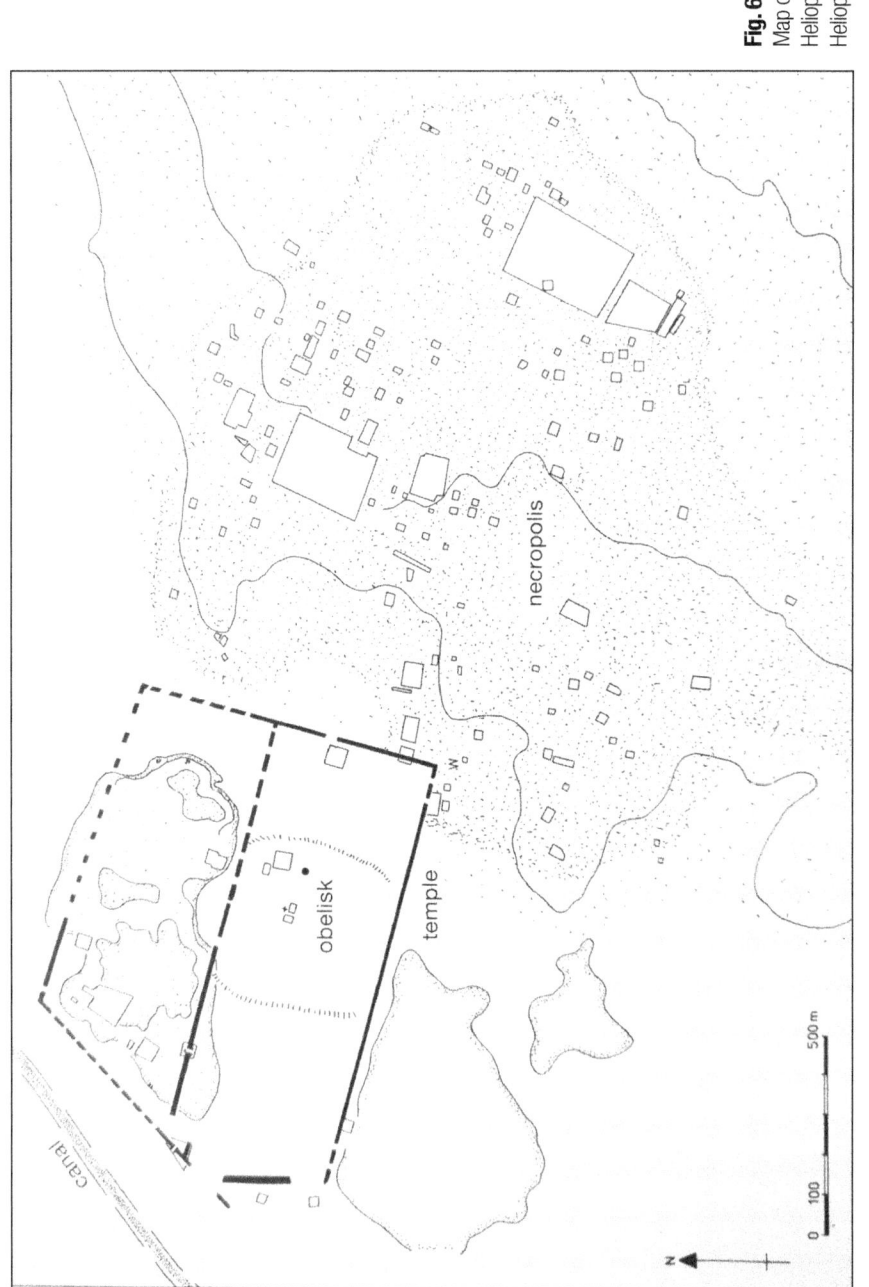

Fig. 6.46 Map of the site of Heliopolis. After Raue, Heliopolis, pl. 4.

model for other religious centers throughout the country, and probably the most intensively quarried for its building material, ancient Heliopolis offers an infinite variety of traces of modification and defacing of images. Erased beards, broken noses, colossi cut into masonry blocks, modification of statues for reuse, traces of burning, and ancient repairs are all visible. The material found in Matariya probably illustrates all the types of mutilations and modifications that one can observe on Egyptian statuary. Heliopolis can be considered one of the most fertile grounds for the study of alteration of sculpture and its motivations. The site offers all types of answers concerning the relationship between people and pharaonic monuments during different periods of history. The material attests to the long life of the city, with several phases of renewed building activity, and a possible devastation and gradual dismantlement and abandonment of the site.[45] Matariya's investigation probably raises more questions than answers concerning the uses, reuses, and destruction of Egyptian statues, but this is precisely what makes research so exciting.

Notes

1. Bleiberg and Weissberg, *Striking Power*.
2. My deep thanks are due to Aiman Ashmawy and Dietrich Raue for inviting me to join their team and to participate in the excavations in Matariya. I am grateful to them for granting me permission to include in this chapter some of the material recently found. The full publication of this material can be found in Ashmawy and Raue, *Heliopolis Report 1.0*. See also http://www.heliopolisproject.org/. See also Raue, *Reise zum Ursprung der Welt*. Further thanks are due to Raue for his valuable comments on the chapter, as well as to the editors of this book for their kind invitation to write and their help with English writing.
3. Tkaczow, *Topography*; Corteggiani, "Aegyptiaca," 25–40; Raue, *Heliopolis*.
4. I thank Paul Stanwick and Nicola Barbagli for their valuable insight concerning the possible role(s) of pharaonica in the classical context of Alexandria.
5. PM VII, 384–85 (with bibliography); Fay, *Louvre Sphinx*, 68, no. 54, pl. 94a–b.
6. Helck, "Ägyptische Statuen im Ausland," 101–15; Scandone Matthiae, "Statuaria regale," 181–88; Warmenbol, "Tombes royales I et II de Byblos," 171; Connor, *Être et paraître*, 151. For another sphinx in anorthositic gneiss, of Menkaure, "beloved of the Baw of Iunu," and therefore also likely to be from Heliopolis, found in Hazor, see Ben-Tor, *Pharaoh in Canaan*, 130–32; Ben-Tor, Zuckerman, Bechar, and Sandhaus, *Hazor 7*, 584–86.
7. For studies concerning reuse of pharaonic blocks in Old Cairo buildings, see, among other publications: Sourouzian, "Headless Sphinx of Sesostris II," 743–54; Raue, *Heliopolis*, 19; Postel and Régen, "Annales héliopolitaines," 229–93, and "Réemplois pharaoniques," 183–218; Pradines and Talaat, "Fortifications fatimides du Caire," 240–41.
8. Cairo JdE 37796–TR 16.2.21.6, graywacke, H. 47; D. 162 cm. Fay, *Louvre Sphinx*, 65, 90, Nb. 26, pl. 85e; Sourouzian, "Headless Sphinx of Sesostris II," 743–54; Raue, *Heliopolis*, 85n3; 373n1; 381n4.
9. Some care should be taken, nevertheless, since solar cults are also attested in Pi-Ramesses, the site that is the main source of monuments for the building of Tanis;

not every mention of Atum, Re-Horakhty, or Khepri necessarily points to Heliopolis. I thank Dietrich Raue for his valuable comments concerning this subject.
10 Jeffreys, "Hekekyan at Heliopolis," 157–68 (specifically 165–68). See also *Description* 1826, vol. 5, pl. 26; 10, 491. According to Hekekyan's drawing, this sphinx must have measured some 11 m to 12 m long and 6 m high.
11 See development of the argumentation in the forthcoming publication of the excavations (Ashmawy and Raue, *Heliopolis Report 1.0*).
12 Current research of Klara Dietze and Federica Ugliano, presented at the International Conference of Egyptologists in Cairo, November 2019. I thank them very much for allowing me to mention their results.
13 Edinburgh 1984.405. Fay, *Louvre Sphinx*, 64, no. 13, pl. 84; Warmenbol, *Sphinx*, 220–21, no. 66 (text by B. Fay). Two elements should be noted which raise questions concerning the dating of the piece (Sixth Dynasty if the statuette was carved during the reign of Merenre). First of all, the material of this piece, steatite, is unusual in sculpture before the late Middle Kingdom; secondly, the type of a sphinx with human arms holding *nw*-vases is, as far as I know, unattested before the Eighteenth Dynasty.
14 Connor, *Statue del Museo Egizio*, 38.
15 New York MMA 12.187.31. Petrie and Mackay, *Heliopolis*, pl. 6; Raue, *Heliopolis*, 398.
16 Petrie and Mackay, *Heliopolis*, pl. 6; Raue, *Heliopolis*, 398, nos. XVIII–XX–5.8.
17 Museum August Kestner, Hanover, 1935.200.128 (= S. 1466). H. 25.6; W. 29.7; D. 31 cm. Petrie and Mackay, *Heliopolis*, 6, pl. 6; Raue, *Heliopolis*, 398–99. I had been looking for this head for quite a long time in museum storage, in the framework of my PhD dissertation, which focused on statuary of the late Middle Kingdom. I was mistakenly expecting to find it in a British collection. This example demonstrates that studying the trajectory of excavation finds and art markets can be particularly revealing. I finally found it, by chance, in December 2018, while researching for a Tutankhamun exhibition in European museums. I had access to the museum's storage, with the kind permission of Christian Loeben. While searching for late Eighteenth Dynasty objects in storage, I saw a big head of dark stone in a showcase's lower shelf. And here it was, the head from Heliopolis! This head, in a relatively good state of preservation, presented quite unusual stylistic features. Its odd appearance may have triggered some doubts in the past concerning its authenticity, perhaps the reason for the head being relegated to storage for decades, unless it was due to its fragmentary state that, understandably, discouraged previous curators from putting it on display.
18 Concerning von Bissing's collection, I refer to Christian Loeben's articles: "Der Ägyptologe Friedrich Wilhelm Freiherr von Bissing," "Die ägyptische Sammlung von Friedrich Wilhelm Freiherr von Bissing," and "1935 Friedrich Wilhelm von Bissing."
19 Connor, *Être et paraître*, 137, 309. Cf. Cairo CG 1200.
20 Ashmawy and Raue, *Heliopolis Report 1.0*.
21 More detailed publication of this series of quartzite sphinxes can be found in El-Mezain and Kacem, "Two Unpublished Sphinxes," as well as Connor and Abou al-Ella, *From Bab el-Nasr to Matariya*.
22 Elephantine 1318. Its bust is Vienna ÄOS 37. Fay, "Amenemhat V," 66–77, pls. 21–23. The quartzite Heliopolitan sphinx of this king was found reused in a postern's masonry in Bab al-Nasr; it is now on display in Matariya's open-air museum.
23 The front part of another quartzite sphinx with human arms holding an offering table

NOTES 109

is on display in Alexandria, Kom al-Dikka (inv. 10). Although very fragmentary, it seems to be a good potential candidate for being part of the same series of sphinxes.

24 Area 251 of Matariya, Egyptian–German excavations.

25 Some of the results of the excavations are published in Ashmawy, Beiersdorf, and Raue, "Thirtieth Dynasty," 13–16; Ashmawy and Raue, "2015 in Heliopolis," 4–9; Ashmawy and Raue, "Héliopolis en 2017," 29–45; Ashmawy and Raue, "Ramesside Dynasties at Heliopolis." A more extensive study of the sculptural material found in Matariya will appear in Ashmawy and Raue, *Heliopolis Report 1.0*.

26 The numbering of the various areas is available at http://www.heliopolisproject.org/

27 The basalt blocks show a procession of Egypt's provinces, ordered by Nectanebo. It has been recently studied by Stephanie Blaschta in Ashmawy, Raue, and von Recklinghausen, *Von Elephantine*.

28 Solkin, "Sphinxes of Amenhotep III."

29 Most of the prostrate statues known today are of small dimensions. Amenhotep III in New York (MMA 66.99.28) is 13.7 cm high; Ramesses II in Cairo (CG 42142, 42143, and 42144) is 27 cm high; Ramesses IX in Edinburgh (A.1965.1) is 20.8 cm high; Osorkon III in Cairo (CG 42197) is 17.5 cm high. A prostrate statue of Thutmose III may have reached some 45 cm in height (head in Brussels E. 2435). Seti I's statue in Cairo (1040 [reused by Osorkon II]) is 123 cm high, while Amasis' statue in Florence (5625) was probably around 160 cm high.

30 Minas-Nerpel, *Chepri*, 397–419.

31 Ramadan, "Was There a Chapel of Nehebkaw," 51–61 and pls. 1–2; Moussa, "Seated Statue of *nḥb-k3w*," 479–83; Abd el-Gelil, Shaker, and Raue, "Recent Excavations at Heliopolis," 138, no. 17; Raue, *Heliopolis*, 357; Massiera, "So-called Statue of Nehebkau." This statue is today on display in the open-air museum of Matariya. The inscription on this life-size statue describes Ramesses II as "beloved of Nehebkaw who dwells in the Great Mansion." Ramadan ("Was There a Chapel of Nehebkaw") and Massiera ("So-called Statue of Nehebkau") consider that this statue should represent the king, and not the deity. Massiera was correct when she argued that the gods' statues can bear such an inscription, with the name of the king beloved of (the name of a deity). Nevertheless, she erred when concentrating the argumentation on the inscription, since the iconography is clearly that of a deity. The statues of kings do not show tripartite wigs, except for rare examples of sphinxes with peculiar iconography (winged sphinx of Amenhotep III in Cairo [CG 42088] and the animal-headed sphinxes of Wadi al-Sebua) and *ka*-statues (wooden statues from the tomb of King Hor [Cairo CG 259 and 1163], and the granite bust of Ramesses II found in December 2019 in Mit Rahina). Tripartite wigs are, however, the most common headdress of deities' representations, both male and female.

32 The long ceremonial beard already appears as the protective deity Dwa-wer ("the great god of the morning") in the *Pyramid Texts*. The cutting off of the beard is perhaps to be compared to the erasure of the uraeus, the other divine attribute that protects the head of the king or god. See Otto, "Duawer"; te Velde, "Zeremonialbart"; Connor, "Mutiler, tuer, désactiver," 161.

33 Abd el-Gelil, Suleiman, Fares, and Raue, "Joint Egyptian–German Excavations," 5–6, pl. 6a–d.

34 See the comments on tool marks.

35. Fay, *Louvre Sphinx*; Abd el-Gelil, Suleiman, Fares, and Raue, "Joint Egyptian–German Excavations," 6, pl. 5a–b.
36. Sourouzian, "Standing Royal Colossi"; Magen, *Steinerne Palimpseste*.
37. The Middle Kingdom and New Kingdom statues found in Tanis, likely to have been previously installed in Pi-Ramesses, show inscriptions that point to various origins, including Memphis or even Upper Egypt (Hill, "Later Life of Middle Kingdom Monuments"). Concerning the practice of reusing or "usurping" statues, see also Eaton-Krauss, "Usurpation."
38. Abd el-Gelil, Suleiman, Fares, and Raue, "Joint Egyptian–German Excavations," 7, pl. 6a–d.
39. This statue is there "by mistake." It was indeed seen and drawn by Rifaud in Tanis, and noticed by Lepsius some twenty years later in Alexandria's harbor. Raue, *Heliopolis*, 359; Sourouzian, "Deux groupes statuaires," 7–8. It is therefore likely that the statue was transported from Heliopolis to Tanis in the Third Intermediate Period.
40. Barbotin, *Statues égyptiennes*, 92–93, no. 41; Petersen and Kehrer, *Ramses*, 104, no. 46.
41. Ashmawy, Connor, and Raue, "Psamtik I in Heliopolis."
42. The abandonment and dismantlement of the pylon cannot be dated with precision, although the two pits in which fragments of the colossus lay contained Old Kingdom, Middle Kingdom, and New Kingdom pottery in the top layers, which could suggest that the statue was destroyed and buried before the Ptolemaic Period.
43. Ashmawy and Raue, *Heliopolis Report 1.0*.
44. As noticed by Raue and Ashmawy, texts by Herodotus and Diodorus mention the construction of buildings with colossal statues during the Twenty-sixth Dynasty (Herodotus II, 153; Diodorus I, 67; see Ashmawy and Raue, "Héliopolis en 2017," 40).
45. For a recent summary of the various phases of occupation and building activity in Heliopolis, see Raue, "Religion et politique."

Bibliography

Abd el-Gelil, Mohammed, Mohammed Shaker, and Dietrich Raue. "Recent Excavations at Heliopolis." *Orientalia* 65 (1996): 136–46.

Abd el-Gelil, Mohammed, Reda Suleiman, Gamal Fares, and Dietrich Raue. "The Joint Egyptian–German Excavations in Heliopolis in Autumn 2005: Preliminary Report." *MDAIK* 64 (2008): 1–9.

Ashmawy, Aiman, Max Beiersdorf, and Dietrich Raue. "The Thirtieth Dynasty in the Temple of Heliopolis." *EA* 47 (2015): 13–16.

Ashmawy, Aiman, Simon Connor, and Dietrich Raue. "Psamtik I in Heliopolis." *EA* 55 (2019): 34–39.

Ashmawy, Aiman, and Dietrich Raue, eds. *Heliopolis Report 1.0*. Propylaeum-DOK, Virtual Library for Classical Studies, University of Heidelberg, online open-access repository. Forthcoming.

———. "Héliopolis en 2017: Les fouilles égypto-allemandes dans le temple du soleil à Matariya/Le Caire." *BSFE* 197 (2017): 29–45.

———. "Matariya 2016: Ramesside Dynasties at Heliopolis." *EA* 50 (2017): 16–21.

———. "2015 in Heliopolis. Die ägyptisch-deutsche Grabung im Sonnentempel von Heliopolis." *Amun* 52 (April 2016): 4–9.

Ashmawy, Aiman, Dietrich Raue, and Daniel von Recklinghausen, eds. *Von Elephantine bis zu den Küsten des Meeres: Die Kulttopographie Ägyptens nach den Gauprozessionen der Spätzeit und der frühptolemäischen Epoche. Soubassementstudien 7*. Studien zur spätägyptischen Religion 24. Wiesbaden: Harrassowitz, 2019.

Barbotin, Christophe, ed. *Les statues égyptiennes du Nouvel Empire: Statues royales et divines*. Paris: Musée du Louvre; Khéops, 2007.

Ben-Tor, Amnon, Sharon Zuckerman, Shlomit Bechar, and Débora Sandhaus. *Hazor VII: The 1990–2012 Excavations, The Bronze Age*. Jerusalem: Hebrew University of Jerusalem, Israel Exploration Society, 2017.

Ben-Tor, Daphna, ed. *Pharaoh in Canaan: The Untold Story*. Jerusalem: Israel Museum, 2016.

Bleiberg, Edward L., and Stephanie Weissberg. *Striking Power: Iconoclasm in Ancient Egypt*. St. Louis, MO: Pulitzer Arts Foundation and the Brooklyn Museum, 2019.

Connor, Simon. *Être et paraître: Statues royales et privées de la fin du Moyen Empire et de la Deuxième Période Intermédiaire (1850–1550 av. J.-C.)*. Middle Kingdom Studies 10. London: Golden House Publications, 2020.

———. "Mutiler, tuer, désactiver les images en Égypte pharaonique." *Perspective: actualité en histoire de l'art* 2018-2 ("Détruire") 2 (2018): 147–66. http://journals.openedition.org/perspective/11431; doi:10.4000/perspective.11431

———. *Le statue del Museo Egizio*. Modena-Turin: Museo Egizio, 2016.

Connor, Simon, and Khaled Abou al-Ella. "From Bab el-Nasr to Matariya: A Tale of Two Wandering Sphinxes." *ZÄS* 147, no. 2 (2020): 141–52.

Corteggiani, Jean-Pierre. "Les Aegyptiaca de la fouille sous-marine de Qaïtbay." *BSFE* 142 (1998): 25–40.

Description de l'Égypte. Commission des monuments d'Égypte, vol. 5. Paris, 1826.

Eaton-Krauss, Marianne. "Usurpation." In *Joyful in Thebes: Egyptological Studies in Honor of Betsy M. Bryan*, edited by Richard Jasnow and Kathlyn M. Cooney, 97–104. Material and Visual Culture of Ancient Egypt 1. Atlanta, GA: Lockwood Press, 2015.

Fay, Biri. "Amenemhat V–Vienna/Assuan." *MDAIK* 44 (1988): 67–77.

———. *The Louvre Sphinx and Royal Sculpture from the Reign of Amenemhat II*. Mainz: Philipp von Zabern, 1996.

Helck, Wolfgang. "Ägyptische Statuen im Ausland: ein chronologisches Problem." *Ugarit-Forschungen* 8 (1976): 101–15.

Hill, Marsha. "Later Life of Middle Kingdom Monuments: Interrogating Tanis." In *Ancient Egypt Transformed: The Middle Kingdom*, edited by Adela Oppenheim, Dorothea Arnold, Dieter Arnold, and Kei Yamamoto, 294–99. New Haven and London: Yale University Press, 2015.

Jeffreys, David. "Joseph Hekekyan at Heliopolis." In *Studies on Ancient Egypt in Honour of H.S. Smith*, edited by Anthony Leahy and John Tait, 157–68. London: EES, 1999.

Loeben, Christian E. "Die ägyptische Sammlung von Friedrich Wilhelm Freiherr von

Bissing, die 'Musea Scheurleer,' das 'Museum Carnegielaan 12' in Den Haag und der Ankauf der Bissingschen Sammlung durch die Stadt Hannover." In *Die Ägypten-Sammlung des Museum August Kestner und ihre (Kriegs-)Verluste*, edited by Christian E. Loeben, 101–13. Rahden: Marie Leidorf, 2011.

———. "Der Ägyptologe Friedrich Wilhelm Freiherr von Bissing: Eine kurze Skizze seiner Biographie und Persönlichkeit." In *Die Ägypten-Sammlung des Museum August Kestner und ihre (Kriegs-)Verluste*, edited by Christian E. Loeben, 93–99. Rahden: Marie Leidorf, 2011.

———. "1935 Friedrich Wilhelm von Bissing." In *Bürgerschätze: Sammeln für Hannover—125 Jahre Museum August Kestner*, edited by Wolfgang Schepers, 88–101. Museum Kestnerianum 19. Hanover: Museum August Kestner, 2013.

Magen, Barbara. *Steinerne Palimpseste: zur Wiederverwendung von Statuen durch Ramses II. und seine Nachfolger*. Wiesbaden: Harrassowitz, 2011.

Massiera, Magali. "The So-called Statue of Nehebkau: A Comparative Study." *Journal of Intercultural and Interdisciplinary Archaeology* 2 (2015): 25–33. doi: urn:nbn:de:bsz:16-jiia-294473

El-Mezain, Mohamed, and Mohamed Mahmoud Kacem. "Two Unpublished Sphinxes of Amenemhat V and Ramses II." *JARCE* 55 (2019): 85–96.

Minas-Nerpel, Martina. *Der Gott Chepri: Untersuchungen zu Schriftzeugnissen und ikonographischen Quellen vom Alten Reich bis in griechisch-römischer Zeit*. OLA 154. Leuven: Peeters, 2006.

Moussa, Ahmed Mahmoud. "A Seated Statue of *nḥb-k3w* from Heliopolis." In *Hommages à Jean Leclant*, edited by Catherine Berger, Gisèle Clerc, and Nicolas Grimal, 479–82. BdÉ 106. Cairo: IFAO, 1994.

Otto, Eberhard. "Duawer." In *LÄ* 1, edited by Wolfgang Helck and Eberhard Otto, col. 1151. Wiesbaden: Harrassowitz, 1975.

Petersen, Lars, and Nicole Kehrer, eds. *Ramses: Göttlicher Herrscher am Nil*. Petersberg: Michael Imhof, 2016.

Petrie, W.M. Flinders, and Ernest Mackay. *Heliopolis, Kafr Ammar, and Shurafa*. BSAE/ERA 24. London: Bernard Quaritch, 1915.

Postel, Lilian, and Isabelle Régen. "Annales héliopolitaines et fragments de Sésostris Ier réemployés dans la porte de Bâb al-Tawfīq au Caire." *BIFAO* 105 (2005): 229–93.

———. "Réemplois pharaoniques à Bâb al-Tawfīq." *BIFAO* 106 (2006): 183–218.

Pradines, Stéphane, and Osama Talaat. "Les fortifications fatimides du Caire: Bāb al-Tawfīq et l'enceinte en briques crues de Badr al-Ǧamālī." *Annales Islamologiques* 41 (2007): 229–76.

Ramadan, Wagdy. "Was There a Chapel of Nehebkaw in Heliopolis?" *GM* 110 (1989): 55–63.

Raue, Dietrich. *Heliopolis und das Haus des Re: Eine Prosopographie und ein Toponym im Neuen Reich*. ADAIK, Ägyptologische Reihe 16. Berlin: Achet, 1999.

———. *Reise zum Ursprung der Welt: Die Ausgrabungen im Tempel von Heliopolis. Unter Mitarbeit von Aiman Ashmawy*. Darmstadt: Philipp von Zabern, 2020.

———. "Religion et politique au cœur de l'ancienne Égypte: Le temple d'Héliopolis." In *Annuaire de l'École pratique des hautes études (EPHE), Section des sciences religieuses: Résumé des conférences et travaux 2016–2017*, 125 (2018): 93–108.

Scandone Matthiae, Gabriella. "La statuaria regale egiziana del Medio Regno in Siria: Motivi di una presenza." *Ugarit-Forschungen* 16 (1984): 181–88.

Solkin, Victor. "The Sphinxes of Amenhotep III in St. Petersburg: Unique Monuments and Their Restoration." In *Actes du neuvième Congrès international des égyptologues: Grenoble, 6–12 septembre 2004*, edited by Jean-Claude Goyon and Christine Cardin, 1713–18. Dudley, MA and Leuven: Peeters, 2007.

Sourouzian, Hourig. "Deux groupes statuaires thébains réassemblées au Musée du Caire." *BSFE* 144 (1999): 6–26.

———. "A Headless Sphinx of Sesostris II from Heliopolis in the Egyptian Museum." In *Studies in Honor of W.K. Simpson* 2, edited by Peter Der Manuelian, 743–54. Boston: Museum of Fine Arts, 1996.

———. "Standing Royal Colossi of the Middle Kingdom Reused by Ramesses II." *MDAIK* 44 (1988): 229–54.

te Velde, Herman. "Zeremonialbart." *LÄ* 6, edited by Wolfgang Helck and Eberhard Otto, col. 1396–97. Wiesbaden: Harrassowitz, 1986.

Tkaczow, Barbara. *The Topography of Ancient Alexandria: An Archaeological Map*. Translated by Iwona Zych. Travaux du Centre d'Archéologie Méditerranéenne de l'Académie Polonaise des Sciences 32. Warsaw: Zakład Archeologii Śródziemnomorskiej, Polskiej Akadmii Nauk, 1993.

Warmenbol, Eugène, ed. *Sphinx: les gardiens de l'Égypte*. Brussels: Fonds Mercator, 2006.

———. "Les tombes royales I et II de Byblos: La puissance et les apparences, Cent notes avec texte." In *Les moyens d'expression du pouvoir dans les sociétés anciennes*, edited by Michèle Broze and Philippe Talon, 157–86. Leuven: Peeters, 1996.

7 Egyptian Stone Vessels Abroad: Reuse and Reconfiguration

Peter Lacovara

THE ANCIENT EGYPTIANS WERE RENOWNED for their facility with stoneworking, from monumental structures, like pyramids and temples, to imposing statues, to vessels of exquisite craftsmanship, elegant in form and made from beautiful materials. Like monuments and sculptures, vessels of stone could be reused and reworked. Even from the earliest periods, stone vessels were recycled from earlier contexts, as in the Step Pyramid complex[1] and the Mycerinus Valley Temple at Giza.[2] Several fragments of an Old Kingdom carinated diorite bowl, inscribed "King of Upper and Lower Egypt . . . Khaf[re]," were found in the Royal Tomb at Amarna.[3]

Vessels that were damaged could be reworked, sometimes obscuring their original design and date. A Middle Kingdom bottle[4] in calcite/travertine or "Egyptian Alabaster" (hereafter, Egyptian alabaster)[5] was found in an early New Kingdom grave (S520) in the South Cemetery at Semna Fort in the Second Cataract.[6] These vessels were often made from two parts joined together, but here no trace of the upper half remained, so it could be that it was reused without it. From another grave in the cemetery (S553) comes an Archaic Period cylinder jar[7] in Egyptian alabaster; the rim was apparently damaged and ground down to the rope molding to make a new rim. Because many altered vases have come into museum collections via the art market (fig. 7.2), it is often difficult to say whether these changes happened in antiquity or were modern interventions to make the pieces more saleable.

The stone vessels from Semna may well have been exported to Nubia, along with a great many others during the Second Intermediate Period, as

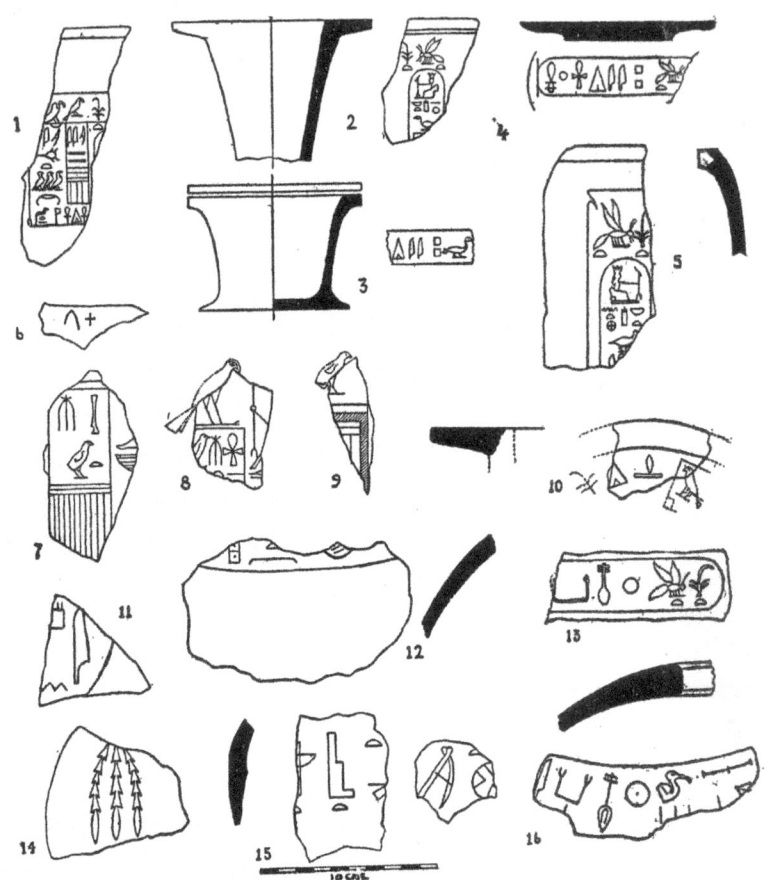

Fig. 7.1. Inscribed Old Kingdom vessel fragments from Kerma. (After Reisner, *Excavations at Kerma IV–V*, 507, fig. 342.)

plunder taken from Egypt by both the Hyksos and the Kingdom of Kerma. At Kerma itself there are a large number of Egyptian stone vessels and fragments dating from the Old Kingdom to the Second Intermediate Period, mirroring the importation of Egyptian sculpture.[8] One bag-shaped vase in travertine or Egyptian alabaster is inscribed for the nomarch Sobeknakht of al-Ka'b[9] and might be directly related to the attack on the town by the Kerma Nubians.[10] While the preponderance of the Egyptian vessels found at the site can be dated to the Second Intermediate Period, there are a significant number of inscribed vases dating to the late Old Kingdom (fig. 7.1).[11]

Most of these fragments come from the area around the Lower or Eastern Defuffa, the great temple in the middle of the ancient city.[12] The vessels are

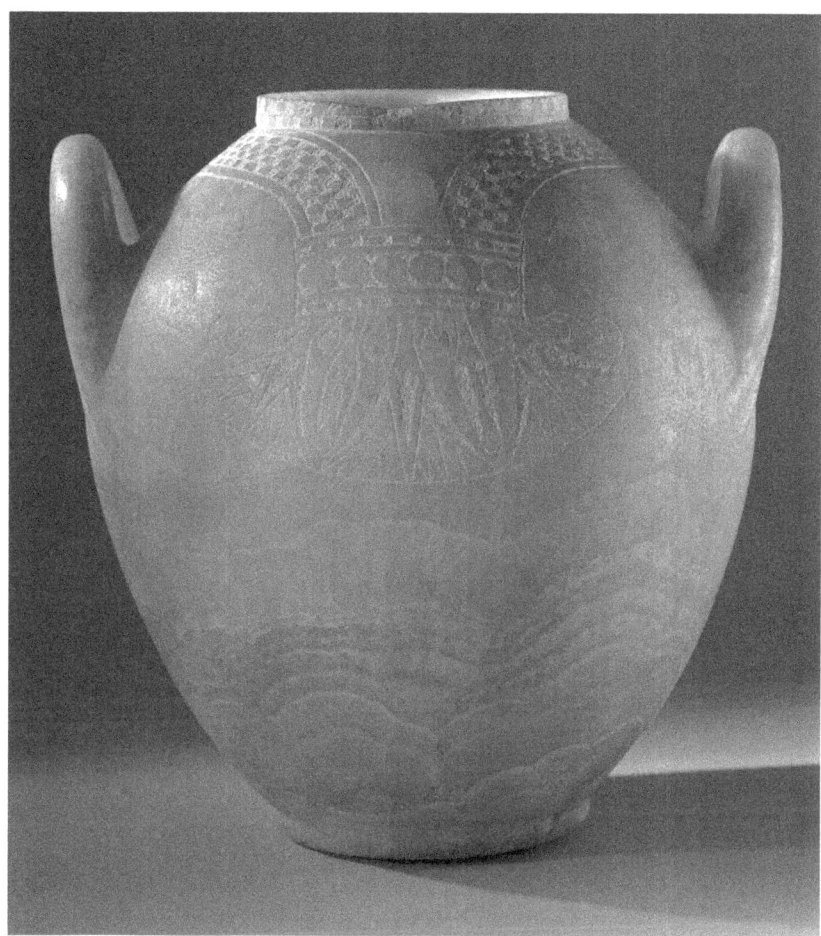

Fig. 7.2. New Kingdom Egyptian alabaster strap-handled amphora with rim and neck cut down. Jar with Floral Collar in Relief, ca. 1292–1190 BCE. Egyptian alabaster, 28.5 × 25 × 28.3 cm (11 1/4 × 9 13/16 × 11 1/8 in). Brooklyn Museum, Charles Edwin Wilbour Fund, 37.386E. Image courtesy of the Brooklyn Museum.

inscribed for Pepi I, Merenre, and Pepi II. As to the question of whether or not they were originally intact or brought as fragments, it is impossible to determine. The area around the *defuffa* was occupied by workshops making stone beads and other objects, so the vessels could well have been intended for some type of reuse.

These vessels can also be associated with others inscribed for these kings found in Second Intermediate Period contexts in Egypt at Deir al-Ballas,[13] in Anatolia at Alalakh, and in Syria-Palestine at Ebla,[14] Ugarit,[15] and possibly

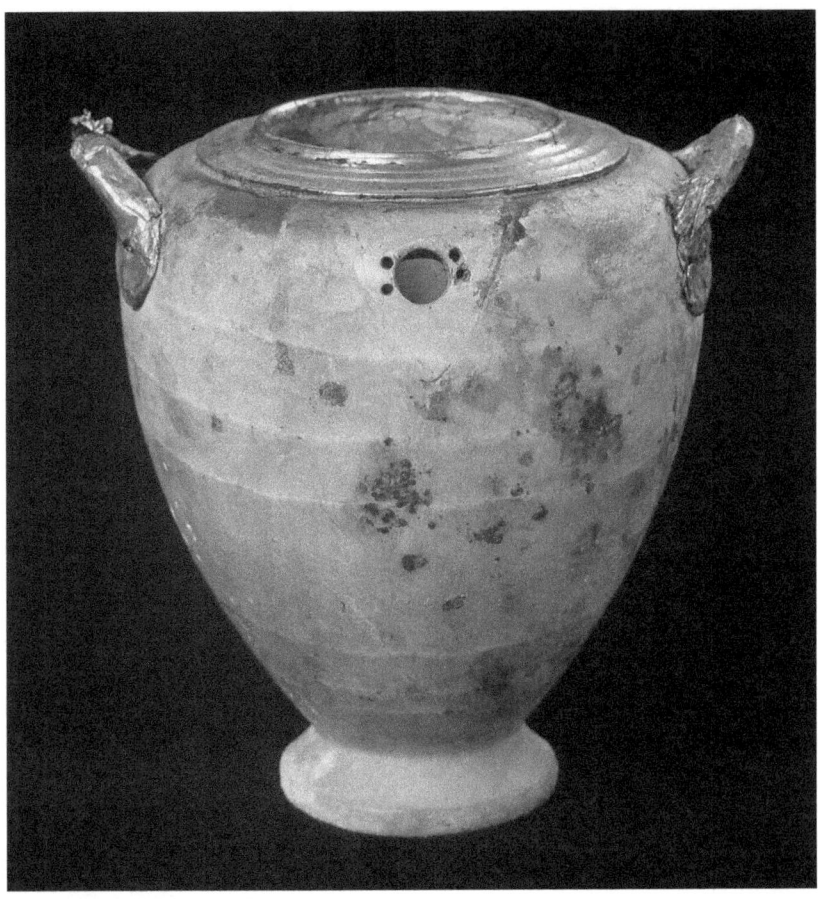

Fig. 7.3. Alabaster vase with gilded handles from Grave V, Grave Circle A, Mycenae. National Archaeological Museum, Athens, Greece, inv. no. P 829. Photograph courtesy of the Department of Collections of Prehistoric, Egyptian, Cypriot, and Near Eastern Antiquities, National Archaeological Museum, Athens.

Lachish.[16] The frequent occurrence of vessels inscribed for rulers of the later Old Kingdom might suggest that at least some of the monuments of these kings may have remained intact until the Hyksos domination of Lower Egypt and were then robbed under their jurisdiction. The vessels with royal names likely had intrinsic value as part of a gift-exchange network,[17] rather than of ordinary commerce. As such, these objects need not have been complete, as, for example, the front paws of a sphinx of Menkaure found recently at Hazor.[18] A large number of Egyptian stone vessels ranging from the Archaic to Second Intermediate periods were also found in Middle Bronze Age levels.[19] As with the stone vessels and sculpture found at Kerma, these have sometimes led scholars to misattribute their importation or even their contexts to the original date of manufacture.[20]

The export of these as gifts appears to reach the Aegean as well, again with the majority of the imported Egyptian vessels in contexts contemporary with the Hyksos occupation in Egypt.[21] While the Egyptian imports have been extensively cataloged,[22] some vessels may have been so altered as to create confusion about their true origin. Many of Warren's "Minoan imitations of Egyptian vases" may well be reworked Egyptian pieces with bases and rims recarved to hide damage or to conform them to Minoan tastes.[23] Many Egyptian squat, shouldered jars, which often had separately made rims,[24] but which have lost them, could be mistaken as "bird's nest bowls,"[25] while others have had their exteriors recarved into "blossom bowls."[26] The fact that many are made from basalt, gabbro, and diorite, stones commonly used in Egypt but rare on Crete,[27] would suggest that many were recycled Egyptian originals. Perhaps the most extreme makeover of all the Aegean vessels was found in Shaft Grave V at Mycenae. A bag-shaped vase of Egyptian alabaster was transformed into a bridge-spouted amphora by capping it, turning it upside down, cutting a hole in the bottom, and adding a gold collar around it, plus wooden strap handles covered in gold. There was a new spout as well, now lost; the recycled vase has a hole where the spout would have been fitted and rivet holes for its attachment (fig. 7.3).[28]

In the same grave, a similar example, also made from a bag-shaped jar[29] of Egyptian alabaster, was found with a hole cut in the bottom.[30] That the shaft grave vase was not only embellished with gold but also held precious metal ornaments,[31] as did an Egyptian alabaster vase found at Qatna,[32] indicates the great value placed on these Egyptian vessels far from home.[33]

Notes

1 Firth, Quibell, and Lauer, *Excavations at Sakkara*, pls. 88–94, 99–104b.
2 Lacovara, "Stone Vessels," 128.
3 Martin, *Royal Tomb*, 96, pl. 57. Now in the Egyptian Museum JdE J59456. I am indebted to Nicholas Reeves for this reference.
4 For the type, see Teasley-Trope, Quirke, and Lacovara, *Excavating Egypt*, 140n.E.
5 On the distinctions, see Harrell, "Review of *Hatnub*," 320.
6 Dunham and Janssen, *Second Cataract*, 81, pl. 118B; now in the Museum of Fine Arts, Boston, 24.718 (24–2–611).
7 Dunham and Janssen, *Second Cataract*, 97, fig. 55, pl. 118A; now in the Museum of Fine Arts, Boston, 24-2-753.
8 Cf. Lacovara, "Review of *Minoan Pottery*," 304–307.
9 Reisner, *Excavations at Kerma*, 57–58, 524.

10 Davies, "Sobeknakht," 3–6.
11 Reisner, *Excavations at Kerma*, 506–508.
12 Bonnet and Valbelle, *Temple Principal*.
13 Lacovara, "Stone Vase," 118–20, fig. 9.
14 Astour, "A Reconstruction," 57–195, 60.
15 Sowada and Grave, *Egypt in the Eastern Mediterranean*, 150–52.
16 Tufnell, *Lachish IV*, 75.
17 Cf. Bleiberg, *Official Gift*, 95–100. Such exchanges of materials may not always seem logical in a strictly economic sense; cf. Liverani, "'Irrational' Elements," 93–105.
18 Ben-Tor, "Sphinx of Mycerinus," 9.
19 Sparks, *Stone Vessels in the Levant*, 46–55.
20 Lacovara, "Stone Vase," 118–28.
21 Bevan, *Stone Vessels*, 101–102; Sparks, "Egyptian Stone Vessels," 49.
22 Cf. Phillips, "Egypt in the Aegean," 319–33; Phillips, "Impact and Implications"; Warren, *Minoan Stone Vases*, 105–14; Warren, "Minoan Crete," 1–18; Pendlebury, *Aegyptiaca*; Reisner, "Stone Vessels," 200–12.
23 Warren, *Minoan Stone Vases*, 74–76.
24 Cf. el-Khouli, *Egyptian Stone Vessels*, 304–20.
25 Warren, *Minoan Stone Vases*, 7–11; cf. "Minoan Bird's Nest Bowl," 1550–1450 BCE, Serpentine 8.1 cm × 15.6 cm (3 3/16 in × 6 1/8 in), 76.AA.22, J. Paul Getty Museum, Villa Collection, Malibu CA, gift of Ira Goldberg.
26 Warren, *Minoan Stone Vases*, 14–17.
27 Warren, *Minoan Stone Vases*, 127–31.
28 Laffineur, "Material and Craftsmanship," 284–85; Sakellarakis, "Mycenaean Stone Vases," 177.
29 On the type, see Lilyquist, *Stone Vessels*, 7–8; figs. 1–2.
30 Schliemann, *Catalog des trésors*, 52.
31 Schuchardt, *Schliemann's Excavations*, 259.
32 Pfälzner, "Royal Funerary Practices," 141–56, especially 151–52.
33 On the value of these imports, see Bevan, *Stone Vessels*, 190–92.

Bibliography

Astour, Michael C. "A Reconstruction of the History of Ebla (Part 2)." In *Eblaitica: Essays on the Ebla Archives and the Eblaite Language*, vol. 4, edited by Cyrus H. Gordon and Gary Rendsburg, 57–195. Winona Lake, IN: Eisenbrauns, 2002.

Ben-Tor, Daphna. "The Sphinx of Mycerinus Found at Hazor." *JAEI* 5, no. 4 (2013): 9.

Bevan, Andrew. *Stone Vessels and Values in the Bronze Age Mediterranean*. Cambridge: Cambridge University Press, 2007.

Bleiberg, Edward L. *The Official Gift in Ancient Egypt*. Norman, OK: University of Oklahoma Press, 1996.

Bonnet, Charles, and Dominique Valbelle. *Le temple principal de la ville de Kerma et son quartier religieux*. Mission archéologique de l'Université de Genève à Kerma. Paris: Errance, 2004.

Davies, William Vivian. "Sobeknakht of Elkab and the Coming of Kush." *Egyptian Archaeology* 23 (2003): 3–6.

Dunham, Dows, and J.M.A. Janssen. *The Second Cataract Forts I: Semna, Kumma.* Boston: Museum of Fine Arts, 1960.

Firth, Cecil M., James Quibell, and Jean-Philippe Lauer. *Excavations at Sakkara: The Step Pyramid II: Plates.* Cairo: IFAO, 1935.

Harrell, James. "Review of Ian Shaw, *Hatnub: Quarrying Travertine in Ancient Egypt.*" *JEA* 98 (2017): 320–23.

el-Khouli, Ali. *Egyptian Stone Vessels: Predynastic Period to Dynasty III.* Mainz: Philipp von Zabern, 1978.

Lacovara, Peter. "Review of Barry J. Kemp and Robert Merrillees, *Minoan Pottery in Second Millennium Egypt.*" *JNES* 47, no. 4 (1988): 304–307.

———. "The Stone Vase Deposit at Kerma." In *Egypt and Africa: Nubia from Prehistory to Islam*, edited by W. Vivian Davies, 118–29. London: British Museum Press, 1991.

———. "Stone Vessels." In *The American Discovery of Ancient Egypt*, edited by Nancy Thomas, 118–28. Los Angeles: Los Angeles County Museum of Art, 1995.

Laffineur, Robert. "Material and Craftsmanship in the Mycenae Shaft Graves: Imports vs Local Production." *Minos* 25–26 (1990–91): 245–95.

Lilyquist, Christine. *Ancient Egyptian Stone Vessels: Khian through Thutmosis IV.* New York: Metropolitan Museum of Art, 1995.

Liverani, Mario. "'Irrational' Elements in the Amarna Trade." In *Three Amarna Essays*, translated by Matthew Jaffe, 93–105. Malibu, CA: Undena, 1979.

Martin, Geoffrey T. *The Royal Tomb at El-Amarna, I.* London: EEF, 1974.

Pendlebury, J.D.S. *Aegyptiaca.* Cambridge: Cambridge University Press, 1930.

Pfälzner, Peter. "Royal Funerary Practices and Inter-regional Contacts in the Middle Bronze Age Levant: New Evidence from Qatna." In *Contextualising Grave Inventories in the Ancient Near East*, edited by Peter Pfälzner, Herbert Niehr, Ernst Pernicka, Sarah Lange, and Tina Köster, 141–56. Supplementa 3. Wiesbaden: Qaṭna-Studien, 2014.

Phillips, Jacke. "Egypt in the Aegean during the Middle Kingdom." In *Akten des vierten internationalen Ägyptologen-Kongresses München 1985*, edited by Sylvia Schoske, 319–33. Hamburg: Helmut Buske, 1991.

———. "The Impact and Implications of Egyptian and 'Egyptianised' Material found in Bronze Age Crete ca. 3000–1100 BC." PhD diss., University of Toronto, 1991.

Reisner, George A. *Excavations at Kerma IV–V.* Harvard African Studies 6. Cambridge, MA: Peabody Museum of Harvard University, 1923.

———. "Stone Vessels Found in Crete and Babylonia." *Antiquity* 5, no. 18 (1931): 200–12.

Sakellarakis, Jannis A. "Mycenaean Stone Vases." *Studi Micenei ed Egeo–Anatolici* 17 (1976): 173–87.

Schliemann, Heinrich. *Catalog des trésors de Mycènes au musée d'Athènes.* Leipzig: F.A. Brockhaus, 1882.

Schuchardt, Carl. *Schliemann's Excavations: An Archaeological and Historical Study.* London: Macmillan and Co., 1891.

Sowada, Karin, and Peter Grave. *Egypt in the Eastern Mediterranean during the Old Kingdom: An Archaeological Perspective.* OBO 237. Fribourg: Academic Press, 2009.

Sparks, Rachael Thyrza. "Egyptian Stone Vessels and the Politics of Exchange (2617–1070 BC)." In *Ancient Perspectives on Egypt*, edited by Roger Matthews and Cornelia Roemer, 39–56. London: Institute of Archaeology, University College London, 2003.

———. *Stone Vessels in the Levant*. Leeds, UK: Palestine Exploration Fund, 2007.

Teasley-Trope, Betsy, Stephen Quirke, and Peter Lacovara, eds. *Excavating Egypt: Great Discoveries from the Petrie Museum of Egyptian Archaeology*. Atlanta, GA: Michael C. Carlos Museum, 2005.

Tufnell, Olga. *Lachish IV: The Bronze Age*. Oxford: Oxford University Press, 1958.

Warren, Peter. "Minoan Crete and Pharaonic Egypt." In *Egypt, the Aegean, and the Levant: Interconnections in the Second Millennium BC*, edited by W. Vivian Davies and Louise Schofield, 1–18. London: British Museum Press, 1995.

———. *Minoan Stone Vases*. Cambridge: Cambridge University Press, 1969.

3 Egyptian Afterlives in Pharaonic Egypt

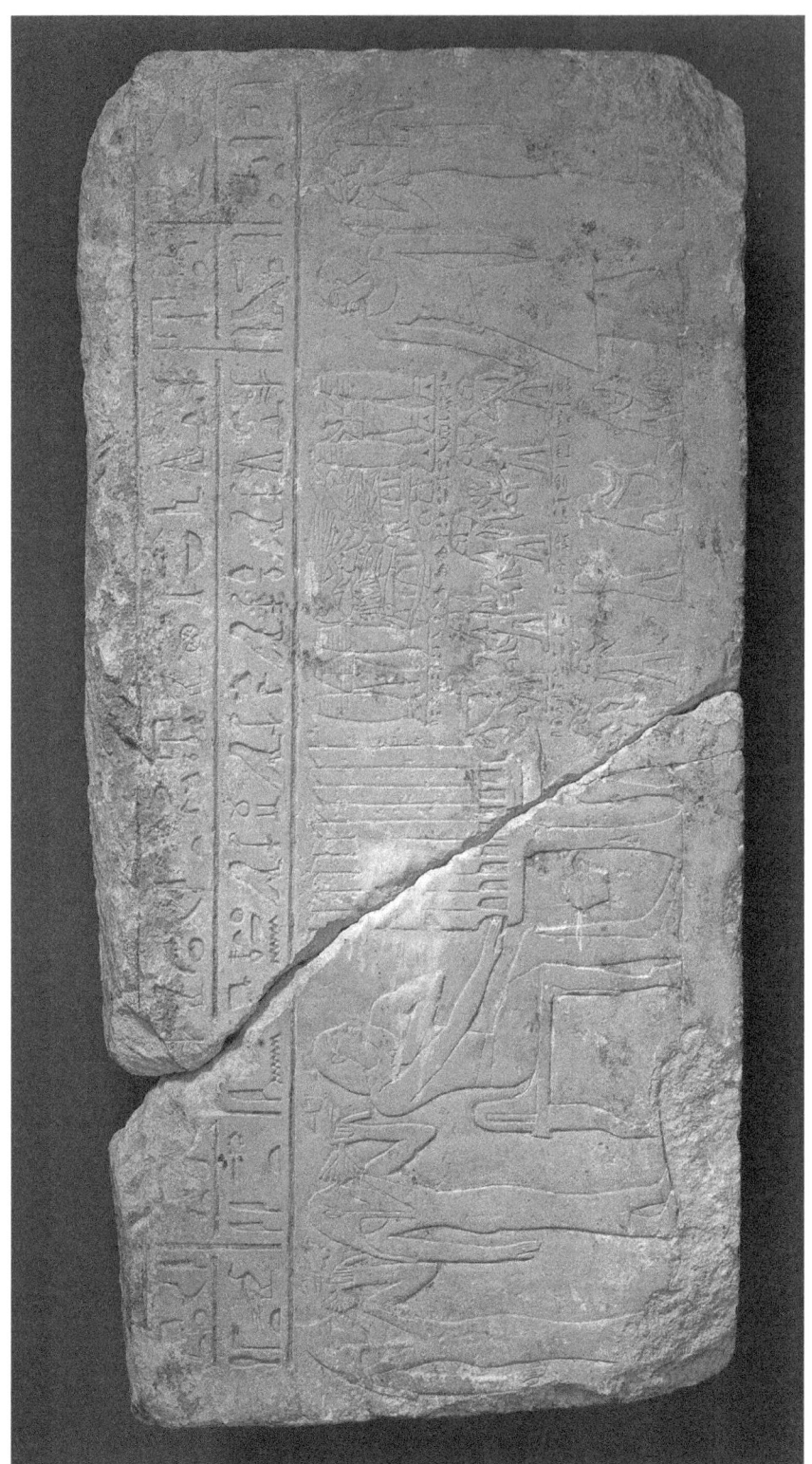

Fig. 8.1. Stela, Royal Ontario Museum 971.289. Photography courtesy of the Royal Ontario Museum.

8 A Late Old Kingdom Stela in the Royal Ontario Museum, Toronto (ROM 971.289)

Ronald J. Leprohon

I DEDICATE THIS STUDY TO Edward ("Eddie") L. Bleiberg, whom I have known for well over forty years as a fellow graduate student, friend, and esteemed colleague. He is truly the embodiment of the expression "a gentleman and a scholar." Given his duties as a museum curator, I hope he will be pleased with the publication of a stela that has long delighted visitors in the Egyptian galleries of the Royal Ontario Museum.

The stela, ROM 971.289 (fig. 1),[1] is made of limestone, with a diagonal break across the piece. There are traces of black color in the incised register lines separating the large hieroglyphs at the top and in the small figures in the middle, as well as traces of blue paint in some of the hieroglyphs. Its horizontal format was perhaps meant to replicate the contents of the central panel between the architrave and the lintel of false doors. The scenes are carved in low raised relief with minimal modeling of the figures, while the texts are in sunk relief, as if the latter were situated on the architrave and the side jambs while the figured representations were inside the aforementioned panel.[2] The scene shows a man seated before a table of offerings; behind him are his wife and daughter. To the right of the offering table are two registers of butchers and offering bearers and a set of offerings in the upper register. Framing the full tableau are two standing figures at the far right.

The stela is 60.5 cm wide, 29.6 cm high, and 4.2 cm thick. Its decoration offers noteworthy measurements, which may give an indication of the ancient craftsman's plan for the design of the decoration. The line beneath the second register of hieroglyphs is 56 cm long, the halfway point of which aligns with the edge of the leftmost jar on the upper register of offerings. From this midpoint to the vertical line on the right, which separates the two offering formulas from the captions identifying the man on the right, is a space that contains the scene of offerings and offering bearers below it. This space measures 16.2 cm, or close to two-sevenths of the total length of this section. The width of the space for the man and woman to his right is 11.5 cm; the vertical line dividing the captions marks the space as 5.5 cm for the man and 6 cm for the woman.

From the measurements found on the left side of the piece, it seems as if the craftsman's measuring rod had shifted about 1 cm to the left of the aforementioned midpoint: the width of the reed leaves on the offering table is 8 cm, and the distance from the reed leaves to the seated man's right shoulder[3] is 8.1 cm. In other words, each of these spaces occupies one-seventh of the full width of the scene, and together they are similar in width to the offering scene. To the left of the seated man, and similar to the right side, the vertical dividing lines are spaced at 5.8 cm for the woman closest to the man and 5.2 cm for her female companion. Interestingly, the proposed leftward shift of the measuring rod is also reflected in the space occupied by the large standing figures, as the distance from the left arm of the woman on the right to the right arm of the woman on the far left is 56 cm.[4]

Some of the measurements obtained seem to suggest divisions of seven in the scene, but units of five are also present. Measurements around 11 cm have already been noted for the widths of the pairs of framing figures; the two hieroglyphic offering formulas in the middle section of the text registers are 33.1 cm wide. Thus, the pairs of outer standing figures occupy first and last fifths, while the main figure, the offering table, and the offering scenes occupy three fifths. Starting from the right and moving leftward, the second fifth ends with the back foot of the last butcher on the bottom register, the third fifth ends with the left edge of the foot of the offering table, and the fourth is the edge of the right shoulder of the seated man.

Vertically, there are also noteworthy elements. The tops of the heads of the three figures on the left align with the top of the reeds on the offering table; the hairline of the seated figure aligns approximately with those of the two figures on the right; and the left elbow of the seated figure roughly aligns with the top of the heads of the upper register of offering bearers.

Additionally, the heights of the two main figures—the seated man before the offering table and the standing woman behind him—agree with the traditional fourteen and eighteen squares, respectively, used for seated and standing figures.[5] The seated figure measures 16 cm from the feet to the hairline and can be divided into five sections: 6.9 cm from the soles of the feet to above the kneecap; 2.6 cm through the right elbow; 2.8 cm to the armpit; 1.7 cm to the neck; and 2 cm to the hairline. The full height of 16 cm means that the fourteen vertical squares required for seated figures roughly occupy 1.14 cm each and the measurements detailed above correspond to the required subdivisions of 6, 3, 2.5, 1.5, and 2 units, respectively, for seated figures. The full height of the woman standing behind the seated man is 16.1 cm from the soles of the feet to her hairline. This height can be divided into six sections: from her feet to her kneecap is 5.3 cm;[6] from there to her buttock is 2.7 cm; up to the waist is another 2.7 cm; from her waist to her armpit is 2.3 cm; up to her neck is 1.3 cm; and from the neck to her hairline is 1.8 cm. These measurements fit perfectly well into the conventional system of 6, 3, 3, 2.5, 1.5, and 2 subdivided units, bottom to top, for standing figures.[7]

At the top of the stela are two registers of hieroglyphs. The texts consist of two offering formulas and two small sections of text on the left and right sides identifying the standing figures below them.

The main figure is the seated man who faces right, a direction indicating higher status.[8] He wears a characteristic Sixth Dynasty shoulder-length wig that leaves the ears uncovered,[9] a broad collar, and a short tight kilt[10] tied at the waist, although no knot is visible. His left hand, closed upon his chest, holds a folded cloth, while his right hand[11] reaches toward the offerings before him.[12] He sits on a low-backed chair with a cushion that covers the backrest.[13] The bottom of the front leg of the chair ends in lions' feet, which replaced bulls' legs later in the Old Kingdom.[14] One significant feature is the top of the rear leg, which projects slightly above the lower edge of the chair, a detail known from late Sixth Dynasty representations at Giza and Saqqara,[15] and from Upper Egyptian sites dated to the First Intermediate Period.[16]

The table has a long stand with a small triangle carved slightly off-center toward the bottom,[17] and has a flat top.[18] On the table are tall, stylized half-loaves of bread represented as outward-curving reeds,[19] a visual pun representing the Field of Offerings *(sḫt ḥtpw)* the deceased wished to visit in the afterlife.[20] In our stela, the reeds reach to the top of the deceased's head,[21] a feature that seems to date back to the early Sixth Dynasty[22] and which can also be found on an Eighth Dynasty false door from Saqqara.[23] Under the table is a ewer deeply nested in its basin,[24] shown floating in space[25] and, to the right of the table stand, a tall *hes* vase.[26]

Above this main scene is a text arranged in two registers, expressing the traditional offering formula on behalf of the deceased. Like the seated man, the hieroglyphs face right, underscoring their relationship. The text reads:

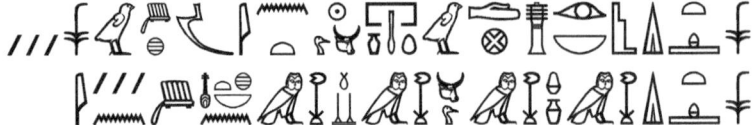

ḥtp-di-nsw wsir nb ḏdw prt-ḫrw t ḥnḳt k3w 3pdw nt im3ḫw [rḫ/sš?] nsw ḥtp-di-nsw ḫ3 m t ḥnḳt ḫ3 m k3w 3pdw ḫ3 m šs mnḫt ḫ3 m ḫt nb(t) nfr(t) n im3ḫw [m]ni

An offering that the king gives, (and) Osiris, lord of Busiris,[27] (consisting of) an invocation offering[28] of bread and beer, oxen and fowl belonging to[29] the honored one,[30] the Royal [///].[31]

An offering that the king gives, (consisting of) a thousand of[32] bread and beer, a thousand of oxen and fowl, a thousand of alabaster (vessels) and clothing, and a thousand of every good thing for[33] the honored one, [Me]ni.[34]

Two women stand behind Meni. They wear traditional tight-fitting dresses with shoulder straps attached below the breasts, tripartite wigs that leave their ears uncovered, and broad collars. Their right arms hang down with the hand opened,[35] while their left hands are raised, holding a lotus flower up to their faces, a traditional Old Kingdom motif especially popular in the Sixth Dynasty.[36] The two are identified by the texts above them.

The woman closer to Meni is

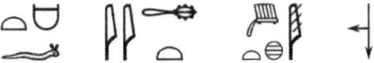

[im3]ḫ(w)t ḫty ḥmt.f, "The honored one, Khety,[37] his wife."

The designation after the name is written below the register line, before her face.

Behind her is

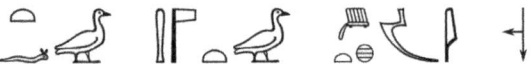

im3ḫ(w)t s3t-ḥm(t)-nṯr s3t.f, "The honored one, Sat-hemet-netjer,[38] his daughter."

The additional epithet is again written directly before the figure.

On the far right of the stela are two more standing figures, both facing left, toward the stela owner.³⁹ The man wears a broad collar and a long kilt and is shown wigless and slightly corpulent, common attributes to indicate advanced age.⁴⁰ Above him are hieroglyphs that designate him as

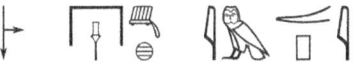

ḫrp pr imȝḫ(w) impi, "The Estate Manager,⁴¹ the honored one Impi."⁴²

The relationship between Impi and Meni is not made clear; perhaps he was simply a favorite subordinate. The woman behind him is essentially identical to the two on the left side of the scene and is identified as

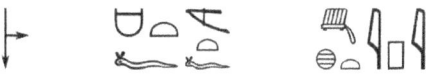

ḥmt.f mrt.f imȝḫ(w)t ipi, "His wife whom he⁴³ loves, the honored one Ipi."⁴⁴

Between the major figure groups, and depicted on a smaller scale, are a number of vignettes that complete the narrative of the monument. The lower register shows three butchers and two offering bearers; the middle register has five offering bearers; and the full scene is topped with an arrangement of offerings.⁴⁵ All the offering bearers face left toward the deceased, while the three butchers face right.⁴⁶ Although the main figures are shown in formal poses and in larger sizes to symbolize higher status,⁴⁷ these minor figures are also significant because they actively perform part of the cult and thus ensure the effectiveness of the monument. The fact that these scenes were not placed on formal register lines may also have been meant to enhance their eternal reiteration of the cultic acts on behalf of the deceased.⁴⁸

On the right side of the lower register are three butchers hard at work.⁴⁹ Unusually, all three face away from the stela owner and the two men butchering the animal face in the same direction, in contrast with the customary stance of butchers facing one another.⁵⁰ Also noteworthy is the space between the butchers and the offering bearers behind them, perhaps to indicate that the two groups had operated within different spaces and perhaps even at different times.⁵¹ Above them are captions that present a conversation between the two butchers. The different legends are separated by incised vertical lines.

The lead man says:

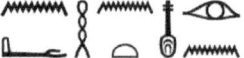

ir n(.i) nfr(t) nt(y) ḥnꜥ(.i), "Do me a favor, partner."[52]

To which the man behind him responds:

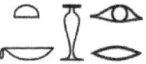

ir(y)(.i) r ḥst.k, "I'll do what'll please you."[53]

Behind them, a third figure, sharpening his knife,[54] declares:

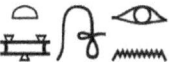

ir n(.i) wꜣt, "Make way for me."[55]

Given the little space the craftsman was given to tell his story, and without any way of ascertaining how much input the patron had over the design of his monument, it is noteworthy that a butchering scene was included in this modest stela. For elite Old Kingdom cult chapels, it has been demonstrated that tomb owners lost their faith in the continuity of actual food offerings over time,[56] which necessitated the use of images that would be helpful in the maintenance of these offerings; butchering scenes were one such set of representations.[57] It is also significant that the butchering scene is at the bottom of the representations, its regular place in the progression of scenes in tomb chapels.[58] Given that ancient Egyptian representations are usually read from the bottom register up,[59] it makes sense to have an animal being butchered in the lower register, followed by the offering of animal parts in the upper ones. Here, lack of space prevented a full presentation of such a sequence, which may explain the different directions in which the butchers and the offering bearers behind them face and the aforementioned space between the two groups of men. The offering bearers face the stela owner; the first holds up a haunch of beef[60] while the man behind him holds what may be a flower in his right hand and a basket on his left shoulder.[61]

Above them, a caption reads:

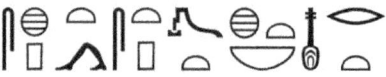

sḥpt stpwt ḥt nb(t) nfrt,
"Bringing choice cuts of meat and every good thing."

In the middle register five figures facing left walk toward the stela owner. From left to right, a man holds up a bird in both hands;[62] the next two carry a bird in their right hands with a basket on their left shoulders;[63] the fourth holds a bouquet in his extended right hand[64] with a basket held on his left shoulder; and the last presents a large papyrus stalk.[65]

Over this line of bearers is a caption in shallow incised hieroglyphs that also faces left, some of which are obscured by incrustations adhering to the surface of the stone.

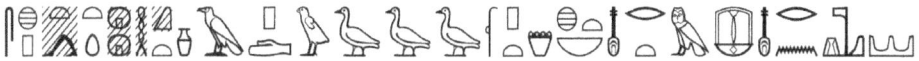

s*ḥ*p[*t*] *t* [*ḥn*]*kt ꜣpdw rnpwt ḫt nb(t) nfrt m ḥb nfr n ḥrty-nṯr*,
"Bringing bread and beer (?), birds and plants, and every good thing on the fine festival of the necropolis."

At the eye level of the deceased, the top register shows two sets of three tall, ovoid jars with conical stoppers, set in ceramic ring stands.[66] The top of the second jar from the right is decorated with blossoms on each side.[67] The heap of offerings between the jars includes meat and various vegetables, the lower strata of which are shown deposited in a basket or on a low table.

Regarding the date of the stela, various criteria would seem to indicate the period of the late Old Kingdom and before the First Intermediate Period. Apart from the stylistic considerations already offered, the writing of the *ḥtp-di-nsw* phrase is consistent with those from the Old Kingdom,[68] while the mention of Osiris in the formula marks it as a later Old Kingdom composition.[69] The writing of Osiris without the seated god determinative (𓀭) is indicative of a Memphite development of avoiding the representation of men and animals close to the body.[70] Begun in the Sixth Dynasty, the practice was moved out of the burial chamber and into the superstructure by the Eighth Dynasty.[71] This phenomenon is more common at Saqqara[72] than at Giza,[73] where older traditions continued for a longer period of time.[74] The designation "Lord of Busiris" for Osiris is mainly seen at Saqqara,[75] but the divine epithet can also be seen on Old Kingdom monuments from Giza[76] and found as far afield as Akhmim,[77] Edfu,[78] and Qubbet al-Hawwa.[79]

The writing of the toponym *ḏdw* with four cross-pieces[80] is common in the Old Kingdom, while three cross-pieces indicate a later date.[81] The writing of the word *nfr* with two bars at the top instead of the usual single bar is also found on Old Kingdom monuments.[82] The unabbreviated writing of the epithet *imꜣḥw*, with the initial reed leaf, is also the usual Old Kingdom and pre–First Intermediate Period orthography.[83] The addition of the words "oxen" and "fowl" in the list of wishes after the *prt ḥrw* invocation is ambiguous in terms of dating; although usually a later feature,[84] it can also be found on Old Kingdom false doors from Saqqara.[85]

For these reasons, I would suggest that the stela is likely to date from the very late Old Kingdom, in the Eighth Dynasty, with a provenance in the Memphite area, most probably Saqqara. It may have been part of a small mastaba erected in the so-called Teti Pyramid Cemetery, where numerous similar monuments were built around the large tombs of already ancient and venerable court officials under whose aegis the devout wished to partake of rituals for eternity.[86] Meni would no doubt have been stunned to know that his modest stela would excite the imagination of people in a faraway land in a time period he could not have imagined.

Notes

1. The piece was first shown in a Sotheby's catalog, sale of 12 July 1971, 17. I would like to thank the late Dr. Nicholas Byram Millet, who years ago gave me permission to publish the stela and shared his preliminary notes, and Dr. Krzysztof Grzymski, the current curator of the Egyptian Department, for honoring the original agreement. Gratitude is also extended to Henry George Fischer for earlier correspondence on the piece, as well as to James P. Allen, Kathlyn M. Cooney, Sherine M. El Sebaie, and Aurore Motte, who have offered helpful comments.
2. Cf. Lacau, "Tableau Central." The same design is also seen on First Intermediate Period false doors from Herakleopolis; see Pérez-Die, "False Door at Herakleopolis Magna," 358–59, 362.
3. Or the vertical line that separates the end of the offering formulae and the captions identifying the wife.
4. Absolute figures should perhaps not be expected from an ancient craftsman using a possibly worn wooden rod and working fairly rapidly when laying out his design. An example of this can be seen with the two registers of text at the top. On the left side, the heights of the two registers are 3 cm and 3.3 cm for the upper and lower registers, respectively, while these measure 3.5 cm and 3.7 cm on the right side. The registers are thus not parallel to one another.
5. Robins, *Proportion and Style*, 61.
6. This particular measurement also happens to align with the top of the heads of the butchers and offering bearers in the lower register to the right.
7. For these divisions within an Old Kingdom context and a useful chart, see Hölzl, *Kultkammer des Ka-ni-nisut*, 39–40.
8. Fischer, *Egyptian Studies* 2, 6–8; Peck, "Ordering of the Figure," 363, 367.
9. Cherpion, *Mastabas et hypogées*, 57, 180.
10. Swinton, *Dating the Tombs*, 84, criterion 26.
11. Depicted as another left hand; for the discrepancy, see Peck, "Ordering of the Figure," 367.

12 The offering meal was the one scene no deceased could avoid in the repertoire of representations on his funerary monuments; see van Walsem, *Iconography*, 94–95.
13 Cherpion, *Mastabas et hypogées*, 29, fig. 7b.
14 Cherpion, *Mastabas et hypogées*, 34n36, points out that lions' legs on chairs were ubiquitous throughout the Old Kingdom, and therefore should not be used as a dating criterion.
15 Fischer, *Inscriptions from the Coptite Nome*, 53–54. For other Saqqara examples, see Ziegler, *Catalogue*, nos. 10 and 45, which date to the late Sixth Dynasty and First Intermediate Period, respectively.
16 Fischer, *Dendera*, 198.
17 Vandier, *Manuel* 4, 93, points out that this small triangle recalled earlier ceramic tripods used for holding objects.
18 Cherpion, *Mastabas et hypogées*, 50, 172, has shown that whether the edges are flat or curved is not a significant dating criterion; see also Swinton, *Dating the Tombs*, 68, §.3.8.4.
19 Brovarski, "Stele of the First Intermediate Period," 5, fig. 3e; Cherpion, *Mastabas et hypogées*, 44, fig. 31; Swinton, *Dating the Tombs*, 85, criterion 38. Swinton, *Dating the Tombs*, 62, has remarked that such reeds do not appear before the Sixth Dynasty, while Cherpion, *Mastabas et hypogées*, 45n60, has cautioned that the variability in the orientation of the reeds makes it an unreliable dating criterion.
20 Vandier, *Manuel* 2, 424; Munro, "Brothälften und Schilfblätter"; Worsham, "Reinterpretation of the So-called Bread Loaves"; Valloggia, "Nouvelle stèle," 324n7; Cherpion, *Mastabas et hypogées*, 45 (e); Ziegler, *Catalogue*, 224; Robins, *Art of Ancient Egypt*, 85; and Pérez-Die, "False Door at Herakleopolis Magna," 365. For an example of these offerings clearly shown as reeds, see the post-reunification Eleventh Dynasty stela of Maaty (MMA 14.2.7), illustrated in Oppenheim, *Ancient Egypt Transformed*, 44.
21 Cherpion, *Mastabas et hypogées*, 45; Kanawati and Abder-Razeq, *Unis Cemetery* 2, pl. 68.
22 Strudwick, *Administration*, 20. Swinton, *Dating the Tombs*, 62, however, has also cautioned that in tombs, the height of the reeds with regard to the tomb owner's head is not an absolute dating criterion.
23 Firth and Gunn, *Teti Pyramid Cemeteries*, 185, pl. 73 (1); Daoud, *Corpus of Inscriptions*, no. 4.1.10, 36–39, pl. 15. For the dating to the late Old Kingdom, see Fischer, "Stela of the Heracleopolitan Period," 36n5.
24 Swinton, *Dating the Tombs*, 87, criterion 47. These were used for washing the hands both before and after the meal; see Hayes, *Scepter of Egypt*, 118; Brovarski, "Stele of the First Intermediate Period," 6; and Pérez-Die, "False Door at Herakleopolis Magna," 367. For a color photograph of a model ewer and basin, see Kanawati et al., *Teti Cemetery*, pl. 63.
25 There seems to have been no guideline regarding the direction in which the ewer faces; here, the ewer faces in the same direction as the seated man, which necessitates the spout facing away from him.
26 Vandier, *Manuel* 4, 155, fig. 51, 84. For a similar arrangement of the objects under the offering table, see Quibell, *Excavations at Saqqara*, pl. 12; and Firth and Gunn, *Teti Pyramid Cemeteries*, pl. 64. For the latter reference, see Brovarski, "False Doors and History: The Sixth Dynasty," 112n404.
27 For the epithet, see Leitz, *LGG* 3, 799 Aa.

28 What looks like a solar sign (Gardiner SL N5) over the bovine and bird determinatives was presumably meant for the elongated bread loaf (Gardiner SL X4).
29 Gardiner, "Tomb of a Much-travelled Theban Official," pls. 8:2 and 9:1; Drioton and Lauer, "Un groupe de tombes à Saqqarah," 231, pl. 20; Lopez, "Rapport préliminaire," 68–77, figs. 7–8, 10–13, 15–16; and Brovarski, "Ahanakht," 25.
30 Fischer, "Marginalia," 22, has noted that being "honored, esteemed" *(im3ḫ)* could also apply to a person who was still alive; cf. the Fifth Dynasty priest Khu-wi-wer who claims to have been *mry it.f, mry mwt.f, im3ḫw ḥr ntyw-ḥnꜥ.f, bnr ḥr snw.f, mry n b3kw.f,* "beloved of his father and mother, esteemed by his companions, kind toward his brethren, and loved by his servants," Hassan, *Gîza* 5, 241, fig. 101a:4; *Urk.* 1, 47:1–4.
31 The stone is unfortunately broken here. The sedge plant sign (Gardiner SL M23) seems clear; given honorific transposition, the title would thus have ended with "of the king." Two choices for a short title here could be *sš nsw* or the ubiquitous *rḫ nsw*.
32 For this Old Kingdom formula, see Barta, *Opferformel*, 26, Bitte 3.
33 The *n* sign is written under the *ḫt nb(t) nfrt* phrase.
34 Ranke, *Personennamen*, 151:2; traces of the *mn* sign (Gardiner SL Y5) remain above the *n*.
35 Cf. Fischer, "Some Early Monuments from Busiris," 15n55.
36 Harpur, *Decoration in Egyptian Tombs*, 134, 469; Brovarski, "False Doors and History: The Sixth Dynasty," 104; Brovarski, *Naga ed-Dêr*, 194.
37 Ranke, *Personennamen*, 277:26.
38 The name is not in Ranke, *Personennamen*, but cf. the Old Kingdom name *ḥm-nṯr*, Ranke, *Personennamen*, 239:22.
39 In this respect, Kanawati, "The Living and the Dead," 219–22, has suggested that the living and the dead rarely face in the same direction in tomb chapels, and that there was usually a "partition" between images of the living and the dead. If Impi and his wife Ipi were indeed meant to be seen as alive here, perhaps the vignettes and heaps of offerings between them and the stela owner could act as this partition.
40 Fischer, "Stela of the Heracleopolitan Period," 23–24; Brovarski, "Unpublished Stele of the First Intermediate Period," 461; Fischer, "Three Stelae from Naga ed-Deir," 64; Brovarski, *Naga ed-Dêr*, 381.
41 The title *ḥrp pr* used without further affiliation is unknown to me; for combinations beginning with these two words, see Jones, *Index*, 713–14, nos. 2601–2605. I had thought of the title *ḥrp zḥ* (Jones, *Index*, 736–37, no. 2682) since such directors of the dining hall were occasionally involved with butchering (Blackman, *Rock Tombs of Meir*, pl. 9; James, *Khentika*, pl. 22[145]; Kanawati et al., *Teti Cemetery*, 2006, pl. 44; for other examples, see Brovarski, *Naga ed-Dêr*, 213), and the three small-scale butchers are shown facing him. However, the title *ḥrp zḥ* is never abbreviated as our example would be, solely written with the *ḥrp* scepter (Gardiner SL S42) and an altered *pr* (Gardiner SL O1) sign, with the latter presumably used instead of the curved-top *zḥ* sign (Gardiner SL O6).
42 Ranke, *Personennamen*, 26:11.
43 Presumably Impi, the man before her.
44 Ranke, *Personennamen*, 22:15.
45 What Cherpion (*Mastabas et hypogées*, 53) delightfully calls a *nature morte*.
46 The captions above the butchers are also written right to left.

47 Robins, *Art of Ancient Egypt*, 21; Woods, "Relief," 221.
48 As suggested by Angenot, "Cadre et organisation," 45.
49 On butchering scenes in general, see Vandier, *Manuel* 5, 128–85; Eggebrecht, "Schlachten"; and a more recent study, Grunert, "Schächtung im Totenopfer."
50 See, for example, Vandier, *Manuel* 5, 144, 171. Examples of both butchers facing the deceased can be found in, for example, Kanawati and Hassan, *Teti Cemetery* 2, pl. 49; Kanawati and Abder-Razeq, *Mereruka*, pl. 70; and Kanawati et al., *Mereruka*, pl. 106. One artistic principle that has been kept, however, is that the animal's head faces toward the deceased to whom it will be offered; see Hassan, *Gîza* 2, 29, fig. 27; 44, fig. 39; 122, fig. 135; Hassan, *Gîza* 3, 65, fig. 57; Hassan, *Gîza* 5, 248, fig. 106; and Ziegler, *Catalogue*, 249, to name only a few examples.
51 On this, see particularly Chauvet, "Entrance-porticoes."
52 Lit., "Do something nice for me, oh one who is with me." The way this caption is worded seems to be unique. The Saqqara mastaba of Akhet-hotep (Davies, *Ptahhetep and Akhethetep*, pl. 23) contains a butchering scene where the man cutting a leg tells his partner, *nḏr*, "Hold fast!," to which the man pulling on the leg responds *ir(.i) r nfrt nty ḥnꜥ(.i)*, "I'll do it right, partner." A faint caption from the Giza mastaba of Nefer-khui (Roth, *Giza Mastaba*, 146 [difficult to see on pl. 106a]) has a man in a butchering scene saying *iry(.i) nfr*, "I'll do well." I wish to thank Aurore Motte for the last reference.
53 This is the expected answer in such circumstances. See Montet, *Scènes*, 38, 172; Edel, *Altägyptische Grammatik*, 369, § 734; Guglielmi, *Reden, Rufe, und Lieder*, 77, 169; Altenmüller, *Wanddarstellungen*, 146; and Motte, "Reden und Rufe," 304.
54 Vandier, *Manuel* 5, 138–39, 157.
55 For the phrase, see Guglielmi, *Reden, Rufe, und Lieder*, 172–73. Examples of the expression used in butchering scenes at Saqqara can be found in James, *Khentika*, pl. 22 (145); Davies et al., *Saqqâra Tombs*, pl. 25; Kanawati and Abder-Raziq, *Teti Cemetery*, pl. 61.
56 Roeten, *Decoration of the Cult Chapel Walls*, 336; Shirai, "Ideal and Reality."
57 On the importance of butchering scenes in general, see Kamrin, *Khnumhotep II*, 130–31; Eyre, *Cannibal Hymn*, 54–55n4; and Chauvet, "Entrance-porticoes," 278.
58 Harpur, *Decoration in Egyptian Tombs*, 71, 82; Roth, *Giza Mastaba*, 45; Angenot, "La formule *m33*," 561; Kanawati et al., *Teti Cemetery*, 43.
59 Smith, *Egyptian Sculpture and Painting*, 343–46; Gaballa, *Narrative*, 53–54, 104–105 (New Kingdom examples); Robins, *Art of Ancient Egypt*, 68; Angenot, "La formule *m33*," 14. Cf. also a Fifth Dynasty scene (Robins, *Art of Ancient Egypt*, 68, fig. 63) where men are trapping birds in a lower register, followed by birds being put in cages in the register above; and an Eighteenth Dynasty representation (Hartwig, *Tomb Painting*, 109) where ducks are being prepared for eating, then placed in amphorae for storage in the register above. In both cases, the actions of the lower registers are necessary for what occurs in the higher register.
60 Vandier, *Manuel* 4, 108, figs. 30, 11.
61 Vandier, *Manuel* 4, 117, figs. 33, 12.
62 Vandier, *Manuel* 4, 108, figs. 30, 10.
63 Vandier, *Manuel* 4, 117, figs. 33, 6.
64 Vandier, *Manuel* 4, 121, figs. 35, 87–89.

65 Vandier, *Manuel* 4, 121, figs. 35, 89.
66 Vandier, *Manuel* 4, 143, figs. 46, 54.
67 Cf. Fischer, *Inscriptions from the Coptite Nome*, 78, pl. 23; Simpson, *Giza Mastabas*, fig. 23. See also stela MMA 12.183.8 (Oppenheim et al., *Ancient Egypt Transformed*, 228, cat. no. 165), which clearly shows green-colored blossoms.
68 Barta, *Opferformel*, 21.
69 Bolshakov, "Princess ḥm.t-rʿ(w)"; Roth, *Giza Mastaba*, 35–36.
70 Firth and Gunn, *Teti Pyramid*, 172–73; Brovarski, *Naga ed-Dêr*, 198. On a related phenomenon, the so-called "Killing of the Glyphs," see Pitkin, "New Perspectives," 106–35.
71 Fischer, "Some Early Monuments from Busiris," 7.
72 Old Kingdom examples from Saqqara are found in Quibell, *Excavations at Saqqara*, pl. 12; Firth and Gunn, *Teti Pyramid*, 184; Daoud, *Corpus of Inscriptions*, no. 4.1.4; Brovarski, "False Doors and History: The Sixth Dynasty," 373n101; but the practice is very common in the First Intermediate Period (Daoud, *Corpus of Inscriptions*, nos. 4.1.1, 4.1.3, 4.1.5, 4.1.6, 4.1.9, and so on, and his remarks, 23, 186).
73 Examples are few but can be found in Hassan, *Gîza* 5, 46; Hassan, *Gîza* 7, 57, 126; Junker, *Gîza* 7, 248; and Junker, *Gîza* 8, 101.
74 See Junker, *Gîza* 4, 45; Junker, *Gîza* 7, 224; Junker, *Gîza* 8, 99–103; and Fischer, "Some Early Monuments from Busiris," 7.
75 Fischer, "Quelques particuliers," 180; Brovarski, "Late Old Kingdom," 50–51, 62; Gourdon, "Éléments de datation," 168; and Brovarski, *Naga ed-Dêr*, 65. Examples can be found in Drioton and Lauer, "Un groupe de tombes," 231, pl. 20; and Badawy, *Nyhetep-Ptah*, 43. See also stelae Berlin 7764 (Schäfer, *Aegyptische Inschriften*, 47); British Museum 718 (James, *Hieroglyphic Texts*, pls. 28–29); Cairo CG 1732 (Borchardt, *Denkmäler*, 162); and Philadelphia University Museum E 15729 (Silverman, *Searching for Ancient Egypt*, 172). A noteworthy example from a false door (Davies et al., *Saqqâra Tombs*, 26n4, pl. 26) reads *wsir nb n ḏdw*, with the additional indirect genitive.
76 Junker, *Gîza* 2, 52; and mastabas of Senedjem-Inti and Senedjem-Mehi, Brovarski, *Senedjemib*, 76, 155, respectively.
77 Louvre C 235 (Ziegler, *Catalogue*, 161–62, cat. no. 24).
78 Tomb of Qar Nefer-mery-Re (*Urk.* 1, 251:17, 252:11).
79 Tomb of Harkhuf (*Urk.* 1, 120:16).
80 The stela is damaged at this point but close examination has yielded four cross-pieces on the sign.
81 Fischer, *Dendera*, 120; "Some Early Monuments from Busiris," 8n13; and "A Parental Link," 18n14.
82 Drioton and Lauer, "Un groupe de tombes," 231, pl. 20; Moussa and Altenmüller, *Nefer and Kahay*, pls. 29, 39; and Ziegler, *Akhethetep*, fig. 32.
83 Fischer, "Some Early Monuments from Busiris," 20; Andreu, "La tombe à l'ouest," 6; Brovarski, "Akhmim," 127; Valloggia, "Une nouvelle stèle," 325. For a useful overview of the various writings of the epithet in this and the succeeding periods, see Pitkin, "New Perspectives," 176–210.
84 Fischer, *Dendera*, 83n359. It would become a feature at Herakleopolis in the First Intermediate Period; see Lopez, "Rapport préliminaire," 68–77, figs. 7–8, 10–13, 15–16.

85 James, *Hieroglyphic Texts*, pls. 28–29 (Fifth Dynasty); Firth and Gunn, *Teti Pyramid*, 184, pl. 72.1. For the dating of the latter monument in the late Old Kingdom, see Brovarski, "False Doors and History: The First Intermediate Period," 373.

86 For similar occurrences at the site of Abydos, see Richards, "Time and Memory."

Bibliography

Altenmüller, Hartwig. *Die Wanddarstellungen im Grab des Mehu in Saqqara*. ArchVer 42. Mainz: Philipp von Zabern, 1998.

Andreu, Guillemette. "La tombe à l'ouest du Mastaba II de Balat et sa stèle funéraire." *BIFAO* 81 (1981): 1–7.

Angenot, Valérie. "Cadre et organisation de l'espace figuratif dans l'Égypte ancienne." In *Cadre, seuil, limite: La question de la frontière dans la théorie de l'art*, edited by Thierry Lenain and Rudy Steinmetz, 21–50. Brussels: La Lettre Volée, 2010.

———. "La formule *m33* (　　　 "regarder") dans les tombes privées de la Dix-huitième Dynastie: Approche sémiotique et herméneutique." PhD diss., Université Libre de Bruxelles, 2003.

Badawy, Alexander. *The Tomb of Nyhetep-Ptah at Giza and the Tomb of Ankhmaahor at Saqqara*. Berkeley: University of California Press, 1978.

Barta, Winfried. *Aufbau und Bedeutung der altägyptischen Opferformel*. Ägyptologische Forschungen Heft 24. Glückstadt: J.J. Augustin, 1968.

Blackman, Aylward M. *The Rock Tombs of Meir, Part IV: The Tomb-Chapel of Pepiaonkh the Middle Son of Sebkḥotpe and Pekhernefert (D, No. 2)*. ASE, EES Twenty-fifth Memoir. London: EES, 1924.

Bolshakov, Andrey O. "Princess ḥm.t-rʿ(w): The First Mention of Osiris?" *CdÉ* 67 (1992): 203–10.

Borchardt, Ludwig. *Denkmäler des Alten Reiches (ausser den Statuen), II*. CG 97. Berlin: Reichsdruckerei, 1964.

Brovarski, Edward. "Ahanakht of Bersheh and the Hare Nome in the First Intermediate Period and Middle Kingdom." In *Studies in Ancient Egypt, the Aegean, and the Sudan: Essays in Honor of Dows Dunham on the Occasion of His 90th Birthday, June 1, 1980*, edited by William K. Simpson and Whitney Davis, 14–30. Boston: Museum of Fine Arts, 1981.

———. "Akhmim in the Old Kingdom and First Intermediate Period." In *Mélanges Gamal Eddin Mokhtar*, vol. 1, edited by Paule Posener-Kriéger, 117–53. BdÉ 97. Cairo: IFAO, 1985.

———. "False Doors and History: The First Intermediate Period and Middle Kingdom." In *Archaism and Innovation: Studies in the Culture of Middle Kingdom Egypt*, edited by David Silverman, William K. Simpson, and Josef Wegner, 359–423. New Haven, CT: Department of Near Eastern Languages and Civilizations, Yale University; Philadelphia: University of Pennsylvania, Museum of Archaeology and Anthropology, 2009.

———. "False Doors and History: The Sixth Dynasty." In *The Old Kingdom Art and*

Archaeology: Proceedings of the Conference, Prague, May 31–June 4, 2004, edited by Miroslav Bárta, 71–118. Prague: Academy of Sciences of the Czech Republic, 2006.

———. "The Late Old Kingdom at South Saqqara." In *Des Néferkarê aux Montouhoteps: Travaux archéologiques en cours sur la fin de la VIe dynastie et la Première Période Intermédiaire*, edited by Laure Pantalacci and Catherine Berger-el Naggar, 31–71. TMO 40. Lyon: MOM, 2005.

———. *Naga ed-Dêr in the First Intermediate Period*. Atlanta, GA: Lockwood Press, 2018.

———. *The Senedjemib Complex, Part 1: The Mastabas of Senedjem Inti (G 2370), Khnumenti (G 2374), and Senedjemib Mehi (G 2378)*. Giza Mastabas 7. Boston: Museum of Fine Arts, 2000.

———. "A Stele of the First Intermediate Period from Naga-ed-Dêr." *Medelhavsmuseet Bulletin* 18 (1983): 3–11.

———. "An Unpublished Stele of the First Intermediate Period in the Oriental Institute Museum." *JNES* 32 (1973): 453–65.

Chauvet, Violaine. "Entrance-porticoes and Portico-chapels: The Creation of an Outside Ritual Stage in Private Tombs of the Old Kingdom." In *Abusir and Saqqara in the Year 2010*, edited by Miroslav Bárta et al., 261–311. Prague: Academy of Sciences of the Czech Republic, 2011.

Cherpion, Nadine. *Mastabas et hypogées d'Ancien Empire: Le problème de la datation*. Brussels: Connaissance de l'Égypte ancienne, 1989.

Daoud, Khaled Abdalla. *Corpus of Inscriptions of the Herakleopolitan Period from the Memphite Necropolis: Translation, Commentary, and Analyses*. BAR-IS 1459. Oxford: Archaeopress, 2005.

Davies, Norman de Garis. *The Mastaba of Ptahhetep and Akhethetep at Saqqareh, Part 2. The Mastaba. The Sculptures of Akhethetep*. ASE, EES Ninth Memoir. London: EES, 1901.

Davies, W. Vivian, et al. *Saqqâra Tombs*. Vol. 1, *The Mastabas of Mereri and Wernu*. ASE, EES Thirty-sixth Memoir. London: EES, 1984.

Drioton, Étienne, and Jean-Philippe Lauer. "Un groupe de tombes à Saqqarah: Icheti, Nefer-khouou-Ptah, Sebek-em-khent, et Ânkhi." *ASAE* 55 (1958): 207–51.

Edel, Elmar. *Altägyptische Grammatik*. AnOr 34. Rome: Pontificum Institutum Biblicum, 1955–64.

Eggebrecht, Arne. "Schlachten." In *LÄ* 5: 4, Fasc. 36, edited by Wolfgang Helck and Eberhard Otto, 638–39. Wiesbaden: Otto Harrassowitz, 1983.

Eyre, Christopher J. *The Cannibal Hymn: A Cultural and Literary Study*. Liverpool: Liverpool University Press, 2002.

Firth, Cecil M., and Battiscombe Gunn. *Teti Pyramid Cemeteries*. 2 vols. Cairo: IFAO, 1926.

Fischer, Henry G. *Dendera in the Third Millennium BC Down to the Theban Domination of Upper Egypt*. Locust Valley, NY: J.J. Augustin, 1968.

———. *Egyptian Studies 2: The Orientation of Hieroglyphs*. New York: Metropolitan Museum of Art, 1977.

———. *Inscriptions from the Coptite Nome: Dynasties VI–XI*. Rome: Pontificum Institutum Biblicum, 1964.

———. "Marginalia." *GM* 122 (1991): 12–30.

———. "A Parental Link between Two Thinite Stelae of the Heracleopolitan Period." *BES* 9 (1988–89): 15–24.

———. "Quelques particuliers enterrés à Saqqâra." In *Études sur l'Ancien Empire et la nécropole de Saqqâra dédiées à Jean-Philippe Lauer*, edited by Catherine Berger and Bernard Mathieu, 177–89. Montpellier: Université Paul Valéry, 1997.

———. "Some Early Monuments from Busiris in the Egyptian Delta." *MMJ* 11 (1976): 5–24.

———. "A Stela of the Heracleopolitan Period at Saqqara: The Osiris Iti." *ZÄS* 90 (1963): 35–41.

———. "Three Stelae from Naga ed-Deir." In *Studies in Ancient Egypt, the Aegean, and the Sudan: Essays in Honor of Dows Dunham, on the Occasion of His 90th Birthday, June 1, 1980*, edited by William K. Simpson and Whitney Davis, 58–61. Boston: Museum of Fine Arts, 1981.

Gaballa, Gaballa A. *Narrative in Egyptian Art*. Mainz: Philipp von Zabern, 1917.

Gardiner, Alan H. "The Tomb of a Much-travelled Theban Official." *JEA* 4 (1917): 28–38.

Gourdon, Yannis. "Éléments de datation d'un groupe de stèles fausses-portes de la Première Période Intermédiaire." In *Des Néferkarê aux Montouhoteps: Travaux archéologiques en cours sur la fin de la VIe dynastie et la Première Période Intermédiaire*, edited by Laure Pantalacci and Catherine Berger-el Naggar, 165–93. TMO 40. Lyon: MOM, 2005.

Grunert, Stefan. "Die Schächtung im Totenopfer: Ritualbestandteil vs. Reflexion allgemeinen Brauchtums." In *Tierkulte im pharaonischen Ägypten und im Kulturvergleich*, edited by Martin Fitzenreiter, 69–82. London: Golden House, 2005.

Guglielmi, Waltraud. *Reden, Rufe und Lieder auf altägyptischen Darstellungen der Landwirtschaft, Viehzucht, des Fisch- und Vogelfangs vom Mittleren Reich bis zur Spätzeit*. TÄB 1. Bonn: Habelt, 1973.

Harpur, Yvonne. *Decoration in Egyptian Tombs of the Old Kingdom: Studies in Orientation and Scene Content*. London and New York: Routledge & Kegan Paul, 1987.

Hartwig, Melinda K. *Tomb Painting and Identity in Ancient Thebes, 1419–1372 BCE*. MonAeg 10, Série IMAGO 2. Turnhout: Brepols, 2004.

Hassan, Selim. *Excavations at Gîza, 1930–1931*. Vol. 2. Cairo: Government Press, 1936.

———. *Excavations at Gîza, 1931–1932*. Vol. 3. Cairo: Government Press, 1941.

———. *Excavations at Gîza, 1933–1934*. Vol. 5. Cairo: Government Press, 1944.

———. *Excavations at Gîza, 1935–1936*. Vol. 7, *The Mastabas of the Seventh Season and Their Description*. Cairo: Government Press, 1953.

Hayes, William C. *The Scepter of Egypt: A Background for the Study of the Egyptian Antiquities in the Metropolitan Museum of Art*. Vol. 1, *From the Earliest Times to the End of the Middle Kingdom*. New York: Metropolitan Museum of Art, 1953.

Hölzl, Regina. *Die Kultkammer des Ka-ni-nisut im Kunsthistorischen Museum Wien.*
Vienna: Kunsthistorisches Museum, 2005.
James, T.G.H. *Hieroglyphic Texts from Egyptian Stelae, Etc., Part I.* 2nd ed. London:
Trustees of the British Museum, 1961.
———. *The Mastaba of Khentika Called Ikhekhi.* ASE, EES Thirtieth Memoir.
London: EES, 1953.
Jones, Dilwyn. *An Index of Ancient Egyptian Titles, Epithets and Phrases of the Old
Kingdom.* 2 vols. Oxford: Archaeopress, 2000.
Junker, Hermann. *Gîza 2: Grabungen auf dem Friedhof des Alten Reiches.* Band 2, *Die
Mastabas der beginnenden V. Dynastie auf dem Westfriedhof.* Vienna and Leipzig:
Hölder-Pichler-Tempsky A.-G., 1934.
———. *Gîza 4: Grabungen auf dem Friedhof des Alten Reiches.* Band 4, *Die Mastaba des
K3jmꜥnḫ (Kai-em-anch).* Vienna and Leipzig: Hölder-Pichler-Tempsky A.-G., 1940.
———. *Gîza 7: Grabungen auf dem Friedhof des Alten Reiches.* Band 7, *Der
Ostabschnitt des Westfriedhofs. Erster Teil.* Vienna and Leipzig: Hölder-Pichler-
Tempsky A.-G., 1944.
———. *Gîza 8: Grabungen auf dem Friedhof des Alten Reiches.* Band 8, *Der
Ostabschnitt des Westfriedhofs. Zweiter Teil.* Vienna and Leipzig: Hölder-Pichler-
Tempsky A.-G., 1947.
———. *Gîza 11: Grabungen auf dem Friedhof des Alten Reiches,* Band 11, *Der
Friedhof südlich der Cheopspyramide. Ostteil.* Vienna and Leipzig: Hölder-Pichler-
Tempsky A.-G., 1953.
Kamrin, Janice. *The Cosmos of Khnumhotep II at Beni Hasan.* Studies in Egyptology.
London and New York: Kegan Paul International, 1999.
Kanawati, Naguib. "The Living and the Dead in Old Kingdom Tomb Scenes." *SAK* 9
(1981): 213–25.
Kanawati, Naguib, et al. *Mereruka and His Family.* Part 3:1. Australian Centre for
Egyptology Report 29. Oxford: Aris and Phillips, 2010.
Kanawati, Naguib, et al. *The Teti Cemetery at Saqqara.* Vol. 8, *The Tomb of Inumin.*
Australian Centre for Egyptology Report 24. Oxford: Aris and Phillips, 2006.
Kanawati, Naguib, and Mahmud Abder-Razeq. *Mereruka and His Family.* Part 2, *The
Tomb of Waatkhethor.* Australian Centre for Egyptology Report 26. Oxford: Aris
and Phillips, 2008.
———. *The Teti Cemetery at Saqqara.* Vol. 6, *The Tomb of Nikauisesi.* Australian
Centre for Egyptology Report 14. Oxford: Aris and Phillips, 2000.
———. *The Unis Cemetery at Saqqara.* Vol. 2, *The Tombs of Iynefert and Ihy (Reused by
Idut).* Australian Centre for Egyptology Report 19. Oxford: Aris and Phillips, 2003.
Kanawati, Naguib, and Ali Hassan. *The Teti Cemetery at Saqqara.* Vol. 2, *The Tomb of
Ankhmahor.* Australian Centre for Egyptology Report 9. Oxford: Aris and
Phillips, 1997.
Lacau, Pierre. "Le tableau central de la stèle-porte égyptienne." *RdÉ* 19 (1967):
39–50.

Leitz, Christian. *Lexikon der ägyptischen Götter und Götterbezeichnungen.* Vol. 3, *p-nbw.* OLA 112. Leuven: Peeters, 2002.

Lopez, Jesus. "Rapport préliminaire sur les fouilles d'Hérakléopolis (1968)." *Oriens Antiquus* 14 (1975): 57–78.

Montet, Pierre. *Les scènes de la vie privée dans les tombeaux égyptiens de l'Ancien Empire.* Strasbourg: Faculté des Lettres de Strasbourg, 1925.

Motte, Aurore. "*Reden und Rufe*, a Neglected Genre? Towards a Definition of the Speech Captions in Private Tombs." *BIFAO* 117 (2017): 293–317.

Moussa, Ahmed, and Hartwig Altenmüller. *The Tomb of Nefer and Kahay.* Archäologische Veröffentlichungen 5. Mainz: Philipp von Zabern, 1971.

Munro, Peter. "Brothälften und Schilfblätter." *GM* 5 (1973): 13–16.

Oppenheim, Adela, et al. *Ancient Egypt Transformed: The Middle Kingdom.* New York: Metropolitan Museum of Art, 2015.

Peck, William H. "The Ordering of the Figure." In *A Companion to Ancient Egyptian Art*, edited by Melinda Hartwig, 360–74. Oxford: Wiley Blackwell, 2015.

Pérez-Die, María del Carmen. "The False Door at Herakleopolis Magna (I): Typology and Iconography." In *Perspectives on Ancient Egypt: Studies in Honor of Edward Brovarski*, edited by Zahi Hawass, Peter Der Manuelian, and Ramadan B. Hussein, 357–93. *ASAE Supplement*, cahier no. 40. Cairo: SCA, 2010.

Pitkin, Melanie L. "New Perspectives for Dating Egyptian False Doors and Funerary Stelae of the First Intermediate Period." PhD diss., Macquarie University, 2017.

Quibell, James E. *Excavations at Saqqara (1905–1906).* Cairo: IFAO, 1907.

Ranke, Herman. *Die ägyptische Personennamen.* Vol. 1, *Verzeichnis der Namen.* Glückstadt: J.J. Augustin, 1935.

Richards, Janet. "Time and Memory in Ancient Egyptian Cemeteries: The Dynamic History of Ancient Sites." *Expedition* 44 (2002): 16–24.

Robins, Gay. *The Art of Ancient Egypt.* Cambridge, MA: Harvard University Press, 1997.

———. *Proportion and Style in Ancient Egyptian Art.* Austin: University of Texas Press, 1994.

Roeten, Leo. *The Decoration on the Cult Chapel Walls of the Old Kingdom Tombs at Giza: A New Approach to Their Interaction.* Leiden: Brill, 2014.

Roth, Ann Macy. *Giza Mastaba Series.* Vol. 6, *A Cemetery of Palace Attendants, Including G 2084–2099, G 2230 + 2231, and G 2240.* Boston: Department of Ancient Egyptian, Nubian, and Near Eastern Art, Museum of Fine Arts, 1995.

Schäfer, Heinrich. *Aegyptische Inschriften aus den Staatlichen Museen zu Berlin.* Vol. 1, *Inschriften von der Ältesten Zeit bis zum Ende der Hyksoszeit.* Leipzig: J.C. Hinrichs'sche Buchhandlung, 1913.

Shirai, Yayoi. "Ideal and Reality in Old Kingdom Private Funerary Cults." In *The Old Kingdom Art and Archaeology: Proceedings of the Conference, Prague, May 31–June 4, 2004*, edited by Miroslav Bárta, 325–33. Prague: Academy of Sciences of the Czech Republic, 2006.

Silverman, David P. *Searching for Ancient Egypt: Art, Architecture, and Artifacts from* the University of Pennsylvania Museum of Art and Anthropology. Ithaca, NY: Cornell University Press, 1997.

Simpson, William K. *Giza Mastabas Series*. Vol. 2, *The Mastabas of Qar and Idu, G 7101 and 7102*. Boston: Department of Ancient Egyptian, Nubian, and Near Eastern Art, Museum of Fine Arts, 1976.

Smith, William Stevenson. *A History of Egyptian Sculpture and Painting in the Old Kingdom*. 2nd ed. Oxford: Oxford University Press, 1949.

Strudwick, Nigel. *The Administration of Egypt in the Old Kingdom*. London and New York: Routledge & Kegan Paul, 1985.

Swinton, Joyce. *Dating the Tombs of the Old Kingdom*. Archaeopress Egyptology 2. Oxford: Gordon House, 2014.

Valloggia, Michel. 1985. "Une nouvelle stèle provenant de Balat." In *Mélanges Gamal Eddin Mokhtar*, vol. 2, edited by Paule Posener-Kriéger, 321–26. BdÉ 97. Cairo: IFAO.

Vandier, Jacques. *Manuel d'archéologie égyptienne*. Vol. 2, *Les grandes époques: L'architecture funéraire*. Paris: Éditions A. et J. Picard et Cie, 1954.

———. *Manuel d'archéologie égyptienne*. Vol. 4, *Bas-reliefs et peintures: Scènes de la vie quotidienne*. Paris: Éditions A. et J. Picard et Cie, 1964.

———. *Manuel d'archéologie égyptienne*. Vol. 5, *Bas-reliefs et peintures: Scènes de la vie quotidienne*. Paris: Éditions A. et J. Picard et Cie, 1969.

van Walsem, René. *Iconography of Old Kingdom Elite Tombs: Analysis and Interpretation, Theoretical and Methodological Aspects*. Leiden: Ex Oriente Lux, 2005.

Woods, Alexandra. "Relief." In *A Companion to Ancient Egyptian Art*, edited by Melinda Hartwig, 219–48. Oxford: Wiley Blackwell, 2015.

Worsham, Charles E. "A Reinterpretation of the So-called Bread Loaves in Egyptian Offering Scenes." *JARCE* 16 (1979): 7–10.

Ziegler, Christiane. *Catalogue des stèles, peintures et reliefs égyptiens de l'Ancien Empire et de la Première Période Intermédiaire, vers 2686–2040 avant J.-C*. Paris: Éditions de la Réunion des musées nationaux, 1990.

———. *Le Mastaba d'Akhethetep (Fouilles du Louvre à Saqqara 1)*. Leuven: Peeters, 2007.

9 A Case Study of Multiple Coffin Reuse in the National Museum of Scotland, Edinburgh

Kathlyn M. Cooney

I HAVE WORKED WITH ED BLEIBERG on a variety of scholarly pursuits, most of them involving coffins in some way, shape, or form. It is the reuse of these coffins that most intrigued us, inspiring many discussions about how and why one human being would reuse the coffin of another. In that spirit, I offer an example of coffin reuse, this one from the Twenty-first Dynasty, when reuse had become de rigueur in elite Egyptian society.

The collection of the National Museum of Scotland in Edinburgh provides a very complicated case study of a reused inner coffin case and lid (1907.569A–B) (fig. 9.1). The coffin pieces came to the museum together but were recently published by Bill Manley and Aidan Dodson separately, with two different catalog entries, to account for the different names found on each piece.

The coffin lid and case seem to have been purchased together as an antiquities-market acquisition at the end of the nineteenth century by Sir Colin Scott-Moncrief, and both lid and case are displayed together in a common vitrine in the museum. Indeed, the color scheme and relative dimensions (for example, the fit between lid and case) seem to indicate that both pieces were crafted, at some point, to fit together for an ancient burial, rather than being an opportunistic match of separate pieces created by antiquities dealers.[1] The coffin is of unknown provenance, but its style and inscriptions suggest a Theban origin,[2] although Andrzej Niwiński published the coffin as potentially finding its origins in Akhmim.[3] Manley and Dodson published the coffin case and the lid separately because their publication, and indeed the field of coffin studies as a whole, prioritizes text over material analysis. Because the coffin lid and case

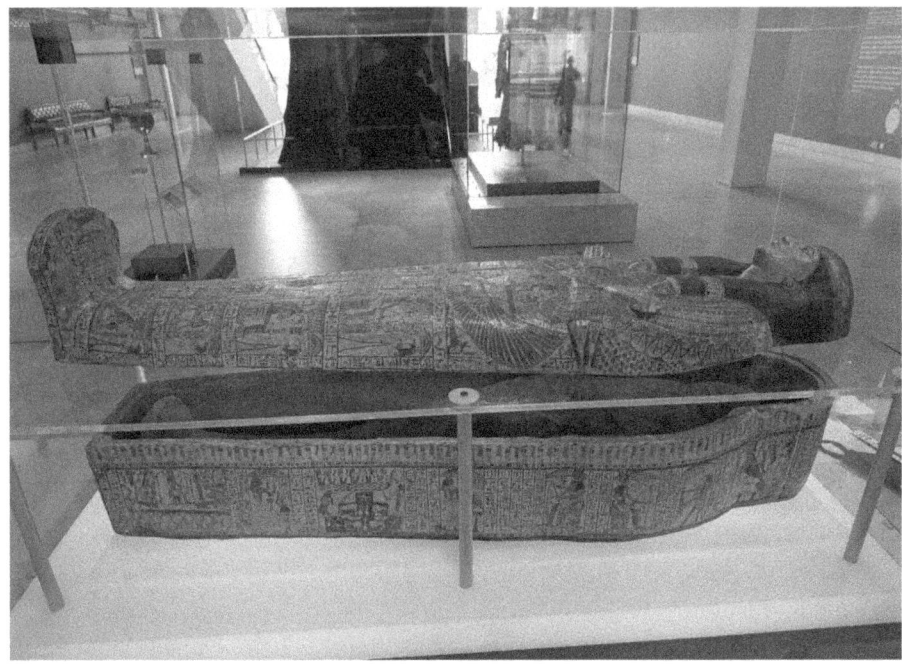

Fig. 9.1. Reused inner coffin case and lid (1907.569A–B) at the National Museum of Scotland in Edinburgh. Photograph by Kathlyn M. Cooney.

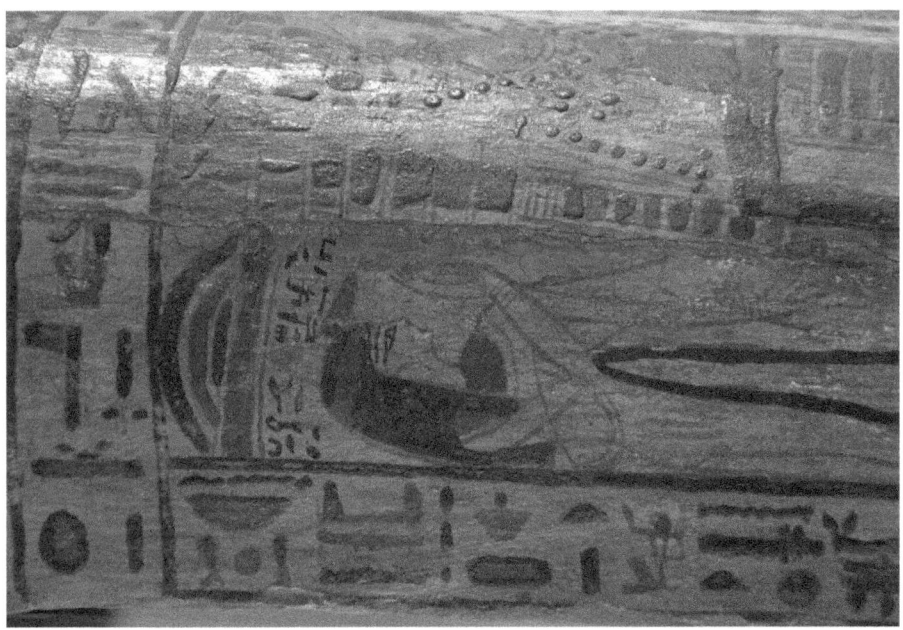

Fig. 9.2. Detail from the inner coffin lid depicting Tjenetweretkat. Photograph by Kathlyn M. Cooney.

inscriptions have separate names, the pieces are automatically assumed not to belong to one another. A close examination of the pieces, however, indicates a very complicated case of reuse—reuse of lid and case separately, and then reuse of lid and case together for another owner when the two were opportunistically modified to fit together. Although Manley and Dodson associate the man mentioned on the coffin-lid inscriptions, a certain Iuefenamen, with the well-known Third High Priest of Amun, known for transferring royal burials in western Thebes, the following analysis will show that both case and lid were decorated for a different priest of Amun who lived earlier in the Twenty-first Dynasty.

The coffin lid is inscribed for a woman, a temple singer named Tjenetweretkat (fig. 9.2), and the lid includes a mélange of different styles from different time periods. The wooden structure of the coffin has carved forearms and elbows, clear elements of the earlier Twenty-first Dynasty, if not the Ramesside Period. The collar on the coffin lid's chest is a short collar, in keeping with coffin-painting style of earlier traditions, rather than the longer collar that became popular later in the Twenty-first Dynasty, once forearms were dispensed with and only hands were shown peeking out of a voluminous *wesekh*. The bottom of the Edinburgh coffin lid's feet is painted and varnished, a decorative element in keeping with the Ramesside Period and early Twenty-first Dynasty. While it seems, at first glance, that the lid is on point with an early Twenty-first Dynasty date, further examination reveals that the rest of the lid's decoration—particularly on the lower body—betrays a later date in the Twenty-first Dynasty or even verging into the early Twenty-second Dynasty.[4] Thus this coffin lid betrays a mix of carpentry and painting actions, blended together, ostensibly, with a final application of varnish over the whole, to match older and newer decorative instances.

Judging a coffin's creation date from decoration alone is flawed.[5] Coffin structure must also be analyzed. Not only are the forearms modeled on the coffin surface, which is an earlier style of coffin-lid construction, but a glance at the underside of the coffin lid shows that it was also later modified. The interior lid seams are rough and unfinished with no plaster, paint, or varnish, and show obvious tool marks, indicating that the lid was cut down for some reason, probably to be reused. If there was any black varnish on the lid's interior, as would be expected if the coffin was originally Ramesside or early Twenty-first Dynasty, it has been cut away. In addition, the coffin lid seams are flat, rather than stepped; the stepped version is what one would expect on an early Twenty-first Dynasty coffin. Thus, it seems this coffin lid may have been modified more than once: first to update it from an early Twenty-first Dynasty style, and a second time for the woman depicted. During one of these modifications, the lid was recarved to fit a case for which it was not originally crafted, likely the same case with which it is currently displayed.

The coffin case is inscribed for a man, a Theban priest, perhaps serving in the Akh-Menu at Karnak, and his figure is visible in two dimensions in the case side decoration. The style of decoration is of early to mid-Twenty-first Dynasty, Type A according to Niwiński's typology.[6] The bottom of the case footend is also painted and varnished, in keeping with earlier Twenty-first Dynasty styles. The case interior shows stepped coffin seams, a characteristic associated with the Ramesside Period and earlier Twenty-first Dynasty, rather than the late Twenty-first and early Twenty-second dynasties when coffin seams, especially of stola coffins, became flat.[7] The case interior also shows traces of previous decoration, including remnants of plaster, removed by means of chiseling. The tool marks are clearly visible, as are the plaster remnants.

I suggest that both lid and case were likely reused separately before they were joined together—given the markers of the Ramesside Period or early Twenty-first Dynasty, such as the stepped ledge of the case's seams and the forearms modeled in the lid's surface. When case and lid were joined, the entirety was likely then redecorated for a priest named Iuefenamen, probably in the early to mid-Twenty-first Dynasty according to the layout and type of the case decoration. After Iuefenamen's use, the entire coffin was redone for a woman in the later Twenty-first Dynasty, but without changing the case sides (for which there are other examples, probably because the lid was a priority and the case would have been what people would notice the least in funerary rites).[8] It is entirely possible that the entire piece was then reused again for the burial of the man currently inside the coffin, without any redecoration of the coffin itself. But it is impossible to know if this mummy really was found in this coffin, or if this was an element added by antiquities dealers who knew that mummies appreciated the value of a coffin.

There are other interesting details on lid and case. The case sides betray a very rough and uneven surface, particularly under raking light, likely because the old decoration was roughly chiseled down for the new decoration of Iuefenamen. There are no clear remnants of earlier decoration underneath the current one of Iuefenamen, but since there are tool marks and remnants of an older plaster layer visible on the interior of the case, we might expect the same treatment of the case exterior. I should note that the coffin was heavily restored in Edinburgh, including even modern repainting to match ancient decoration in many places, complicating a thorough examination of use and reuse. Nonetheless, coffin case sides should, ideally, be smooth and finished, not rough and uneven. This is a circumstantial marker, to be sure, but when

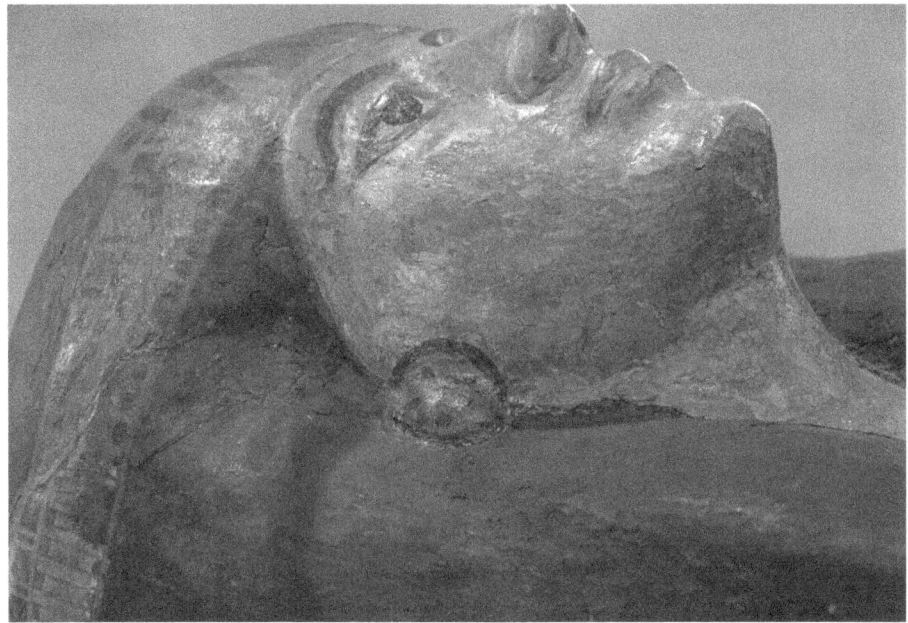

Fig. 9.3. Detail of the face of the inner coffin lid. Photograph by Kathlyn M. Cooney.

analyzed in combination with removal of interior decorative layers, it is likely a marker of reuse.

There are also clues that the coffin lid was modified for the female gender. Breasts and earrings were added in plaster, as cracks around and through them show. The earrings do not lie flat on the wig as traditionally done, but were folded into the angle between the face and headcloth (fig. 9.3). Upon close examination it is possible to see how the plaster for the earrings was inserted in between the face and headdress. It seems possible that these plaster additions were meant to cover up the ears, traditionally shown on a male coffin. The cracks around the earrings are especially telling of a later modification, rather than matching the original work. The flat female-style hands are thick and uneven, even turning up at the attachment point, a sign that they were not part of the original coffin-lid modeling. There are stars painted onto the fingers of the hands, seemingly added in one of the last reuses in the late Twenty-first Dynasty, when such baroque embellishments had become more common. Except for the short collar and modeled forearms, the lid decoration seems late Twenty-first Dynasty in date, much later in style than the case sides. The left lid seam inscription reads: *inḏ n Wsir nbt pr šmꜥyt n imn-rꜥ nswt nṯrw ṯnt-wrḥ(-k3t) ḏd t3-mwt*. Another circumstantial marker of (yet another?) reuse are

Fig. 9.4. Detail from the inner coffin case depicting Iuefenamen. Photograph by Kathlyn M. Cooney.

the name and title labels in monochrome black ink added around the female figure in two dimensions, but there is no evidence that there was another name under that of Tjenetweretkat.

A final point on the sculptural style of this coffin lid, though a very tendentious one: a glance at the face plate, from the side or straight on, reminds one of the coffin of Nysuamen now in Leeds, which dates to the late Twentieth or early Twenty-first Dynasty.[9] Based on this craft comparison, I would suggest that the coffin lid of Tjenetweretkat was made at the same time or even in a similar late Ramesside craft context, then it was decorated and sculpted *before* it was given a gender modification to be reused by Tjenetweretkat.

In their catalog, Manley and Dodson suggest that the woman Tjenetweretkat was the grandmother of Iuefenamen. However, her decoration is much *later* than his, not earlier. Even if lid and case were not used together for Tjenetweretkat, the decoration style suggests a late Twenty-first Dynasty date for the reuse of this earlier coffin lid. If lid and case were reused together for this woman, then that reuse was incompletely done, gender modifications being made only to the lid and not to the case. According this hypothesis, she, not he, is the later reuser of the coffin set. Her reuse left the case sides as they were, which would be a common reuser's method, a short cut, if you will. If the pieces were not reused together as lid and case, then the case still shows remnants of reuse on its own for Iuefenamen, indicating that he was not the first one to use this coffin case. His reuse likely dates to the early to mid-Twenty-first Dynasty.

This brings us to Manley and Dodson's problematic identification of the priest Iuefenamen as the Third High Priest of Amun at Karnak, son of Nespakashuty of the Twenty-second Dynasty, living around the time of King Sheshonq I (fig. 9.4). First, as the authors themselves state, the titles on the coffin do not match the known titles of this Third High Priest. Second, the stylistic date of the case side decoration is early to mid-Twenty-first Dynasty, not early Twenty-second Dynasty. Third, one might expect this important Twenty-second Dynasty high priest to have been buried in a stola-type coffin with the red crossed bands on the chest, and this is not a stola coffin. Furthermore, stola coffins were always crafted with flat coffin seams; this coffin case has stepped ledges. In the end, Manley and Dodson use unusual iconography on the case sides to argue that the case dates to the early Twenty-second Dynasty. Finally, Manley and Dodson link the coffin date to the mummy now inside, claiming it was likely Iuefenamen, which is also problematic. Just because there is a mummy in this trough does not mean it is that of Iufenamen himself. As already mentioned, dealers often put mummies inside coffins to make a better sale. Reusers used coffins for new mummies with no modifications to the coffin at all. Both of these options are more plausible. The male mummy brought to the museum with the coffin was estimated to have died at forty years of age. The mummy has spiral bandaging and packing associated with late Twenty-first Dynasty mummification. But even though the date of this mummification matches (most of) the decoration of the female coffin lid, it does not necessarily match that of the earlier coffin decoration of Iuefenamen. On the whole, there is no compelling evidence to think the male mummy was necessarily found inside this coffin, and a lack of identification on the mummy wrappings makes identification impossible.

In conclusion, this lid and case, displayed together at the National Museum of Scotland in Edinburgh, tell a compelling and complicated story about coffin reuse. This funerary assemblage reminds us that archaeological objects need holistic examination lest we prioritize certain elements, like text and typology, and fail to take into account all of the available evidence.

Notes

1   Discussions with curators revealed that while lid and case do fit with one another, the fit is not exact. This imprecise fit is exactly what one would expect if lid and case were originally made independently to fit other pieces but were later opportunistically brought together for reuse.

2 Manley and Dodson, *Life Everlasting*, 36–38, 47–51.
3 Niwiński, *Twenty-first Dynasty Coffins from Thebes*, entry 183.
4 Although Manley and Dodson note this inconsistency (page 36), they do not connect it with reuse or a mix of styles.
5 See Cooney, "Ancient Egyptian Funerary Arts as Social Documents." It was van Walsem who first critiqued Niwiński's typology as flawed because it prioritized surface decoration over wooden structure and form: van Walsem, "The Study of 21st Dynasty Coffins from Thebes," 13.
6 Manley and Dodson, *Life Everlasting*. But note that in their attempts to make this coffin fit with the Third High Priest of Amun Iuefenamen, they write (page 50): "The decoration of this coffin trough corresponds to Niwiński's Type A, but as he himself points out, classification of coffin troughs is far more problematic than that of their associated lids. Even then typology is of little use for dating purposes, as most coffin trough types have a broad span of use." They instead use an unusual funerary vignette to date the coffin to the last part of the Twenty-first Dynasty and thus to the lifetime of the Third High Priest of Amun.
7 van Walsem, *Coffin of Djedmonthuiufankh*.
8 For another coffin in which only the lid was changed but case decoration was left as is, see Florence 7450, a Ramesside coffin with Twenty-first Dynasty redecoration. See Niwiński, *Twenty-first Dynasty Coffins from Thebes*, entry 188. For more on coffin reuse, see Cooney, "Coffin Reuse in the 21st Dynasty: How and Why Did the Egyptians Reuse the Body Containers of Their Ancestors?"; "Ancient Egyptian Funerary Arts as Social Documents"; "A 21st Dynasty Coffin Fragment in Private Collection in Oegstgeest"; "Reuse of Egyptian Coffins in the 21st Dynasty: Ritual Materialism in the Context of Scarcity"; "Coffin Reuse in Dynasty 21: A Case Study of the Coffins in the Rijksmuseum van Oudheden"; "Coffin Reuse in Dynasty 21: A Case Study of the Coffins in the British Museum"; "Coffin Reuse in the 21st Dynasty: A Case Study of the Bab El-Gasus Coffins in the Egyptian Museum of Florence"; and "Evidence for Coffin Reuse in the 21st Dynasty Coffins of the Royal Cache Deir El Bahari 320."
9 The coffin of Nysuamen is now in the City Museum in Leeds (D.1960.426.1–3). See Osburn, *An Account of an Egyptian Mummy*; Schmidt, *Sarkofager, Mumiekister, og Mumiehylstre i det gamle Aegypten*, figs. 670–73; David and Tapp, *The Mummy's Tale*; Niwiński, *Twenty-first Dynasty Coffins from Thebes*, entry 2200; van Walsem, "Deir El Medina as the Place of Origin of the Coffin of Anet in the Vatican"; Cooney, *Cost of Death*, 470–75; and Cooney, "Changing Burial Practices at the End of the New Kingdom," 25.

Bibliography

Cooney, Kathlyn M. "Ancient Egyptian Funerary Arts as Social Documents: Social Place, Reuse, and Working Towards a New Typology of 21st Dynasty Coffins." In *Body, Cosmos, and Eternity: New Research Trends in the Iconography and Symbolism of Ancient Egyptian Coffins*, edited by Rogério Sousa, 45–66. Archaeopress Egyptology 3. Oxford: Archaeopress, 2014.

———. "Changing Burial Practices at the End of the New Kingdom: Defensive Adaptations in Tomb Commissions, Coffin Commissions, Coffin Decoration, and Mummification." *JARCE* 47 (2011): 3–44.

———. "Coffin Reuse in the 21st Dynasty: A Case Study of the Bab El-Gasus Coffins in the Egyptian Museum of Florence." In *The Tomb of the Priests of Amun: Burial Assemblages in the Egyptian Museum of Florence*, edited by Rogério de Sousa, 492–514. Leiden and Boston: Brill, 2018.

———. "Coffin Reuse in Dynasty 21: A Case Study of the Coffins in the British Museum." In *Ancient Egyptian Coffins: Craft Traditions and Functionality*, edited by John Taylor and Marie Vandenbeusch, 295–322. Leuven: Peeters, 2018.

———. "Coffin Reuse in Dynasty 21: A Case Study of the Coffins in the Rijksmuseum van Oudheden." In *The Coffins of the Priests of Amun: Egyptian Coffins from the 21st Dynasty in the Collection of the National Museum of Antiquities in Leiden*, edited by Lara Weiss, 69–95. Leiden: Sidestone Press, 2018.

———. "Coffin Reuse in the 21st Dynasty: How and Why Did the Egyptians Reuse the Body Containers of Their Ancestors?" *ARCE Bulletin* 203 (2013): 48–51.

———. *The Cost of Death: The Social and Economic Value of Ancient Egyptian Funerary Art in the Ramesside Period*. Leiden: Egyptologische Uitgaven 22, 2007.

———. "Evidence for Coffin Reuse in the 21st Dynasty Coffins of the Royal Cache Deir El Bahari 320." In *The Proceedings of the Second Vatican Coffins Conference July 2016*, edited by Alessia Amenta. Vatican City: Edizioni Musei Vaticani, forthcoming.

———. "A Late 21st–Early 22nd Dynasty Coffin Fragment from Thebes in a Private Collection in Oegstgeest, the Netherlands." In *A Workman's Progress: Studies in the Village of Deir El-Medina and Other Documents from Western Thebes in Honour of Rob Demarée*, edited by Ben Haring, Olaf Kaper, and Réne van Walsem, 21–32. Leiden: Egyptologische Uitgaven, Netherlands Institute of the Near East; Leuven: Peeters, 2014.

———. "Reuse of Egyptian Coffins in the 21st Dynasty: Ritual Materialism in the Context of Scarcity." In *The First Vatican Coffins Conference, 19–22 June 2013: Conference Proceedings*, edited by Alessia Amenta, 87–98. Vatican City: Edizoni Musei Vaticani, 2017.

David, A. Rosalie, and Edmund Tapp. *The Mummy's Tale: The Scientific and Medical Investigation of Natsef-Amun, Priest in the Temple at Karnak*. London: Michael O'Mara Books, 1992.

Manley, Bill, and Aidan M. Dodson, eds. *Life Everlasting: National Museums Scotland Collection of Ancient Egyptian Coffins*. Edinburgh: National Museums Scotland, 2010.

Niwiński, Andrzej. *Twenty-first Dynasty Coffins from Thebes: Chronological and Typological Studies*. Mainz: Philipp von Zabern, 1988.

Osburn, William. *An Account of an Egyptian Mummy, Presented to the Museum of the Leeds Philosophical and Literary Society by the Late John Blayds. With an Appendix*

Containing the Chemical and Anatomical Details of the Examination of the Body. Leeds, UK: Leeds Philosophical and Literary Society, 1928.

Schmidt, Valdemar. *Sarkofager, Mumiekister, og Mumiehylstre i det gamle AEgypten: Typologisk Atlas.* Copenhagen: J. Frimodts, 1919.

van Walsem, Réne. *The Coffin of Djedmonthuiufankh in the National Museum of Antiquities at Leiden.* Leiden: Nederlands Instituut voor het Nabije Oosten, 1997.

———. "Deir El Medina as the Place of Origin of the Coffin of Anet in the Vatican (Inv.: Xiii.2.1, Xiii.2.2)." In *Deir El Medina in the Third Millennium AD: A Tribute to Jac J. Janssen,* edited by Robert Demarée and Arno Egberts, 337–49. Egyptologische Uitgaven 14. Leiden: Peeters, 2000.

———. "The Study of 21st Dynasty Coffins from Thebes." *Bibliotheca Orientalis* 50 (1993): 9–92.

10 A New Version of Book of the Dead 30B: Art Institute Chicago Heart Scarab 1894.1359

Emily Teeter

WHILE CATALOGING EGYPTIAN OBJECTS in the collection of the Art Institute of Chicago, a fine heart scarab and its inscription caught my eye.[1] It is in honor of Ed Bleiberg's long museum career, in commemoration of his personal anniversary, and also to remind him of the joys of "discovering" unusual objects in museum storage areas, that I present these comments.

In 1894, the Art Institute of Chicago acquired nearly two thousand Egyptian objects from the collection of the Rev. Chauncey Murch of the Presbyterian Mission in Luxor. This lot included a wide variety of materials, including architectural elements, sculpture, stelae, amulets, jewelry, canopic equipment, and a Book of the Dead. The details of this transfer are somewhat unclear. In 1894, Charles L. Hutchinson, the first director of the Art Institute, and his friend and museum trustee Martin A. Ryerson traveled to Egypt to secure more material for their growing Egyptian collection,[2] armed with letters of introduction to "responsible agents and dealers," including Murch.[3] In an arrangement, the terms of which are unclear today, Murch loaned the Art Institute more than two thousand objects. These were later, "at the close of the exhibition," purchased by Hutchinson and Henry H. Getty, another museum trustee and friend of the Ryerson family.[4] Among the objects was a collection of 667 scarabs and seals.[5] With all of these additions, the collection was regarded as being of "great rarity and value, sufficient, with the loans of Mr. Murch, to form a collection respectable in quantity, and more than respectable in quality."[6]

Unfortunately, it is not known where Murch acquired most of the scarabs, much less most of the other items in the lot. Some objects came from Saqqara,

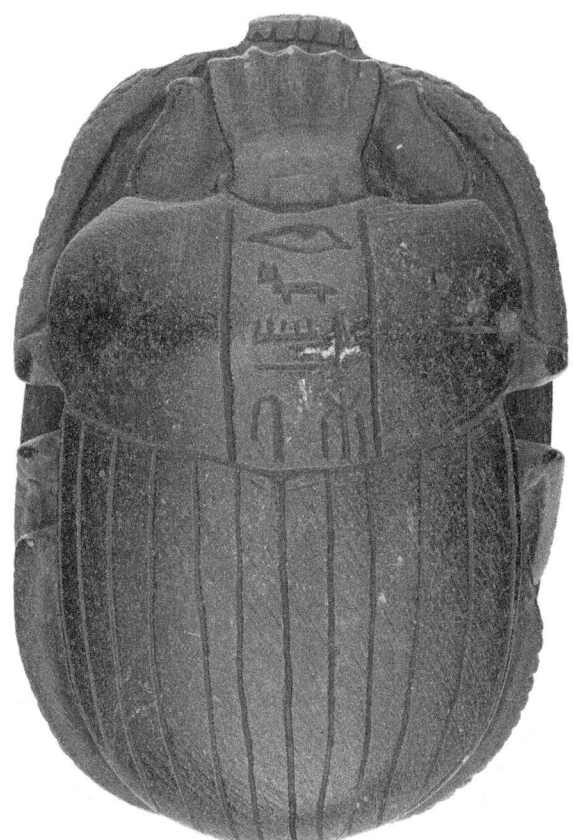

Fig. 10.1. Back of Art Institute of Chicago 1894.1359.

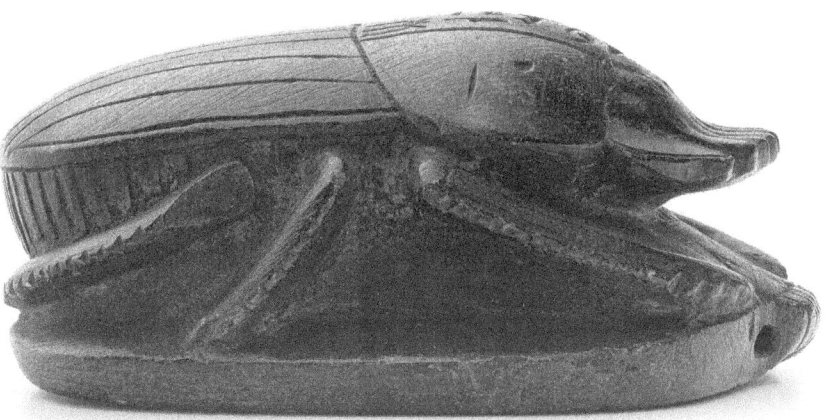

Fig. 10.2. Side view of Art Institute of Chicago 1894.1359.

such as a lintel from the tomb of Iniuia and Yui,[7] while others are from Thebes, such as a fragment of a stela of Neferhotep from Deir el Medina, and a Book of the Dead of a Theban Singer of Amun,[8] indicating that Murch, like many of his fellow dealers, had a very far-flung and often clandestine network for acquiring antiquities.[9]

Among the many scarabs in the 1894 acquisition were nine heart scarabs.[10] Although not a large collection, they display a range of variations. Two (AIC 1894.1935–1936, now OIM E 18777, E18778) have faked inscriptions. Another is inscribed in ink (1894.1937) rather than being incised. One other, including the example presented here, has a text that varies from the standard Spell 30B.[11]

The scarab presented here measures 7 cm × 4.4 cm × 2.5 cm (2 5/8 in × 1 3/4 in × 1 in) and is of a dark brown fine-grained stone. Until now, it has remained unpublished.[12]

The back is finely detailed (fig. 10.1). A curved line divides the prothorax from the elytra. The elytra is scored with lines, dividing each wing case into six sections.[13] A vertical line of text naming the owner of the scarab, *Wsir Imn-ms*, "The Osiris Amenmesse," is centered on the prothorax, running from the clypeus to the line of the elytra. The text is framed by a single vertical line on each side. The clypeus has five ruffles and the eyes are deeply indented. Visible-induced luminescence shows traces of Egyptian blue in some of the incised lines.[14]

A small bale extends from the top of the base under the head. It is pierced to allow the scarab to be suspended from a cord or wire, presumably from the neck of the mummy.[15] Because the text on the base runs the full width of each register, it is unlikely that the scarab was mounted in a frame as it would have covered the signs.[16]

The sides of the hindquarters of the body are marked with vertical lines. The legs are carved in high relief and have notches along their lengths and ends to indicate feathering. As seen from the side (fig. 10.2), the front and middle legs have space between them as they emerge from the junction of the prothorax and elytra. The hind legs are positioned well behind the junction of the middle legs where they descend from the body. The scarab sits on a thick base.

The base of the scarab has eight lines of text (fig. 10.3). Traces of Egyptian blue can be seen in the hieroglyphs when viewed with visible-induced luminescence.[17] The text is a variant of Book of the Dead Spell 30B:

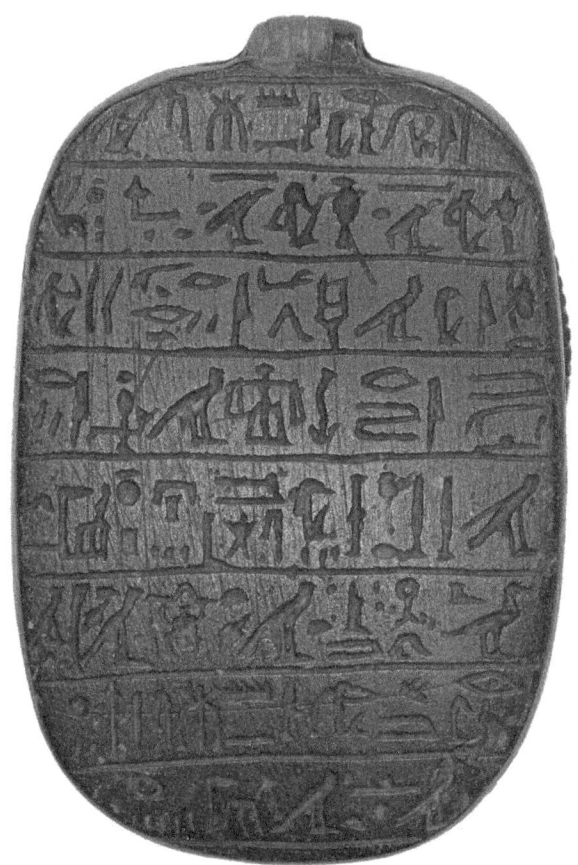

Fig. 10.3. Base of Art Institute of Chicago 1894.1359.

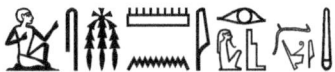 1. *ḏd mdw in Wsir Ỉmn-ms*
Words said by the Osiris Amenmesse:

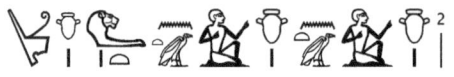 2. *ib.i n mwt.(i) ib.i [a] n mwt.(i) ḥȝt n*
Heart of (my) mother! Heart of (my) mother! Heart of

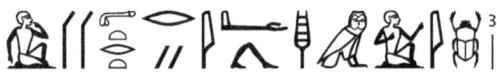 3. *ḫpr(w).i [b] m ꜥḥꜥ ir.i [c] (m) mtr*
my form(s)! Do not stand against me as witness

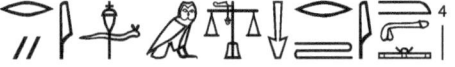 4. *m-bȝḥ iry [d] mḫȝt m ḫsf ir.i*
before the guardian of the balance, do not oppose me

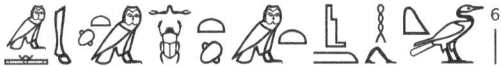 5. *m ḏ3ḏ3w m sb3wᵉ nw ḥrt-nṯr nn*
before the magistrates in the portals of the necropolis, without

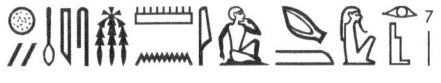 6. *ꜥḳ.(i) ḥtmᶠ mwt.(i) n ḫpr mwt.(i) (m) wḥm*
my entering into destruction when I die, my death not occurring again.

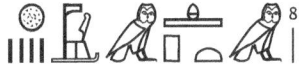 7. *Wsir sḏm-ꜥš ᵍ 'Imn-ms m3ꜥ ḫrw sp sn*
The Osiris, the worker Amenmesse, truly justified

8. *m ḥtp m ḥrt-nṯr sp-4*
being one who rests in the necropolis, 4 times (= forever).

Notes to the Inscription

a. Here, the sign, which should be *ib*, looks much more like a *hes* vase with its flat top. The artist's intent is unclear, especially considering the other errors in the text.

b. Here, *ḫpr* is singular rather than the expected plural. The first-person singular suffix is written with the reed leaf.[18]

c. *iry* written here (and in line four) for *r.i*, with the preposition *r* written *ir*,[19] and the double slashes being for the first-person singular, which are easily confused through the hieratic.[20]

d. For the coil rather than the two strokes in *iry* through confusion from the hieratic original.[21]

e. The stroke determinative below the *pr* and the following *nw* is much broader than the example in line two (after *ib*), looking more like a *p*. The artist's/sign carver's intention is unclear.

f. The walking legs in *ḥtm* may be a mistake through hieratic for the bread loaf *t*, or for the preposition *r* that would be expected after *ꜥḳ*.[22] An alternative reading, which, however, requires more emendation of the text, is to disregard the *ḥ* and read *nn ꜥḳ.(i m) st m mwt*, giving "Without my entering the place (= the necropolis) as a dead one . . ."

g. The man with hand to mouth for *ꜥš* in the title *sḏm-ꜥš*. The same abbreviated title is applied to Pentaweret and Nebnefer, well-attested workers, who otherwise have the fully written title *sḏm-ꜥš* at Deir el Medina.[23]

Commentary

This text shows apparent errors from copying from the hieratic original of the text, transposition and omission of some phrases that are found in the standard version of spell 30B, and the addition of entirely new text.

In lines three to five, the expected text "do not oppose me before the tribunal, do not outweigh me . . ." has been completely omitted, leaving the phrase "do not stand against me as witness" to continue with "before the guardian of the balance." In lines four and five, the reference to the balance comes before that to the magistrates, the reverse of the usual order.

Lines five and six introduce entirely new text after "the magistrates," continuing with the elaboration "in the portals of the necropolis," followed by additional unknown text which might be read "without my entering into destruction when I die, and my death not happening again . . ." or, "without my entering the place as a dead one and my death not happening again . . ."

All of line seven is given over to the name and title of the deceased with "Osiris" and ending with "justified," which here is quantified as "twice over." This personal data takes over the space that would have been used for the phrases found in the standard text, "You are my *ka* which is in my body, Khnum who makes my limbs firm."[24]

This emphasis upon the name of the deceased is striking. In the examples of heart scarabs where the name is inserted to personalize it, the name is usually written once in the first line.[25] Only rarely is the name incised on the back.[26] The Chicago scarab has the very unusual feature of having the name on the back and twice on the base.[27] The inclusion of the personal name within the body of the text confirms that the scarab was specially commissioned by Amenmesse.

I have not been able to locate the source of the new text in lines five and six. It is not found in other versions of Spell 30B or 30C,[28] nor is it in BD Spells 21–30 or 64A that can be associated with 30B.[29] Yet the vocabulary and phrases are very familiar from other religious texts. The verb ꜥk, "entering," in line six is very commonly used for the passage of the deceased through portals and gates that mark transitions in the liminal world.[30] In contrast, the phrase ḏꜣḏꜣw m sbꜣw nw ḥrt-nṯr, "magistrates in the portals of the necropolis," is not common, as opposed to magistrates in/of the "portals of the west" or "portals of the *dwꜣt*." However, the phrase appears in the Solar Liturgy in the context of the deceased coming and going unhindered,[31] and also in Spell 134 of the Book of the Dead of Gautseshen (Twenty-first Dynasty).[32]

The introduced text in lines five and six refers to the overarching themes of the freedom of movement ("my entering") and with the deceased not dying again that are standard elements of funerary literature.

The deviations from the standard text, and especially replacing the expected text with Amenmesse's name, title, and funerary epithets in line seven, may be another reflection that the scarab was especially commissioned by him rather than it being the product of a standardized production of heart scarabs. Perhaps the amulet maker (or should such an artisan who worked in hard stone be referred to as a sculptor?) making a custom product was less tied to copying the standard version of the religious text. Certainly, the heart scarab, being incised, was produced apart from the scribes who copied Book of the Dead papyri, perhaps leaving more latitude for innovation.[33] The many errors in the text suggest that it was copied from a hieratic original.

Provenance, Date, and Ownership

The title *sḏm-ʿš* in line seven indicates that the scarab is from Deir el Medina in western Thebes.[34] The use of that title indicates that the scarab must date from the end of the Eighteenth Dynasty to the end of the Twentieth, the interval during which that particular title was used.

The date of the scarab may be refined further by the stripes on its elytra. Malaise commented that heart scarabs with this feature are known from the Eighteenth Dynasty,[35] while Petrie dates examples with this characteristic[36] from the late Eighteenth Dynasty into the early Nineteenth Dynasty.[37]

Unfortunately, Amenmesse, the name of the owner of the scarab, is not an uncommon name. Of the nearly dozen men of that name attested in Thebes, there are only two who held the title "worker" in Deir el Medina during the time that the scarab can be stylistically dated: Amenmesse iii and Amenmesse vii, both of whom are attested in the first half of the Nineteenth Dynasty,[38] which accords with the date of the scarab's production. The first Amenmesse (iii) was the son of Pashedu (i) and Mekhay-ib (i).[39] Amenmesse is shown in his parent's tomb (TT 292) as well as on stelae in London and Turin.[40] The other candidate, Amenmesse (vii), was the son of Nebenmaat (i) and Hotepty (iii).[41] He is shown on the southern wall of the chapel of his parent's tomb (TT 218), along with other members of the family.[42] Both of these men came from prominent families with the resources that would allow such a beautiful heart scarab to be produced.

Unfortunately, there is no way of determining which of these two Amenmesses may have been the owner of the Chicago scarab. What we do know is that the scarab dates to the first half of the reign of Ramesses II; it is from Deir el Medina; and it belonged to an Amenmesse who commissioned an inventive version of Book of the Dead Spell 30B, and who thought well enough of himself to give his name unusual prominence upon it.

Notes

1. I thank Peter F. Dorman, Malcolm Mosher, and Foy Scalf for their very helpful comments on the scarab text.
2. This was their second trip to Egypt. The first was in 1892, during which Hutchinson and Ryerson purchased 232 objects from dealers in Cairo and Luxor. See Hilliard, *The Prime Mover*, 60–61, and Alexander, "From Plaster to Stone," 23–24. See also "History of the Collection [of the Art Institute]" in Teeter, forthcoming. Hutchinson and Ryerson were close personal friends and benefactors of the Art Institute who made numerous buying trips to Europe.
3. Hilliard, *The Prime Mover*, 60–61.
4. Hilliard, *The Prime Mover*, 61; Hutchinson, Dole, Sprague, et al., "Report of the Trustees," 17. The British Museum also bought a large collection of scarabs from Murch in 1906; in 1910, Murch sold another 3,370 objects to the Metropolitan Museum of Art: see Mace, "Murch Collection."
5. Examples with royal and non-royal names were published by Pier, "Historical Scarab Seals," 75–94.
6. Hutchinson, Dole, Sprague, et al., "Report of the Trustees," 17.
7. AIC 1894.246.
8. Stela of Neferhotep (AIC 1894.579); Book of the Dead of Tayu-henut-Mut (AIC 1894.180).
9. See Hagen and Ryholt, *Antiquities Trade in Egypt*, 122–30, for letters that record roughly contemporary dealers' travels through the Nile Valley to collect objects that they would sell, and for the precautions that had to be observed to prevent seizure by agents from the Antiquities Service. See, for example, a letter from Murch to E.A. Wallis Budge (1899): "Native boats were searched [by agents from the museum] as they passed the Nagʽ Hammadi Bridge. Natives were watched and searched when they got off the cars at Luxor," in Hagen and Ryholt, *Antiquities Trade in Egypt*, 126–27, and Ismail, *Wallis Budge*, 381.
10. Registered as AIC 1894.1933–39 and 1894.1359. Six of them (1894.1933–36, 1894.1938–39) were transferred to the Oriental Institute Museum in 1950, along with a group of 441 scarabs and seals, as the Art Institute reduced the number of its archaeological, as opposed to "art," holdings. The heart scarabs are registered at the Oriental Institute in sequence from E18775–18780. Two of the Murch heart scarabs (1894.1937 and 1894.1359) were retained by the Art Institute. A third (1894.1358; Allen, *Handbook of the Egyptian Collection*, 150) was withdrawn from the collection. Two heart scarabs were acquired earlier, in 1892 (1892.169, 1892.173, now OIM E18349). For the transfer of objects between the collections, see Arico and Teeter, "Collecting Ancient Egypt."
11. The scarab (1894.1938, now OIM E18779) bears a *ḥtp di nsw* formula in favor of Aba, a priest of Bastet.
12. It is listed in Allen, *Handbook of the Egyptian Collection*, 150, erroneously as a scarab with holes around the edge to attach it to a mummy.
13. See other examples with this feature: Brussels E.5697, E.4246, E.4348 in Malaise, *Scarabées de coeur* (unnumbered plate); BM EA 29626 in Taylor, *Journey through the Afterlife*, 44–45; HAUM Aeg S 42 (Ramesses II "or later") in Tinius, *Altägypten in Braunschweig*, 179–80. See Malaise, *Scarabées de coeur*, 49, for the striped elytra being

characteristic of some Eighteenth Dynasty scarabs, a feature that becomes more rare in the Nineteenth and Twentieth dynasties, and totally disappears in the Twenty-second Dynasty but is revived in the Twenty-sixth Dynasty. Taylor, *Journey through the Afterlife*, 44, dates BM 29626 to the Eighteenth and Nineteenth dynasties. See also an example in Tübingen ("probably" the Twenty-sixth Dynasty) in Brunner-Traut and Brunner, *Ägyptische Sammlung*, 187n1155, pl. 104.

14 Personal communication from Ashley F. Arico, 2 July 2019.

15 For general remarks about attaching heart scarabs to the mummy, see Malaise, *Scarabées de coeur*, 62–66. See also the further (unnumbered) plate in that volume with a heart scarab of Cha (Dynasty 18) and BM EA 29626 in Taylor, *Journey through the Afterlife*, 44–45, on a cord or wire. Stone heart scarabs that are pierced through the length (or width) of the body are rare. BM 7925 has two transverse borings, while OIM E18776 (ex AIC 1894.1934 in Scalf, *Book of the Dead*, 187–88) has a single hole drilled through the width.

16 Cf. to BM EA 29626 in Taylor, *Journey through the Afterlife*, 44–45, which has a margin around the text to accommodate its surrounding gold frame.

17 Personal communication from Ashley F. Arico, 2 July 2019.

18 Gardiner, *Egyptian Grammar*, §34.

19 *Wb* I.103.6.

20 Möller, *Hieratische Paläographie*, no. 33.

21 Möller, *Hieratische Paläographie*, no. 183.

22 See Möller, *Hieratische Paläographie*, nos. 575, 91.

23 See Teeter, "A 'New' Stela of the Vizier To (OIM E14655)," forthcoming.

24 See Leiden L.II.1 in Schneider, *Life and Death under the Pharaohs*, 144, no. 211, scarab of Seb, where the usual text that did not fit on the base was incised on the right elytra. See also Hodjash, *Ancient Egyptian Scarabs*, nos. 698 and 707, where three full lines on the base are given over to the name, title, and epithets of the deceased, and Hodjash, *Ancient Egyptian Scarabs*, nos. 717 and 722, where about half of the text on the base consists of the owner's name and epithets.

25 In numerous examples, the space where the name would have been inserted has been left blank. See examples in Hodjash, *Ancient Egyptian Scarabs*, nos. 695, 696, and 715 (with "Osiris" before the blank space), 719, 721, 731, 732, 740, 741; Teeter, *Scarabs, Seals, and Seal Impressions*, 126–27, no. 202; BM EA 29626 (space in second line) in Taylor, *Journey through the Afterlife*, 44–45. For another example where the name is given special prominence, see Hodjash, *Ancient Egyptian Scarabs*, no. 739, where, like the Chicago scarab, it appears in the first and last lines. A few scarabs with very short texts give the name almost as much room as the spell itself. See Hodjash, *Ancient Egyptian Scarabs*, nos. 717, 722, and Teeter, *Scarabs, Seals, and Seal Impressions*, 129, no. 204.

26 Leiden AO 1a in Roehrig, *Hatshepsut*, 214 (General Djehuty); Louvre E3369 in Gombert-Meurice and Payraudeau, *Servir les dieux*, 155 (Khaemwaset). Rarely, text other than the name may appear on the back. See for example, Bruyère, *Rapport sur les fouilles*, 53, pl. 7 (Sennefer), with four lines of funerary texts; BM EA 7925 in Parkinson, *Cracking Codes*, 139 (Iuy), with four lines of funerary texts; Hodjash, *Ancient Egyptian Scarabs*, nos. 712(?), 722; Schneider, *Life and Death under the Pharaohs*, 144, no. 211 (Leiden L.II.), scarab of Seb, where the continuation of BD 30B is written on the wing case.

27 See Hodjash, *Ancient Egyptian Scarabs*, no. 739, for another example where the name is given twice on the base.
28 Mosher, *Book of the Dead* 2, 428–31.
29 Lüscher, *Mund- und Herzsprüche*; Mosher, *Book of the Dead* 2, 415.
30 For example, BD 125c (S6–7).
31 Assmann, *Sonnenhymnen*, 192 (150.19).
32 Allen, *The Book of the Dead*, 110 (T9).
33 As Mosher, *Book of the Dead* 2, 415, writes, "[T]he texts on scarabs and other media could have been produced in different workshops [from the papyri], possibly with different versions of the text."
34 Although it has been suggested that this title also was used for workers in Saqqara who were "seconded" from the Theban area, this is now doubtful. See Davies, *Life within the Five Walls*, 196, with references.
35 Malaise, *Scarabées de coeur*, 49.
36 Petrie, *Scarabs and Cylinders*, pl. 47, nos. 13, 15, 16.
37 Other examples with this feature remain without date, or are assigned vaguely to the "New Kingdom." In many cases, dates are not even ventured. See, for example, Hodjash, *Ancient Egyptian Scarabs*, nos. 712, 722, 725, where none of the heart scarabs are assigned a date.
38 Davies, *Who's Who at Deir el-Medina*, 8–9, 224.
39 Davies, *Who's Who at Deir el-Medina*, 222, charts 14, 24.
40 Davies, *Who's Who at Deir el-Medina*, 222nn255–56.
41 Davies, *Who's Who at Deir el-Medina*, 237, chart 21.
42 Davies, *Who's Who at Deir el-Medina*, 237n448.

Bibliography

Alexander, Karen. "From Plaster to Stone: Ancient Art at the Art Institute of Chicago." In *Recasting the Past: Collecting and Presenting Antiquities at the Art Institute of Chicago*, edited by Karen Alexander, 15–39. Chicago: Art Institute of Chicago, 2012.

Allen, T. George. *The Book of the Dead or Going Forth by Day: Ideas of the Ancient Egyptians Concerning the Hereafter as Expressed in Their Own Terms*. SAOC 37. Chicago: Oriental Institute Press, 1974.

———. *A Handbook of the Egyptian Collection*. Chicago: University of Chicago Press, 1923.

Arico, Ashley, and Emily Teeter. "Collecting Ancient Egypt in Chicago." *Kmt* 29, no. 4 (2018–19): 63–73.

Assmann, Jan. *Sonnenhymnen in Thebanischen Gräber: Theben I*. Mainz: Philipp von Zabern, 1983.

Brunner-Traut, Emma, and Hellmut Brunner. *Die Ägyptische Sammlung der Universität Tübingen*. Mainz: Philipp von Zabern, 1981.

Bruyère, Bernard. *Rapport sur les fouilles de Deir el Médineh (1928)*. FIFAO 6/2. Cairo: IFAO, 1929.

Davies, Benedict. *Life within the Five Walls: A Handbook to Deir el-Medina*. Wallasey, UK: Abercromby Press, 2018.

———. *Who's Who at Deir el-Medina: A Prosopographic Study of the Royal Workmen's Community*. Egyptologische Uitgaven 13. Leiden: NINO, 1999.

Gardiner, Alan. *Egyptian Grammar*. 3rd ed. Oxford: Griffith Institute, 1957.

Gombert-Meurice, Florence, and Frédéric Payraudeau. *Servir les dieux d'Égypte: Divines adoratices, chanteuses, et prêtres d'Amon à Thèbes*. Paris: Somogy éditions d'Art, 2018.

Hagen, Fredrick, and Kim Ryholt. *The Antiquities Trade in Egypt 1880–1930: The H.O. Lange Papers*. Scientia Danica. Series H, Humanistica 4, vol. 8. Copenhagen: Det Kongelige Danske Videnskabernes Selskab, 2016.

Hilliard, Celia. *The Prime Mover: Charles L. Hutchinson and the Making of the Art Institute of Chicago*. Museum Studies 36, 1. Chicago: Art Institute of Chicago, 2010.

Hodjash, Svetlana. *Ancient Egyptian Scarabs: A Catalog of Seals and Scarabs from Museums in Russia, Ukraine, the Caucasus and the Baltic States*. Moscow: Vostochnaya Literatura, 1999.

Hutchinson, Charles L., James H. Dole, Albert A. Sprague, et al. "Report of the Trustees." In *The Art Institute of Chicago, Annual Report of the Trustees, June, 1894*, 9–19. Chicago: Art Institute of Chicago, 1894.

Ismail, Matthew. *Wallis Budge: Magic and Mummies in London and Cairo*. Kilkerran: Hardinge Simpole, 2011.

Lüscher, Barbara. *Die Mund- und Herzsprüche (Tb 21–30)*. TbT 9. Basel: Orientverlag, 2016.

Mace, Arthur. "The Murch Collection of Egyptian Antiquities." *BMMA* 6 (January 1911): 1–28.

Malaise, Michel. *Les scarabées de coeur dans l'Égypte ancienne*. MRE 4. Brussels: Fondation Égyptologique Reine Élisabeth, 1978.

Möller, Georg. *Hieratische Paläographie*. Vol. 2, *Von der Zeit Thutmosis III. bis zum Ende der einundzwanzigsten Dynastie*. Leipzig: Hinrichs, 1909.

Mosher, Malcolm. *The Book of the Dead, Saite through Ptolemaic Periods: A Study of Traditions Evident in Versions of Texts and Vignettes 2 (BD Spells 16, 18–30)*. SPBD Studies 2. Prescott, AZ: SPBD Studies, 2016.

Parkinson, Richard. *Cracking Codes: The Rosetta Stone and Decipherment*. Berkeley: University of California Press, 1999.

Petrie, W.M. Flinders. *Scarabs and Cylinders with Names*. London: British School of Archaeology, 1917.

Pier, Garrett Chatfield. "Historical Scarab Seals from the Art Institute Collection, Chicago." *American Journal of Semitic Languages and Literatures* 23, no. 1 (October 1906): 75–94.

Roehrig, Catherine, ed. *Hatshepsut: From Queen to Pharaoh*. New York: Metropolitan Museum of Art; New Haven, CT: Yale University Press, 2005.

Scalf, Foy, ed. *The Book of the Dead: Becoming God in Ancient Egypt*. Oriental Institute Museum Publications 39. Chicago: Oriental Institute, 2017.

Schneider, Hans, ed. *Life and Death under the Pharaohs: Egyptian Art from the National Museum of Antiquities in Leiden, the Netherlands*. Perth: Western Australian Museum, 1996.

Taylor, John, ed. *Journey through the Afterlife: Ancient Egyptian Book of the Dead*. Cambridge, MA: Harvard University Press, 2010.

Teeter, Emily. *History of the Egyptian Collection of the Art Institute, Chicago*. Forthcoming.

———. "A 'New' Stela of the Vizier To (OIM E14655)." Festschrift edited by Friedhelm Hoffmann, Gabi Pieke, et al. Ägypten und Altes Testament 97, in press, 2021.

———. *Scarabs, Seals, and Seal Impressions from Medinet Habu*. OIP 118. Chicago: Oriental Institute, 2003.

Tinius, Iris. *Altägypten in Braunschweig: Die Sammlungen des Herzog Anton Ulrich-Museums und des Städtischen Museums*. Wiesbaden: Harrassowitz, 2011.

11 The *Ba*-bringer and Other Fun(erary) Texts: pBrooklyn Museum 37.1783E

Yekaterina Barbash

I know Ed Bleiberg as a man of great integrity, compassion, curiosity, and an open mind. He always encourages these qualities in his colleagues, and inspires us to do Egyptology, to think deeply, and to not shy away from difficult topics. The wondrous papyrus presented here could not have been edited without an open mind or with a fear of difficulties, and I thank Ed for his encouragement in all such endeavors. I cannot imagine a better supervisor, colleague, and friend than Ed.

Description

Originally listed in museum records as a Book of the Dead (BD) papyrus, pBrooklyn 37.1783E consists of eleven texts, most of which occur more than once. Some texts, namely the Invocation to the *Ba*-bringer, BD 30B, the Ptah-Sokar-Osiris hymn, and the offering formulae, are well attested in other sources. The other texts, addressing mortuary themes and utilizing phrases familiar from funerary and Osirian rituals, are strikingly rare, with scarce parallels on sarcophagi and other funerary equipment. Burkhard Backes recently published the only other three manuscripts that have a selection of texts similar to those found in pBrooklyn.[1]

The owner of pBrooklyn is Takhabes, who has no titles in this text. The name of her father, Sereshu, appears to be of an elusive foreign origin.[2] Her mother, Lady of the House, Isisakhbit, has a typical Egyptian name.[3]

There are two large monochromatic outline vignettes placed between the text columns. One depicts the deceased praising Horakhty, Isis, Nephthys, and Hor-sa-wsir. The other shows Takhabes before Osiris, Isis, Hor-sa-wsir, and Nephthys. A smaller, largely broken vignette, placed above some of the text columns, comprises a series of mummiform crouching gods. The empty spaces above other text columns suggest that the decoration was not finished. The vignettes differ in style and content from those in the parallel manuscripts.[4]

pBrooklyn is composed of three large fragments attached to a modern paper backing.[5] Together the fragments measure about 3 m in length and slightly less than 20.3 cm in height.[6] The manuscript is inscribed in black and red ink in vertical columns of cursive hieroglyphs, delineated by a single line. Despite a deceptively careful handwriting, many words are written "unetymologically,"[7] with highly unusual and problematic orthography, which was rightfully described as corrupt and at times untranslatable. Our scribe had a preference for phonetic spelling and commonly omitted determinatives. For example, 𓅱𓊃𓂋 stands for *wsr*, "power;" and 𓈎 for *qrr*, "cavern." Such "unetymological" writing is a feature of Demotic that was in popular use during the time when pBrooklyn was compiled. The predilection for alphabetic spelling in the Late and Ptolemaic Periods may be explained as archaism, based on the monoconsonantal signs and suppressed determinatives in some Old Kingdom texts.[8] Other explanations highlight an intentional move away from etymological Egyptian and toward phonetic hieroglyphs in the Late Period.[9]

A selection of orthographic peculiarities follows.

The texts contain numerous omissions of phonemes and suffix pronouns as well as superfluous *w*'s, *n*'s, and *t*'s.[10] The consonants *t*, *d*, and *ḏ* are often interchangeable, as are *s* and *z*.

𓉺 "O!"

𓏇 stands for *mi*, "like," on two occasions, but is spelled normally as 𓏇𓇋 in others.[11]

𓉱𓉐, 𓉐𓏺, and 𓉱𓉐 all spell *ḥr.t-nṯr*, "necropolis."

𓐠 with occasional phonetic complements, is consistently used for *sṯ3*, "to extend."

𓎡𓂋𓐠 *ḳrs*, "burial."

𓈋 stands for *ḏw*, "mountain."

𓇾 stands for *t3*, "land."

The content, paleography, orthography, and names of the owner of pBrooklyn and her parents all point to a Late Period Greco-Roman date.[12] The peculiarities of our manuscript closely parallel the three abovementioned papyri.[13]

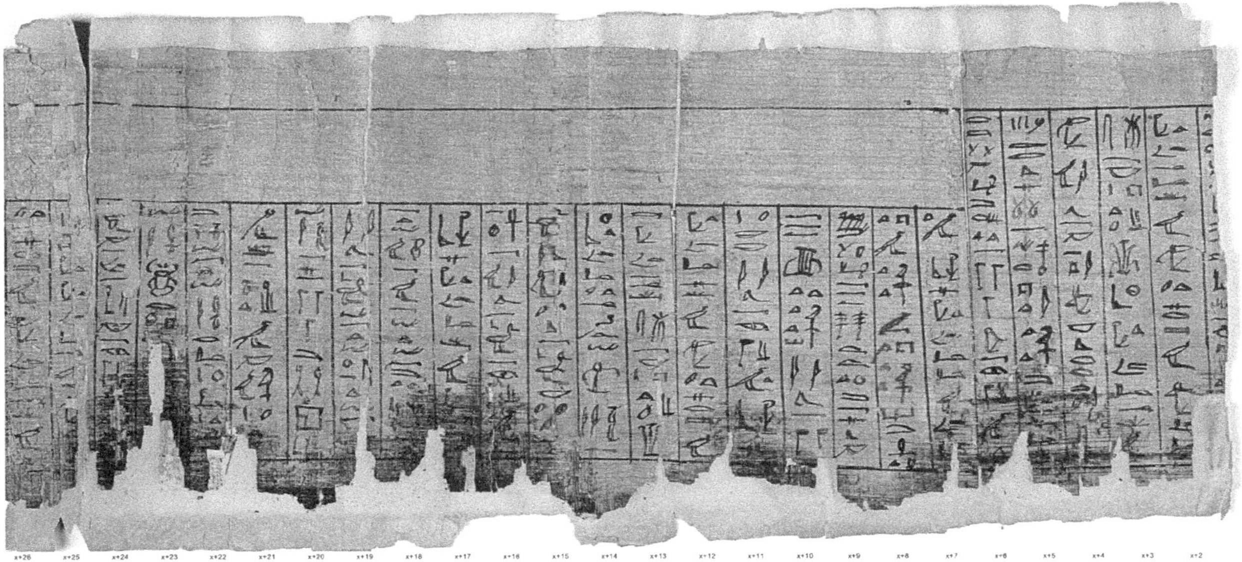

Fig. 11.1a. pBrooklyn 37.1783E, fragment 1. Image courtesy of the Brooklyn Museum; edited by Elena Sakevich.

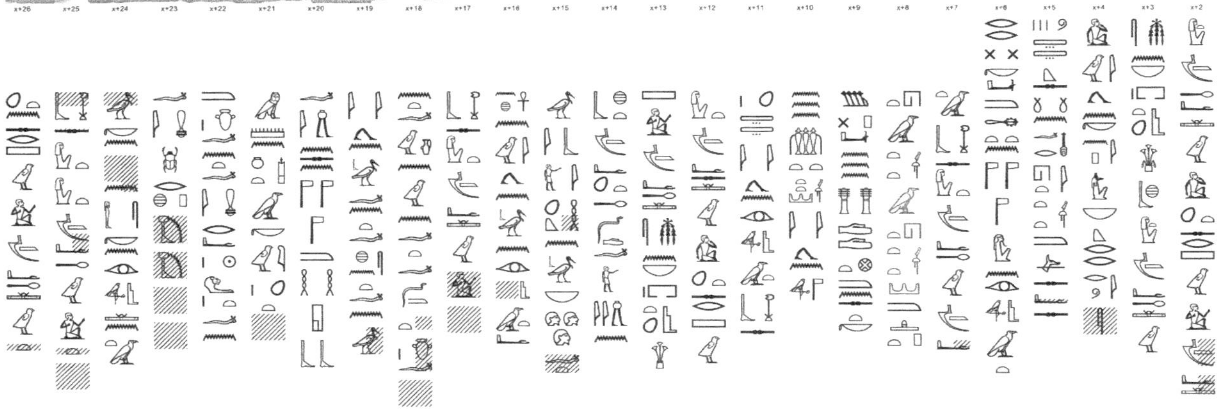

Fig. 11.2a. Hieroglyphic transcription of pBrooklyn 37.1783, fragment 1.

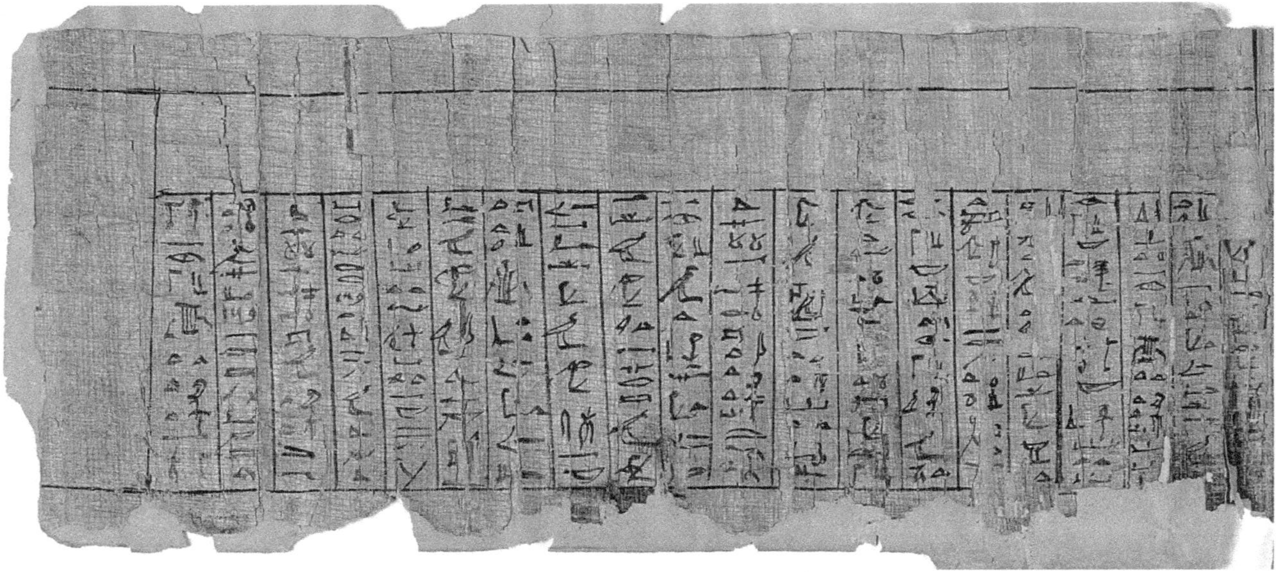

Fig. 11.1b. pBrooklyn 37.1783E, fragment 1, continued. Image courtesy of the Brooklyn Museum; edited by Elena Sakevich.

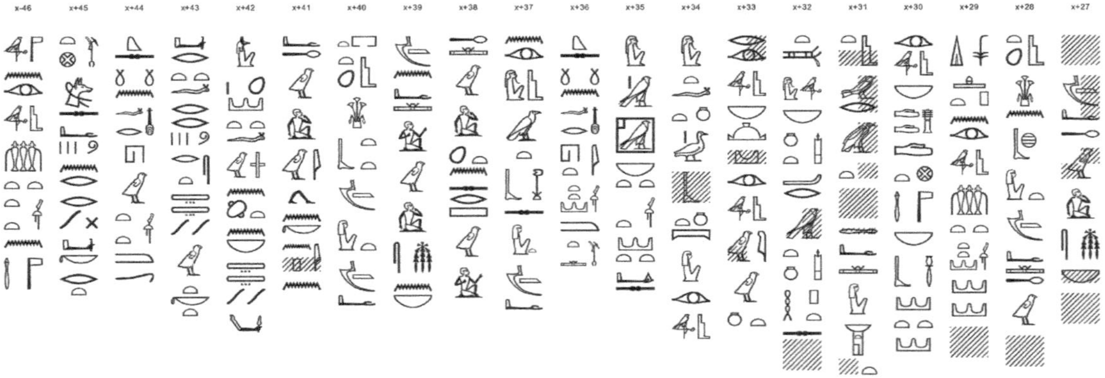

Fig. 11.2b. Hieroglyphic transcription of pBrooklyn 37.1783, fragment 1, continued.

Fig. 11.3. pBrooklyn 37.1783E, fragment 2. Image courtesy of the Brooklyn Museum; edited by Elena Sakevich.

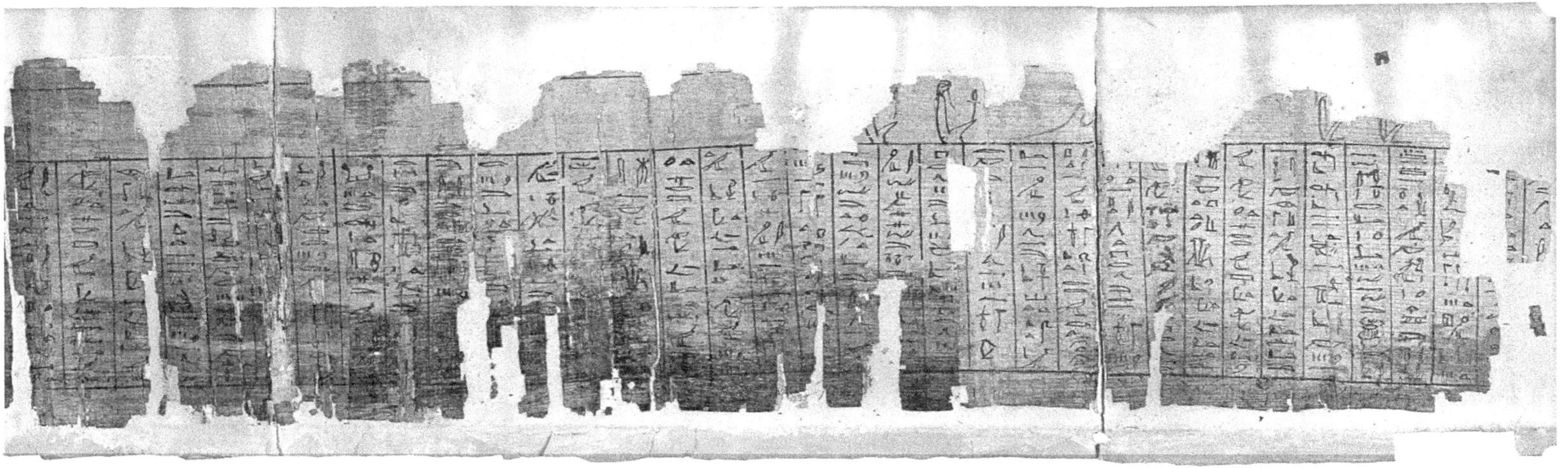

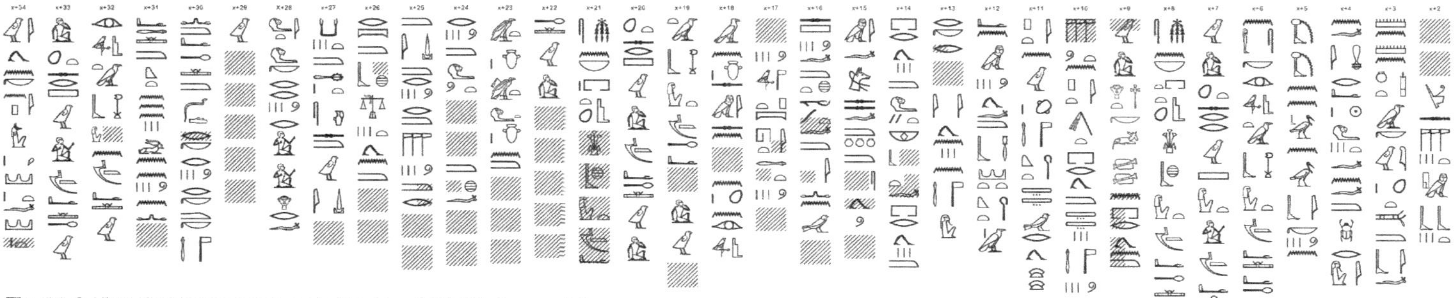

Fig. 11.4. Hieroglyphic transcription of pBrooklyn 37.1783, fragment 2.

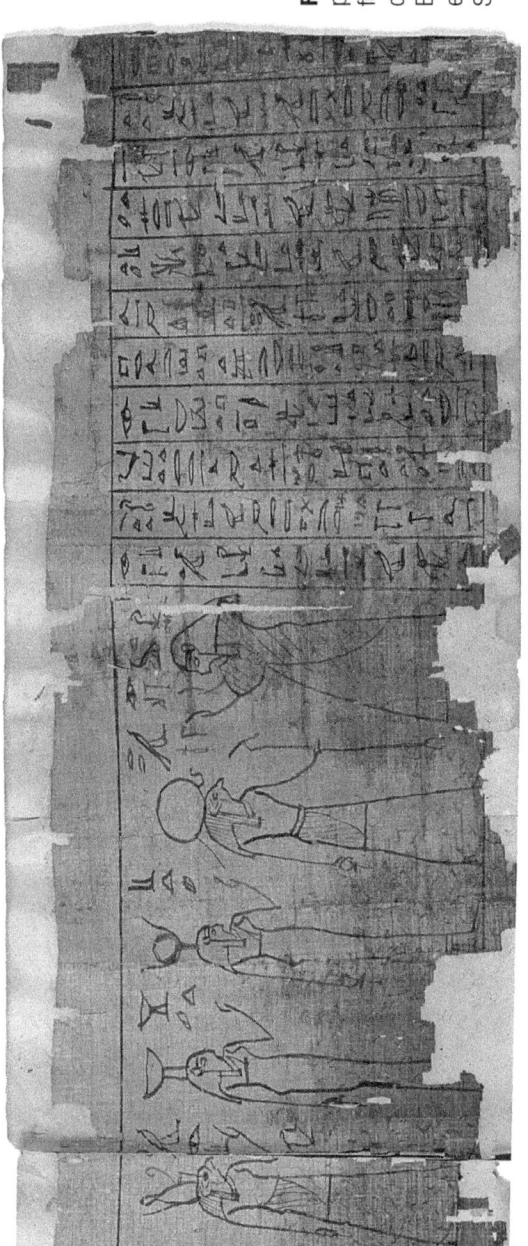

Fig. 11.5a. pBrooklyn 37.1783E, fragment 3. Image courtesy of the Brooklyn Museum; edited by Elena Sakevich.

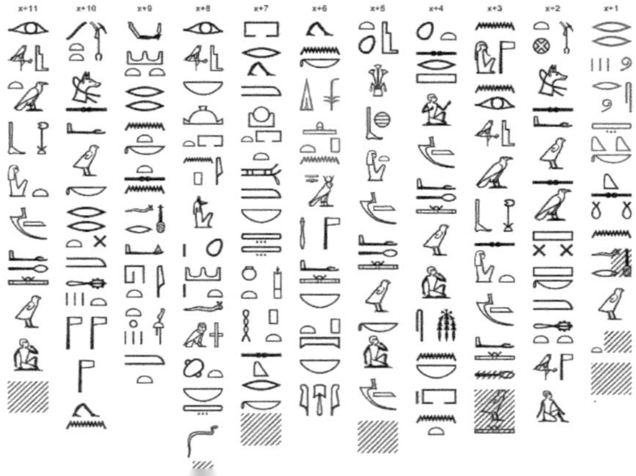

Fig. 11.6a. Hieroglyphic transcription of pBrooklyn 37.1783, fragment 3.

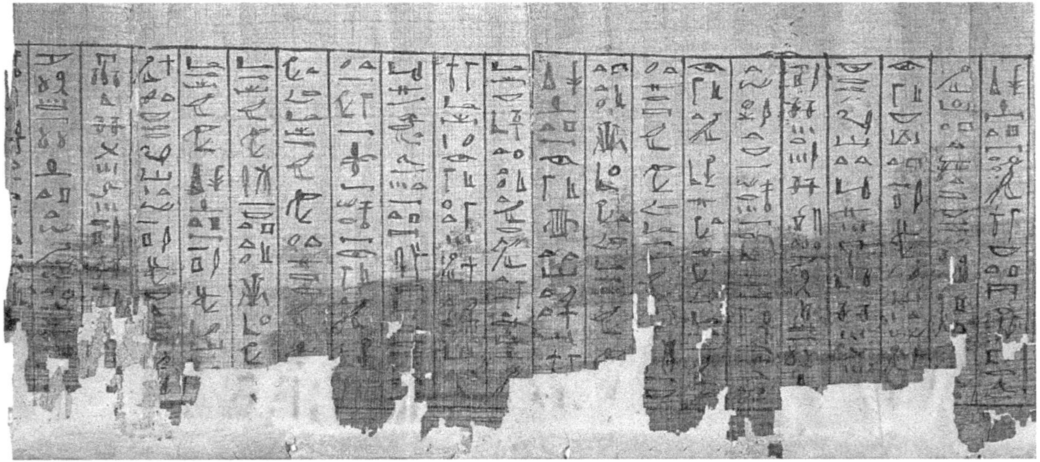

Fig. 11.5b. pBrooklyn 37.1783E, fragment 3, continued. Image courtesy of the Brooklyn Museum; edited by Elena Sakevich.

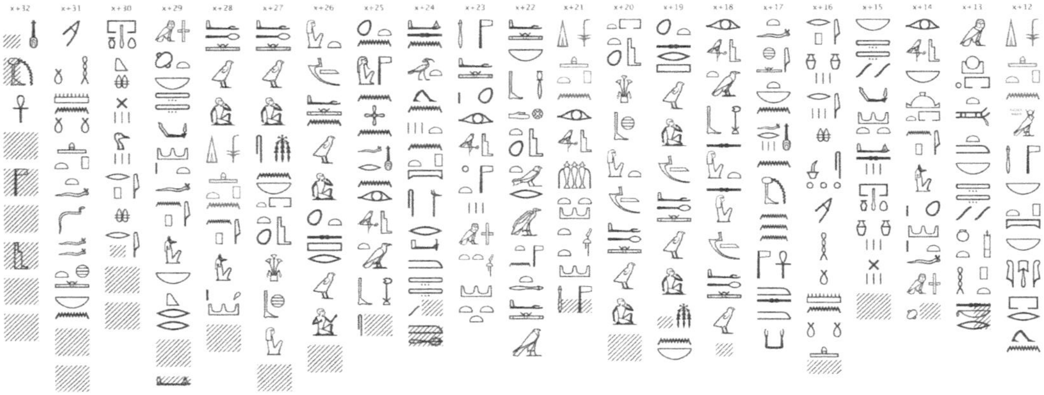

Fig. 11.6b. Hieroglyphic transcription of pBrooklyn 37.1783, fragment 3, continued.

Translation
Fragment 1 (figs. 11.1a–b, 11.2 a–b)

. . . ⁽ˣ⁺²⁾(Takhabes), justified, daughter of Sereshu, justified, ⁽ˣ⁺³⁾born of the Lady of the House Isisakhbit, justified.

Arrival of Anubis
⁽ˣ⁺⁴⁾Anubis, lord of caverns,[14] comes to you to make (you) powerful ⁽ˣ⁺⁵⁾(on) earth[15] and a good burial.

Invocation to the West-B
O, West in (Thebes),[16] her arm(s) stretch ⁽ˣ⁺⁶⁾toward you in the necropolis for Osiris Ta-(!)⁽ˣ⁺⁷⁾-Takhabes, justified.

Invocation to the West-A
⁽ˣ⁺⁸⁾O, West, **O West**,[17] welcome! ⁽ˣ⁺⁹⁾May (you) be received as the One of Busiris.[18] May she moor you ⁽ˣ⁺¹⁰⁾like Khenti-Amentiu.

Arrival of the Deceased as God
The god has come, ⁽ˣ⁺¹¹⁾protector of the lands.[19] Here comes Osiris Takhabes, ⁽ˣ⁺¹²⁾justified, daughter of Sereshu, ⁽ˣ⁺¹³⁾justified; born of the Lady of the House, Isisakhbit, justified.

Invocation to the Ba-*bringer*
⁽ˣ⁺¹⁴⁾He[20] says, O, Bringer of ⁽ˣ⁺¹⁵⁾*Ba*(s), O one who cuts off *Ba*(s),[21] lords[22] who are above ⁽ˣ⁺¹⁶⁾the living. Come (and br)ing the *Ba* of Osiris Ta- ⁽ˣ⁺¹⁷⁾khabes, justified, ⁽ˣ⁺¹⁸⁾to his(!) body[23] that it may unite (with) it(!), that he may rejoice, ⁽ˣ⁺¹⁹⁾that his *Ba* may come to his body, that his body may embrace his *[B]a*.[24] ⁽ˣ⁺²⁰⁾May the gods in the Benben temple ⁽ˣ⁺²¹⁾that stands (in) Heliopolis, bring them[25] (at) your moment,[26] Shu, son of At⁽ˣ⁺²²⁾um. His heart is his like Re. His heart is (his) ⁽ˣ⁺²³⁾like Khepri. Pu[rity, purity] … … ⁽ˣ⁺²⁴⁾(for) [yo]ur *Ba*, for (your) [shadow?] for your mummy, for Osiris of Takhabes, ⁽ˣ⁺²⁵⁾Osiris Takhabes, justified, ⁽ˣ⁺²⁶⁾daughter of Sereshu, justified-⁽ˣ⁺²⁷⁾justified(!), born of the Lady (of the House), ⁽ˣ⁺²⁸⁾Isisakhbit, justified.

Offering Formula to Osiris-Khenti-Amentiu
⁽ˣ⁺²⁹⁾Offering which the king gives to Osiris, Khenti-Amentiu; ⁽ˣ⁺³⁰⁾Osiris, lord of Busiris, great god, lord of Abydos; ⁽ˣ⁺³¹⁾Isis, the great, excellent . . . mother; Nephthys; ⁽ˣ⁺³²⁾Atum, lord of Heliopolis; Horus of Heliopolis; Ptah-Sokar-⁽ˣ⁺³³⁾

Osiris, lord of the sanctuary, Osiris, Shu, ^(x+34)Tefnut, Geb, Nut, Osiris, ^(x+35) Horus, Hathor, lady of the West. May th(ey) give (to you) ^(x+36)a good burial.[27]

Invocation to the West-B
O, West in Thebes ^(x+37)to Osiris Takhabes ^(x+38)justified, daughter of Sereshu, ^(x+39)justified, born of Lady of the ^(x+40)House, Isisakhbit, justified.

Arrival of Anubis
^(x+41)Anubis, ^(x+42)upon his mountain, the embalmer, lord of the necropolis comes to you ^(x+43)that he may make you powerful (on) earth (and) ^(x+44)a good burial.

Invocation to the West-B
O, West in ^(x+45)Thebes, she stretches the arms to place(?) you (in) the necropolis ^(x+46)to Osiris, Khenti-Amentiu, great god.

Fragment 2 (figs. 11.3, 11.4)
Invocation to the Ba-*bringer*
^(x+2) . . . gods of the Benben temple ^(x+3)that stands[28] in Heliopolis . . . at your moment, Shu, son of Atum. His heart ^(x+4)is his like Re, his heart is his like Khepri. ^(x+5)Purity, purity for the *Ba*, for your *Ba*, your heart, ^(x+6)for your mummy, Osiris Takhabes, justified, ^(x+7)daughter of Sereshu, justified, ^(x+8)born of Lady of the House, Isisakhbit, justified.

Ptah-Sokar-Osiris Hymn
^(x+9)Hail to you, heir who came from ^(x+10)these gods; the flail[29] that came from the land;[30] these great gods ^(x+11)who assess; the great god, ruler of Ta-wer, who appears crowned ^(x+12)when he comes from Abydos;[31] ruler of Aker.[32] ^(x+13)The great god arrived, ^(x+14)having come from the front of the flood,[33] that came ^(x+15)from it.[34] He extends from Nut as . . . . . . [35] ^(x+16)His fol(low)ers are behind him as the u(nwea)rying (stars). ^(x+17)sky . . . greatly rejoicing . . . [36] ^(x+18)about it(!) . . . to protect Osiris ^(x+19)Takhabes, justified, ^(x+20)daughter of Sereshu, justified, ^(x+21)born of Lady of the House Isisakhbit, justified . . .

Heart Spell
. . . . . . ^(x+23)(my) mother, heart of (my) mother, (my for)ms ^(x+24)in front . . . Do not oppose . . . ^(x+25)in court. Do not act against (me) be(fore) the gods. Do not . . . . . . ^(x+26)the balance-keeper . . . . . . ^(x+27)(my) Ka in (my) body, Khnum who makes whole . . . ^(x+28)O, your heart, against the people upon it(?)[37] ^(x+ 29) . . . . ^(x+30)justified(?). Do not speak or act against me before(!) the great god. ^(x+31)

Look, (you) are assessed as (you) exist . . . ³⁸ ⁽ˣ⁺³²⁾Osiris Takhabes, justified, ⁽ˣ⁺³³⁾daughter of Sereshu, justified.

Arrival of Anubis
⁽ˣ⁺³⁴⁾Anubis upon his mountain, comes to you ⁽ˣ⁺³⁵⁾to make for you a good burial.

Invocation to the West-B
O, West ⁽ˣ⁺³⁶⁾in Thebes, she stretches her arms (to) you . . . ⁽ˣ⁺³⁷⁾in the necropolis, to Osiris Takhabes.

> *A scene with the deceased praising gods identified as Osiris, Isis, Horus-son-of-Osiris, and Nephthys follows. Behind Nephthys, "Osiris Takhabes" is again inscribed.*

*Traversing the Sky*³⁹
⁽ˣ⁺³⁸⁾ **. . . your heart** of your mother [**comes? to you**] . . . ⁽ˣ⁺³⁹⁾it, upon its place⁴⁰ in the belly, like those who come to ⁽ˣ⁺⁴⁰⁾the mooring post(?) . . . so that you may traverse the sky in peace and see⁴¹ Re ⁽ˣ⁺⁴¹⁾Re(!) in the horizon, as Re goes forth forever and ever for Osiris ⁽ˣ⁺⁴²⁾Takhabes, justified, ⁽ˣ⁺⁴³⁾(daugh)ter of Sereshu, justified; born of the Lady of the ⁽ˣ⁺⁴⁴⁾House, Isisakhbit, justified.⁴²

Invocation to the West-A
⁽ˣ⁺⁴⁵⁾O West, O west . . . ⁽ˣ⁺⁴⁶⁾May you be received as the Djed-pillar. May she moor you like (Khenty)-Amentiu. ⁽ˣ⁺⁴⁷⁾Here comes⁴³ Osiris Takhabes ⁽ˣ⁺⁴⁸⁾Takhabes, justified, daughter of Sereshu, ⁽ˣ⁺⁵³⁾justified, born of the Lady of the House, (Isis)akhbit . . .

Arrival of Anubis
⁽ˣ⁺⁵⁴⁾Here comes to you Anubis, upon his mountain, . . . lord of caverns, ⁽ˣ⁺⁴⁹⁾the embalmer, lord of the necropolis; Anubis, lord of caverns; ⁽ˣ⁺⁵⁰⁾Anubis, lord of the White Land;⁴⁴ Anubis, ⁽ˣ⁺⁵¹⁾lord of the sanctuary; Anubis, foremost of the god's booth; ⁽ˣ⁺⁵²⁾Anubis, lord of burials, powerful one⁴⁵ ⁽³, ˣ⁺¹⁾to make you powerful (on) earth and a good burial.

Fragment 3 (figs. 11.5a–b, 11.6a–b)
Invocation to the West-B
O [West in] ⁽ˣ⁺²⁾Thebes, she stretches her arms (to) conceal you in the necropolis, ⁽ˣ⁺³⁾Osiris Takhabes, justified, ⁽ˣ⁺⁴⁾daughter of Sereshu, justified, born of Lady of the House, ⁽ˣ⁺⁵⁾Isisakhbit, justified of your voice, true . . . ⁽ˣ⁺⁶⁾You have come.

Offering Formula to Re-Horakhty
Offering which the king gives to Re-Horakhty, great god, lord of the sky, colorful of plumes, (x+7)who came forth from the horizon; Atum, lord of the two lands, Heliopolitan; Ptah-Sokar-(x+8)-Osiris, lord of the sanctuary; Anubis, upon his mountain, the embalmer, lord of the necropolis, (x+9)making for you a good burial.[46]

Invocation to the West-B
O, West in (x+10)Thebes, she stretches your(!) arm to (you) in the necropolis. Here comes (x+11)Osiris Takhabes, justified.

A scene with Takhabes praising gods identified as (Re)-Horakhty, the great god; Isis; Nephthys; and Horus-son-of-Osiris, follows.

Offering Formula to Re-Horakhty
(x+12)Offering which the king gives to Re-Horakhty, great god, lord of the sky, colorful of plumes, who came forth (x+13)from the horizon; Atum, lord of the two lands, the Heliopolitan; Ptah-(Sokar)-(x+14)Osiris, lord of the sanctuary; Anubis, upon his mountain, the [embalmer], (x+15)lord of the necropolis. May they give voice offerings, bread, beer . . . (x+16)wine, milk, incense, oil, linen, alabaster, offerings, provis(ions), (x+17)all good and pure things on which a god lives for the Ka of (x+18)Osiris Takhabes, justified, (x+19)daughter of Sereshu, justified, born of Lady of the (x+20)House, Isisakhbit, justified.

Offering Formula to Osiris-Khenti-Amentiu
(x+21)Offering which the king gives to Osiris, Khenti-Amentiu, great god, (x+22)lord of Abydos; Isis, the great, excellent divine mother; Horus, (x+23)great god, son of Osiris; the Ennead which is in the West.[47] (x+24)May they cause effectiveness in the sky, power on earth and in the necropolis,[48] (x+25)and a good existence for Osiris Takhabes, (x+26)justified, daughter of Sereshu, (x+27)justified, born of the Lady of the House, Isisakhbit, (x+28)justified.

Offering Formula to Anubis[49]
Offerings which the king gives to Anubis, upon his mountain, (x+29)the embalmer, lord of his necropolis. Anubis, lord of caverns. [May he give] (x+30)voice offerings, beer, fowl, wine, milk . . . (x+31)oil, linen. May he offer provisions of every good [and pure] thing (x+32)on which a god lives . . .

Discussion

Rather than providing a detailed commentary on specifics of the texts,[50] the purpose of this chapter is to introduce pBrooklyn 37.1783E and to highlight its role in the continuity and revival of Egyptian religious traditions. This manuscript comprises several peculiar texts, a number of which are repeated up to six times. Some of these texts closely follow conventional patterns of mortuary literature, some deviate in adventurous ways, while others convey traditional concepts in unconventional forms. As a whole, the compilation represents the beliefs and practices of its time[51] and, I believe, serves as evidence for a thoughtful and intentional revision of the rituals. The selection of texts is uncommon even for the time period, when a wide variety of mortuary texts were used. Nevertheless, each text belongs to a longstanding tradition.

Because the three parallel papyri include several texts and vignettes typical to BD, Backes sees them as part of the corpus of late mortuary texts that incorporated BD with new texts appended at the end.[52] As he points out, the selection of texts exhibits a strong connection with equipment that would ideally be included in a burial. I would like to expand on the notion that these papyri record texts that were otherwise omitted due to reduced space in the cramped and reused group interments typical of later periods.[53] I argue that these manuscripts were intended to perform the function of burial equipment and tomb decoration that could not be physically provided.[54] Akin to the abbreviation of tombs and offerings to coffin decoration, or to mere symbols of offerings,[55] the texts of pBrooklyn are a concentrated version of everything the deceased might have needed in his or her transition to the hereafter. Together, the texts appear to correspond to the standard burial set of the Late Period and early Ptolemaic Period, when "well-provisioned" tombs included an anthropoid coffin; stela; with funerary offerings;[56] and a Ptah-Sokar-Osiris figure.[57]

Accordingly, pChester Beatty IV paints writing as the only true lasting and functional memory for the dead: "Better is a book than a graven stela, than a solid [tomb-enclosure]. They (= books) act as chapels and tombs in the heart of him who speaks their name."[58]

The first complete text of pBrooklyn is the *Arrival of Anubis*. From the time of the Old Kingdom, Anubis was responsible for providing a "good burial" in tomb inscriptions and offering formulae.[59] However, the significance of the "good burial," emphasized throughout the manuscript, seems particularly meaningful for a period when fewer people had individual graves and mortuary equipment.[60] The text occurs at least four times in our manuscript,[61] likely in connection with the four Anubises known from the seventh hour of the night in *Stundenwachen*, and from Glorifications I: "O, these four Anubises before the Temple of Osiris."[62]

The *Invocation to the West-B* (= *Invocation to the West in Thebes*) follows the *Arrival of Anubis* in every occurrence of the latter and twice more in other contexts.[63] Inscriptions on the legs of Ptolemaic cartonnages frequently relate these two texts.[64] Thus, Louvre N. 2627 reads, "Anubis, the embalmer, foremost of the god's booth, comes to you that he may give you a burial in the west of Thebes."[65] The "west in/of Thebes"[66] refers to the Goddess of the West, who personifies the necropolis from the Old Kingdom onward.[67] In almost every instance of the text in pBrooklyn, she extends her arms to receive and welcome the deceased.[68] On one occasion, the goddess extends her arms to conceal *(št3)* the deceased as an act of protection.[69] Another example in pBrooklyn names Osiris Khenti-Amentiu, rather than Takhabes, perhaps pointing to the invocation's role in Osirian temple rituals. The *Invocation to the West-A* continues the same themes.[70] Together, the invocations to the west and *Arrival of Anubis* serve as the decoration on cartonnage legs; they assure divine acceptance of the deceased and protection of their place of burial. Already in the Third Intermediate Period, the coffin functioned as "the tomb and temple," creating a safe transition and sustaining and protecting the deceased.[71] The next step in reducing expensive burial equipment was the incorporation of texts that typically adorned contemporary elite containers for bodies into more affordable papyri.

The *Arrival of the Deceased as God* similarly belongs to a long tradition of mortuary rituals. Equating the deceased king with god and announcing his arrival occurs in PT 422: "The god comes, the god comes, N comes to the throne of Osiris."[72] The statements eventually evolve into a part of Glorifications II.[73]

The *Invocation to the* Ba-*bringer* is familiar to Egyptology. Because it was appended to some late BD, Allen identified it as BD 191.[74] However, several scholars have since demonstrated that the text, more commonly attested on sarcophagi and stelae, does not belong to the BD corpus.[75] Titled "Spell for Bringing the *Ba* to the Body" in some sources, it was intended to reunite the body and *Ba* for a successful existence in the afterlife.[76] This text was sometimes placed on the breast and belly of late anthropoid coffins—presumably the location where the *Ba* (re)unites with the body—and in conjunction with representations of the human-headed bird with outstretched wings.[77] Thus, the text functioned to ensure the return of the *Ba* and simultaneously represented the breast portion of the cartonnage decoration.

The *Heart Spell*, recorded once on pBrooklyn, is first attested on heart scarabs dating to the late Middle Kingdom.[78] Because the main objective of this text was securing a successful Osirian judgment, in the New Kingdom it was associated with judgment scenes.[79] In late BD this spell was typically combined with 30A, resulting in BD 30.[80] The survival of the isolated BD 30B in late compilations is remarkable. Although Passalacqua does not explicitly discuss the contents (or location) of the Theban tomb where he found the parallel papyri, the presence of the *Heart Spell* on our papyrus may have functioned in place of a heart scarab and its inscription.

The *Ptah-Sokar-Osiris Hymn* is known almost exclusively from Type IV (late Ptolemaic) Ptah-Sokar-Osiris statues, where corrupt language and "a predilection for Ptolemaic signs" are also common.[81] The slightly altered hymn in our manuscript was certainly intended to perform the same function as the Ptah-Sokar-Osiris figure. The appearance of offering formulae addressed to gods of the solar and Osirian cycles on Ptah-Sokar-Osiris figures[82] further connects pBrooklyn with them. There are three offering formulae in pBrooklyn.[83] The formula addressed to Osiris-Khenti-Amentiu lists an unprecedented pantheon, while the parallel papyri include at most three gods.[84] The first version of the offering formula to Re-Horakhty veers off course quite quickly, ending with the wish for a good burial rather than the expected list of offerings. Its second version is considerably more elaborate and standard. Lastly, the *Offering to Anubis* is not paralleled in the papyri published by Backes although, already in the Fourth Dynasty, Anubis is a prevalent addressee of offering formulae.[85] Known from stelae, coffins, and tomb walls from the Old Kingdom onward, offering formulae provide crucial sustenance for the spirit. Subsequently, the offering formula not only listed provisions for the deceased Takhabes, but also allowed the enumerated deities to be included in her burial despite the presumable lack of her own space/tomb/sarcophagus.[86] These offering texts functioned much like the stelae placed in burials.

A hitherto unknown text, *Traversing the Sky*, compiles concepts and phrases familiar from a number of sources. For instance, the clause "your heart of your mother," commonly known from BD 30, appears already in the Coffin Texts: "Your heart from your mother is given to you."[87] Replacing the heart to "its place in the belly" hearkens to embalming procedures and is known from PT 595: "I bring to you your heart and place it in your belly for you."[88] Finally, the wish to traverse the sky and see Re is common in offering formulae and throughout the BD.[89]

In sum, the texts discussed above belong to ancient funerary traditions, some of which were copied verbatim while others underwent numerous editions and iterations. Each text was chosen to perform a specific function in Takhabes' afterlife: Anubis' protection of her mummy and burial, admission into the necropolis and protection by the Goddess of the West, acceptance into the company of the gods (in particular, Ptah-Sokar-Osiris), unification of her *Ba* and body, success in the Osirian judgment, joining Re in his journey, and receiving the necessary provisions.

While the essence of these ritual texts barely changed throughout millennia, their expression has taken new forms. Finally, the extremely complicated orthography of pBrooklyn 37.1783E and its three known parallels also belong to a continuing tradition that has been reworked and reinterpreted over millennia. While Backes reasonably concluded that the papyri he published were made in one workshop and belonged to members of the same family, the handwriting and style of vignettes of pBrooklyn suggest that it was inscribed and decorated by a different scribe and draftsman. The lack of color and simplified decoration may point to it being a "cheaper" version.[90] Clearly, this composition was not just the work of one scribe who created the *Drei Totenpapyri*. Rather than being untranslatable and corrupt,[91] the four manuscripts may point to the existence of a distinct and peculiar workshop, perhaps with a regional dialect, that gave new life to old traditions.

Notes

1. Composed for one Theban family, pBerlin P. 3158, pBerlin P. 3159, and pAberdeen ABDUA 84023 also include BD spells 79, 80, 85, 86, and 89 (Backes, *Totenpapyri*). Each of the two Berlin papyri were found between the feet of mummies in a Theban tomb, according to Passalacqua (*Catalogue raisonné et historique*, 170n1). See also Curtis, Munro, and Kockelmann, "Collection of Book of the Dead Manuscripts," and reviews by Vittmann and Bojowald.
2. A similar Egyptian name, *srwš*, and Greek names like Seras, Sirios, Sorous, and so on, are listed at www.trismegistos.org. Schneider, *Asiatische Personennamen*, 190, identifies the Ramesside-period Asiatic names *s3-rw-s3* and *s3-r-sw*.
3. For the spelling of Isisemakhbit without the *m*, see Ranke, *Personennamen*, 4.
4. The painted vignettes in parallel papyri include the Weighing of the Heart and vignettes for BD 15 and 162, among others.
5. It was originally collected by Dr. Henry Abbott.
6. Fragment 1 measures 87.6 cm.; fragment 2 joins fragment 3, together measuring 2 m, 10 cm. The height compares well to the parallels, which measure 16.5–17 cm.
7. Smith, "Bodl. MS. Egypt," 151–53, identifies "unetymological" writing as "any orthography of a word which differs in some manner from the traditional one."
8. Der Manuelian, *Living in the Past*, 389–90, presents an overview of earlier theories on Saite alphabetic writing, including Greek influence and archaism, while questioning the notion that alphabetic writing was preferred at this time.
9. Schweitzer, "Zur Herkunft," believes that late alphabetic writing was rather related to creation of new signs and word values. Engsheden, "Verge of Ptolemaic Egyptian," 39, discusses the use of bi-consonantal signs for one phoneme as a Thirtieth Dynasty innovation. Stadler, "Demise of Egyptian Writing," 167 and 172, suggests that the increasing popularity of phonetic writing was driven by the Libyan elite, citing the ideas of Leahy, "Libyan Period," and Vittmann, *Ägypten und die Fremden*, 10. Stadler also notes the desire

to reflect proper pronunciation and to add additional meaning as reasons for phonetic writing. Widmer, "Words and Writing," 135 and 142, distinguished unetymological, "nonstandard" orthography in Demotic from phonetic writing, and saw it as intentional wordplay rather than an attempt to capture a correct pronunciation.

10 Engsheden, "Verge of Ptolemaic Egyptian," 37.
11 The parallel papyri use the more common ⟨⟩.
12 Backes, *Totenpapyri*, 3–4 and 28, discusses the similarly peculiar spellings (along with vignettes and offering formulae) on Type III–IV Late Period funerary stelae; Munro, *Totenstelen*, 43–61 and 233.
13 Backes, *Totenpapyri*, 14–18 and 27–30.
14 The epithet *nb krrt* (*LGG* 3, 760–61), known from the Middle Kingdom onward, does not appear in the parallels. The very similar *nb krst*, Lord of Burials, is a more common title of Anubis (*LGG* 3, 761).
15 Backes, *Totenpapyri*, 48, interprets *wsr t3* as *sm3-t3* and reads the entire phrase *sm3-t3*(=k) *krs.t nfr*, "um deine Bestattung und ein schönes Begräbnis auszuführen." Nevertheless, our scribe consistently uses the spelling *wsr-t3 krs.t nfr*, closely matching a construction common in offering formulae of the Middle Kingdom and later: *3ḫ m pt wsr m t3 m3ʿ-ḫrw m ḫr.t-nṯr*, "Being Akh in the sky, powerful on earth, and justified in the necropolis." See Ilin-Tomich, "Changes in the *ḥtp-di-nsw*," 25, and Barta, *Opferformel*, 59–60. The phrase should, thus, perhaps be taken at face value, merely omitting the preposition *m*. Quirke, *Going Out in Daylight*, 561, translates this clause as "to cause your two lands to become powerful with a perfect burial."
16 The phrase *m w3st* is omitted erroneously, as all parallels except for pBerlin P. 3159 include it. See Bojowald, "Review," 109, for the substitution of the preposition *m* for *n*.
17 Text in bold indicates that the text in the original papyrus was written in red ink, rather than black.
18 Backes, *Totenpapyri*, 46, and Quirke, *Going Out in Daylight*, 561, translate the word as "*Djed*-pillar" due to the lack of ⊗ in the parallels, although *ḏd.t* is a well-attested epithet of Osiris (*LGG* 7, 677–83).
19 Quirke, *Going Out in Daylight*, 561, translates *s3-t3* as "son of the earth."
20 The pronoun likely refers to the deceased mentioned in the preceding text. Some parallels begin with *ḏd mdw in wsir NN . . . ḏd=f* (Backes, *Totenpapyri*, 40).
21 While Backes' papyri all have some version of *ḥsk b3*, other instances of this text use *ḥsk šwt*. See Assmann, *Totenliturgien 3*, 215; Allen, "Additions," 180; Schneider, "Bringing the *Ba* to the Body," 359. The *Ba*-bringer has the capacity to bring or destroy the *Ba* / shadow (Backes, *Totenpapyri*, 40; George, *Vorstellungen vom Schatten*, 1970, 92–97).
22 Most parallels agree on *nṯr.w ipw nb tpiw ʿnḫ*, with *nb* modifying "gods." However, Assmann, *Totenliturgien 3*, 213, interprets *nb* as a noun: "o ihr Götter, Herren der lebendigen Köpfe/Köpfe der Lebenden."
23 The group ⟨⟩ may be interpreted as *n=f*, "to him" (Schneider, "Bringing the *Ba* to the Body," 359f; Quirke, *Going Out in Daylight*, 558; Assmann, *Totenliturgien 3*, 213), or as *n (ḏ)t=f*, "to his body," commonly spelled without ⟨⟩ by this scribe. Cf. the parallels in Backes, *Totenpapyri*, 41.
24 The parallels differ slightly, *sḫn b3=f n ḏt=f* (*n ib=f*), allowing for the more common interpretation, "his *Ba* may rest in his body (at his heart)." See Schneider, "Bringing the *Ba* to the Body," 359–60; Backes, *Totenpapyri*, 42; *Wb* 4, 253.

25 The plural *sn* must refer to the body and heart. Most parallels incorporate a dative *n=f*, "to him."
26 Backes, *Totenpapyri*, 42, reads *3t=k* as a visual and phonetic stand-in for *gs=k*, which appears in some parallels (Schneider, "Bringing the *Ba* to the Body," 359–61). However, reading the signs at face value also results in the conceivable request that the *Ba* be provided to the deceased at the correct moment. The second-person pronoun identifies the deceased with Shu, much like in PT §1870a: "This Osiris N is Shu, Atum's son. You are the eldest and senior son of Atum" (Allen, *Pyramid Texts*, 272).
27 The parallels express an alternative wish: *di=sn 3ḫ m pt wsr m t3 m ḥr.t-nṯr wnn-nfr n wsir NN*.
28 Note the staggering difference in orthography between the phrase here and in lines 1, x+20–21.
29 The flail represents Osiris in a ritual offering at Edfu (Wilson, *Lexikon*, 538). The word is variously interpreted as *nḫḫ*, "spittle" (Raven, "Papyrus-Sheaths," 277) or "child" (Backes, *Totenpapyri*, 56). However, the presence of 𓌅 unquestionably results in "flail." Cf. Bojowald, "Review," 109, with further bibliography.
30 Cf. pBerlin P. 3159: *nḫ3ḫ3 pr m itm <nb> t3wy* . . . (Backes, *Totenpapyri*, 56; Quirke, *Going Out in Daylight*, 563).
31 Cf. the standard PSO formula, *ḥꜥ m i3dt m i3bt* (Raven, "Papyrus-Sheaths," 277).
32 The standard PSO hymn has *igrt* (Raven, "Papyrus-Sheaths," 277), while pBerlin 3159 matches pBrooklyn.
33 PSO hymn also has *ḫbbt*. Cf. pBerlin P. 3159: *nṯr-ꜥ3 pr m ḥ3.t wsḫt*.
34 Cf. *ḥk3(.n)=f pr im=f* (Raven, "Papyrus-Sheaths," 277).
35 The parallels diverge: pBerlin P. 3159, 85, reads *st3=f m ib m sꜥḥ.w* (Backes, *Totenpapyri*, 57), while the PSO hymn reads *psd=f m nwt m s3ḥ* (Raven, "Papyrus-Sheaths," 277). The Brooklyn version is an oddly logical combination of the two versions.
36 Cf. Backes' translation of pBerlin: "Lauter Jubelruf ist in ihrem Herzen darüber als der Ruf, Schutz der Erde!" Cf. Raven, "Papyrus-Sheaths," 277: "He supports the heaven which is rejoicing under her master."
37 Backes, *Totenpapyri*, 34, refers to this line in pABDUA: "Nicht mehr übersetzbar."
38 This line, omitted from pABDUA, is typical in BD versions of 30B (Quirke, *Going Out in Daylight*, 100).
39 This text is not paralleled in the papyri published by Backes.
40 Cf. the speech of Thoth in the Weighing of the Heart vignette of pLouvre 3079 and pTurin 1791: *imm n=f ib=f m st=f n wsir NN st=f*. "Its place" may designate the scales in this context, as the text within a similar vignette of the Third Intermediate Period, pBM10008, reads: *rdi.tw ib=s r mḫ3t* (Seeber, *Totengerichts*, Abb. 23, 25, 16).
41 For 𓌢 as a determinative of *m33*, see *Wb* 2, 7.
42 I am indebted to Burkhard Backes for his suggestions on the translation of this passage.
43 This phrase does not occur in any attested parallel.
44 Probably Gebelein. See Kees, "Kulttopographische und mythologische Beiträge." El Gabri, "Unpublished Stela," 176–77, reviews various locations of *t3-ḥd* and its translations.
45 The fragment with lines x+49–52 was attached in this location in modern times and thus may not belong here.

46 A typical list of offerings follows in most parallel papyri. Some, however, insert a convoluted *iri srk=k/krs=k* after Anubis' epithets (Backes, *Totenpapyri*, 50). This version of the offering formula may result from a confusion of this text with the *Arrival of Anubis*.
47 The list of gods varies: cf. line 1, x+29–36, and Backes, *Totenpapyri*, 51.
48 Wishes of power on earth and in the underworld are common in funerary texts throughout Egyptian history and normally insert $m3^c$-hrw before $hr.t$-ntr, "justification in the necropolis" (Ilin-Tomich, "Changes in the *htp-di-nsw*," 25; Barta, *Opferformel*, 59–60, 111–12).
49 This formula is not paralleled in the papyri published by Backes.
50 Backes, *Totenpapyri*, offers a brilliant and detailed commentary on the parallel texts.
51 Original texts, frequently titled *sm3-t3 nfr*, were often included with Books of Breathing (Herbin, *Books of Breathing*, 3–4; Backes, *Totenpapyri*, 102n477).
52 Backes, *Totenpapyri*, 101–104, notes that our papyri do not conform.
53 A drastic reduction of burial equipment began in the Twentieth Dynasty, while its function was transferred to texts and images on coffins or papyri (Taylor, "Changes in the Afterlife," 225–34; Cooney, "Changing Burial Practices"). Aston, "Theban West Bank," 157ff, discusses the lack of new tomb construction among Late Period Theban burials.
54 Cf. the elite Late and Ptolemaic sarcophagi (for example, GEM 2756–57) decorated with the Invocation to the *Ba*-bringer, BD 89, images of the sons of Horus, and BD 154 vignette (Leitz, Mahrous, and Tawfik, *Catalogue of Late and Ptolemaic Period Anthropoid Sarcophagi*, 15–57).
55 Assmann, *Death and Salvation*, 411; Smith, *Traversing Eternity*, 48–49. Cooney, "Changing Burial Practices," 17–36n59, points to increased preference for image decoration over text on coffins.
56 Munro, *Totenstelen*, 43–50.
57 Snape, *Tombs*, 253–54. According to Aston, "Theban West Bank," 162, typical Theban burials immediately preceding the Ptolemaic Period also include *shabti*s, amulets, a hypocephalus, and a canopic box. The function of the latter would be covered by the text regarding the sons of Horus, which does not appear among the surviving parts of pBrooklyn but does occur in the papyri published by Backes, *Totenpapyri*, 43–45.
58 Verso 3, 1; Lichtheim, *Ancient Egyptian Literature*, 2, 177.
59 Barta, *Opferformel*, 39, Bitte 4; Lichtheim, *Autobiographies*, 10, 38, and 136; and Herbin, *Books of Breathing*, 145, offer a selection of further references and examples. A similar phrase, *sm3-t3 nfr*, is common on the verso of funerary papyri (Backes, *Totenpapyri*, 50; Goyon, *Le papyrus du Louvre N. 3279*, 83–85).
60 Snape, *Tombs*, 253–58.
61 The parallels record it up to four times (Backes, *Totenpapyri*, 48–49). The initial text of the Berlin papyrus is the title "Beginning of Spells of Going Forth by Day" (Backes, *Totenpapyri*, 32).
62 The four Anubises are connected with the embalming ritual (Junker, *Stundenwachen*, 18, 119; Pries, *Stundenwachen im Osiriskult*, 313–14). For Glorifications I, 5, 43–47, see Assmann, *Totenliturgien 3*, 51 and 61.
63 This text also appears numerous times in the parallel papyri (Backes, *Totenpapyri*, 49–50).

64 For example, see Myers and Fairman, "Excavations at Armant," 225–28, pls. lv–lvi; Herbin, "Texte de glorification," 172n11. Refai, "Westgöttin," 246–50, discusses the connection of the Goddess of the West and Anubis.
65 Herbin, *Books of Breathing*, 145.
66 The examples of this text not on papyri omit *m*, suggesting a genitive sense.
67 von Falck and Martinssen-von Falck, "Neues zur Göttin," 93–94; Refai, "Westgöttin,"145.
68 The (Goddess of the) West giving her arm/hand to the deceased is known from tomb inscriptions as early as the Sixth Dynasty (Refai, *Göttin des Westens*, 25; Barta, *Opferformel*, 20; Herbin, *Books of Breathing*, 119, with further examples).
69 See von Falck and Martinssen-von Falck, "Neues zur Göttin," 95–100, for the development of this goddess' function over time.
70 For another translation, Quirke, *Going Out in Daylight*, 561.
71 Cooney, "Changing Burial Practices."
72 Most parallels repeat *iy nṯr*, akin to the original PT.
73 Assmann, *Totenliturgien 3*, 267–68.
74 Allen, "Additions." For example, Allen's 191–92 in pRyerson are followed by the Arrival of Anubis (Quirke, *Going Out in Daylight*, 560).
75 Goyon, "Véritable Attribution," 118ff and n10; Schneider, "Bringing the *Ba* to the Body," 356f. Assmann, *Totenliturgien 3*, 212–15, views this text as belonging to the embalming context and formally outside the scope of Glorifications, although he includes it in Spell 15 of Glorifications I.
76 Quirke, *Going Out in Daylight*, 558; Schneider, "Bringing the *Ba* to the Body," 357. The importance of the unification of *Ba* and body is emphasized already in CT (Assmann, *Death and Salvation*, 95–96; Žabkar, *Study of the Ba-Concept*, 106–12).
77 Allen, "Additions," 186.
78 Lüscher, *Mund- und Herzsprüche*, ix–xii ff.
79 Seeber, *Totengericht*, 10–16.
80 Verhoeven, *Iahtesnacht*, 124. Some Ptolemaic BD record this spell in a sequence with the Invocation to the *Ba*-bringer (Quirke, *Going Out in Daylight*, 97–99 and 558). Few Ptolemaic manuscripts separate this text from other BD spells (Backes, *Totenpapyri*, 32–33).
81 Raven, "Papyrus-Sheaths," 276–87, provides a synopsis of the hymns on Ptah-Sokar-Osiris statues. See also Rindi, "Tradition and Transformation," 461–62; and Budka, "Ptah-Sokar-Osiris-Statuetten," 34–35, who argue for a slightly earlier date.
82 Raven, "Papyrus-Sheaths," 275.
83 The *Ba*-bringer text and four offering formulae follow regular BD texts in the Ptolemaic pRyerson, OIM 9787, Mosher, "Catalog No. 14," 202–204.
84 Backes, *Totenpapyri*, 56–57.
85 Barta, *Opferformel*, 8.
86 Smith, *Traversing Eternity*, 48, discusses the functions of a traditional tomb, identified by Assmann, *Totenliturgien 2*, 36, as concealing the body, providing a venue for offerings, perpetuating the identity and status of the deceased, and enabling proximity to gods. Smith argues that Greco-Roman afterlife texts were mainly concerned with the latter two functions.
87 CT 1, 56c.

88 Cf. CT 1, 265e.
89 Barta, *Opferformel*, Bitte 30 and 89. Cf. BD 100 and 131.
90 I am grateful to Burkhard Backes for his very valuable comments and suggestions.
91 Mosher, "Book of the Dead Traditions," 172, describes Late Ptolemaic BD as poorly copied and frequently "unintelligible . . . indicating that the copyists had no idea what the texts meant."

Bibliography

Allen, James. *The Ancient Egyptian Pyramid Texts*. Atlanta, GA: Society of Biblical Literature, 2005.

Allen, T. George. "Additions to the Egyptian Book of the Dead." *JNES* 11 (1952): 177–86.

Assmann, Jan. *Altägyptische Totenliturgien 2: Totenliturgien und Totensprüche in Grabinschriften des Neuen Reiches*. Heidelberg: Universitätsverlag Winter, 2005.

———. *Altägyptische Totenliturgien 3: Osirisliturgien in Papyri der Spätzeit*. Heidelberg: Universitätsverlag Winter, 2008.

———. *Death and Salvation in Ancient Egypt*. Translated by David Lorton. Ithaca, NY, and London: Cornell University Press, 2005.

Aston, David. "The Theban West Bank from the Twenty-fifth Dynasty to the Ptolemaic Period." In *The Theban Necropolis: Past, Present, and Future*, edited by Nigel Strudwick and John Taylor, 138–66. London: British Museum Press, 2003.

Backes, Burkhard. *Drei Totenpapyri aus einer thebanischen Werkstatt der Spätzeit (pBerlin P. 3158, pBerlin P. 3159, pAberdeen ABDUA 84023)*. Wiesbaden: Harrassowitz, 2009.

Barta, Winfried. *Aufbau und Bedeutung der altägyptischen Opferformel*. Glückstadt: J.J. Augustin, 1968.

Bojowald, Stefan. "Review of *Drei Totenpapyri aus einer thebanischen Werkstatt der Spätzeit (pBerlin P. 3158, pBerlin P. 3159, pAberdeen ABDUA 84023)*." *JSSEA* 40 (2013–14): 107–109.

Budka, Julia. "Ptah-Sokar-Osiris-Statuetten aus Grab VII im Asasif." In *Das Alte Ägypten und seine Nachbarn: Festchrift zum 65. Geburtstag von Helmut Satzinger; mit Beitragen zur Ägyptologie, Koptologie, Nubiologie, und Afrikanistik*, edited by Monika Hasitzka, Johannes Diethart, and Günther Dembski, 32–42. Kremser wisssenschafliche Reihe 3. Krems: Österreichisches Literaturforum, 2003.

Cooney, Kathlyn M. "Changing Burial Practices at the End of the New Kingdom: Defensive Adaptations in Tomb Commissions, Coffin Commissions, Coffin Decoration, and Mummification." *JARCE* 47 (2011): 3–44.

Curtis, Neil, Irmtraut Munro, and Holger Kockelmann. "The Collection of the Book of the Dead Manuscripts in Marischal Museum, University of Aberdeen, Scotland: A Comprehensive Overview." *BIFAO* 105 (2005): 49–73.

Engsheden, Åke. "On the Verge of Ptolemaic Egyptian: Graphical Trends in the 30th Dynasty." *Abgadiyat* 1 (2006): 35–41.

El Gabri, Dina. "An Unpublished Stela in the Grand Egyptian Museum, Cairo CG 20151." In *Joyful in Thebes: Egyptological Studies in Honor of Betsy M. Bryan*, edited by Richard Jasnow and Kathlyn M. Cooney, 171–81. Atlanta: Lockwood Press, 2015.

George, Beate. *Zu den altägyptischen Vorstellungen vom Schatten als Seele*. Bonn: Habelt, 1970.

Goyon, Jean-Claude. *Le papyrus du Louvre N. 3279*. BdÉ 42. Cairo: IFAO, 1966.

———. "La véritable attribution des soi-disant chapitres 191 et 192 du Livre des morts." In *Studia aegyptiaca: Recueil d'études dédiées à Vilmos Wessetzky à l'occasion de son 65e anniversaire*, 117–27. Budapest: ELTE, 1974.

Herbin, François. *Books of Breathing and Related Texts*. London: British Museum Press, 2008.

———. "Un texte de glorification." *SAK* 32 (2004): 171–204.

Ilin-Tomich, Alexander. "Changes in the ḥtp-di-nsw Formula in the Late Middle Kingdom and the Second Intermediate Period." *ZÄS* 138 (2011): 20–34.

Junker, Hermann. *Die Stundenwachen in den Osirismysterien: nach den Inschriften von Dendera, Edfu und Philae*. Vienna: A. Hölder, 1910.

Kees, Hermann. "Kulttopographische und mythologische Beiträge." *ZÄS* 71 (1935): 150–55.

Leahy, Anthony. "The Libyan Period in Egypt: An Essay in Interpretation." *Libyan Studies* 16 (1985): 51–65.

Leitz, Christian, et al., eds. *Lexikon der ägyptischen Götter und Götterbezeichnungen (LGG)*. Dudley, MA: Peeters, 2002.

Leitz, Christian, Zeinab Mahrous, and Tarek Tawfik, eds. *Catalogue of Late and Ptolemaic Period Anthropoid Sarcophagi in the Grand Egyptian Museum*. Grand Egyptian Museum–Catalogue Général 1. Cairo: Ministry of Antiquities, 2018.

Lichtheim, Miriam. *Ancient Egyptian Autobiographies Chiefly of the Middle Kingdom: A Study and an Anthology*. Freiburg: Universitätsverlag Freiburg Schweiz, 1988.

———. *Ancient Egyptian Literature*. Vol. 2, *The New Kingdom*. Berkeley, Los Angeles, and London: University of California Press, 1976.

Lüscher, Barbara. *Die Mund- und Herzsprüche (Tb 21–30)*. Totenbuchtexte 9. Synoptische Textausgabe nach Quellen des Neuen Reiches. Basel: Orientverlag, 2016.

Manuelian, Peter Der. *Living in the Past: Studies in Archaism of the Egyptian Twenty-sixth Dynasty*. London and New York: Kegan Paul International, 1994.

Mosher, Malcolm. "Catalog No. 14." In *Book of the Dead: Becoming God in Ancient Egypt*, edited by Foy Scalf, 202–204. Chicago: Oriental Institute of the University of Chicago, 2017.

———. "Theban and Memphite Book of the Dead Traditions in the Late Period." *JARCE* 29 (1992): 143–72.

Munro, Peter. *Die spätägyptischen Totenstelen*. Glückstadt: J.J. Augustin, 1973.

Myers, Oliver, and Herbert Fairman. "Excavations at Armant, 1929–31." *JEA* 17 (1931): 223–32.

Passalacqua, Joseph. *Catalogue raisonné et historique des antiquités découvertes en Égypte*. Paris: A la Galerie d'Antiquités Égyptiennes, 1826.

Pries, Andreas. *Die Stundenwachen im Osiriskult: eine Studie zu Tradition und späten Rezeption von Ritualen im Alten Ägypten*. Wiesbaden: Harrassowitz, 2011.

Quirke, Stephen. *Going Out in Daylight—prt m hrw—The Ancient Egyptian Book of the Dead: Translations, Sources, Meanings*. London: Golden House Publications, 2013.

Ranke, Hermann. *Die ägyptischen Personennamen*. Glückstadt: J.J. Augustin, 1935.

Raven, Martin. "Papyrus-Sheaths and Ptah-Sokar-Osiris Statues." *OMRO* 59–60 (1978–79): 251–96.

Refai, Hosam. *Göttin des Westens in den thebanischen Gräbern des neuen Reiches: Darstellung, Bedeutung und Funktion*. Berlin: Achet, 1996.

———. "Die Westgöttin nach dem Neuen Reich." *SAK* 35 (2005): 245–60.

Rindi Nuzzolo, Carlo. "Tradition and Transformation: Retracing Ptah-Sokar-Osiris Figures from Akhmim in Museums and Private Collections." In *(Re)productive Traditions in Ancient Egypt: Proceedings of the Conference held at the University of Liège, 6th–8th February 2013*, edited by Todd Gillen, 445–74. Aegyptiaca Leodiensia 10. Liège, Belgium: Presses Universitaires de Liège, 2017.

Schneider, Hans. "Bringing the *Ba* to the Body: A Glorification Spell for Padinekhtnebef." In *Hommages à Jean Leclant IV*, edited by Catherine Berger, Gisèle Clerc, and Nicholas Grimal, 355–62. BdÉ 106, no. 4. Cairo: IFAO, 1994.

Schneider, Thomas. *Asiatische Personennamen in ägyptischen Quellen des Neuen Reiches*. Freiburg, Switzerland: Universitätsverlag; Göttingen: Vandenhoeck & Ruprecht, 1992.

Schweitzer, Simon. "Zur Herkunft der spätzeitlichen alphabetischen Schreibungen." In *Basel Egyptology Prize 1: Junior Research in Egyptian History, Archaeology, and Philology*, edited by Susanne Bickel and Antonio Loprieno, 371–86. AH 17. Basel: Schwabe & Co., 2003.

Seeber, Christine. *Untersuchungen zur Darstellung des Totengerichts im Alten Ägypten*. MÄS 35. Munich and Berlin: Deutsche Kunstverlag, 1976.

Smith, Mark. "Bodl. MS. Egypt.a.3(P) and the Interface between Temple Cult and Cult of the Dead." In *Ägyptische Rituale der griechisch-römischen Zeit*, edited by Joachim Friedrich Quack, 145–55. Orientalische Religionen in der Antike 5. Tübingen: Mohr Siebeck, 2014.

———. *Traversing Eternity: Texts for the Afterlife from Ptolemaic and Roman Egypt*. New York: Oxford University Press, 2009.

Snape, Stephen. *Ancient Egyptian Tombs: The Culture of Life and Death*. Oxford: Blackwell Publishing, 2011.

Stadler, Martin. "On the Demise of Egyptian Writing: Working with a Problematic Source Basis." In *The Disappearance of Writing Systems: Perspectives on Literacy and Communication*, edited by John Baines, John Bennet, and Stephen Houston, 157–81. London: Equinox, 2008.

Taylor, John. "Changes in the Afterlife." In *Egyptian Archaeology*, edited by Willemina Wendrich, 220–40. Chichester, UK and Malden, MA: Wiley-Blackwell, 2010.

Verhoeven, Ursula. *Das saitische Totenbuch der Iahtesnacht: P. Colon. Aeg. 10207.* Vol. 1, *Papyrologische Texte und Abhandlungen*. Bonn: Habelt, 1993.

Vittmann, Günter. *Ägypten und die Fremden im ersten vorchristlichen Jahrtausend*. Mainz: Philipp von Zabern, 2003.

———. "Review of *Drei Totenpapyri aus einer thebanischen Werkstatt der Spätzeit (pBerlin P. 3158, pBerlin P. 3159, pAberdeen ABDUA 84023)*." *Wiener Zeitschrift für die Kunde des Morgenlandes* 101 (2011): 495–97.

von Falck, Martin, and Susanne Martinssen-von Falck. "Neues zur Göttin des Westens." In *Diener des Horus: Festschrift für Dieter Kurth zum 65. Geburtstag*, edited by Wolfgang Waitkus, 93–108. Aegyptiaca Hamburgensia 1. Gladbeck: PeWe-Verlag, 2008.

Widmer, Ghislane. "Words and Writing in Demotic Ritual Texts from Soknopaiu Nesos." In *Ägyptische Rituale der griechisch-römischen Zeit*, edited by Joachim Friedrich Quack, 133–44. Orientalische Religionen in der Antike 5. Tübingen: Mohr Siebeck, 2014.

Wilson, Penelope. *A Ptolemaic Lexikon: A Lexicographical Study of the Texts in the Temple of Edfu*. OLA 78. Leuven: Peeters, 1997.

Žabkar, Louis V. *A Study of the Ba-concept in Ancient Egyptian Texts*. Chicago: University of Chicago Press, 1968.

www.trismegistos.org